About the Book and Editor

Assessing the social impact of rural development projects, the contributors to this book develop a cultural model based on theories of political economy and apply that model to a consideration of such factors as geography, language, economics, religion, and cultural patterns of domination. They focus on the interrelationship between cultural factors and social stratification. Their model serves as a means for moving from abstract discussions of political economy toward a practical application of social impact assessment.

The book begins with theoretical essays developing the conceptual model, followed by a review of the relevant social impact assessment literature and case studies of rural projects that have affected such socially disadvantaged groups as laborers, women, ranchers, and ethnic minorities. In the final two chapters, the authors apply and test the cultural model, using the findings of the case studies, and draw new conclusions about the differential effects of rural resource development projects.

Pamela D. Elkind-Savatsky is associate professor of sociology at Eastern Washington University.

Dedicated to Rhonda-T and Stacey Hara Savatsky
and to all the children of the contributors

Differential Social Impacts
of Rural Resource
Development

Social Impact Assessment Series
C. P. Wolf, General Editor

What Happened to Fairbanks? The Effects of the Trans-Alaska Oil Pipeline on the Community of Fairbanks, Alaska, Mim Dixon

Social Impact Assessment and Monitoring: A Cross-Disciplinary Guide to the Literature, Michael J. Carley and Eduardo S. Bustelo

Integrated Impact Assessment, edited by Frederick A. Rossini and Alan L. Porter

Public Involvement and Social Impact Assessment, edited by Gregory A. Daneke, Margot W. Garcia, and Jerome Delli Priscoli

Applied Social Science for Environmental Planning, edited by William Millsap

Guide to Social Impact Assessment: A Framework for Assessing Social Change, Kristi Branch, Douglas A. Hooper, James Thompson, and James Creighton

Social Impact Analysis and Development Planning in the Third World, edited by William Derman and Scott Whiteford

Differential Social Impacts of Rural Resource Development, edited by Pamela D. Elkind-Savatsky

A Systems Approach to Social Impact Assessment: Two Alaskan Case Studies, Lawrence A. Palinkas, Bruce Murray Harris, and John S. Petterson

Differential Social Impacts of Rural Resource Development

Editor
Pamela D. Elkind-Savatsky

Associate Editor
Judith D. Kaufman

LONDON AND NEW YORK

First published 1986 by Westview Press, Inc.

Published 2018 by Routledge
52 Vanderbilt Avenue, New York, NY 10017
2 Park Square, Milton Park, Abingdon, Oxon OX14 4RN

Routledge is an imprint of the Taylor & Francis Group, an informa business

Copyright © 1986 Taylor & Francis

All rights reserved. No part of this book may be reprinted or reproduced or utilised in any form or by any electronic, mechanical, or other means, now known or hereafter invented, including photocopying and recording, or in any information storage or retrieval system, without permission in writing from the publishers.

Notice:
Product or corporate names may be trademarks or registered trademarks, and are used only for identification and explanation without intent to infringe.

Library of Congress Catalog Card Number: 86-51103
ISBN 13: 978-0-367-00631-0 (hbk)
ISBN 13: 978-0-367-15618-3 (pbk)

Contents

Contributors xi
Series Editor's Preface, C. P. Wolf xiii
Acknowledgments xvii

Introduction
Pamela D. Elkind-Savatsky........................ 1

PART 1: THE CONCEPTS

1   The American Society/Environment
    Relationship: Challenging Prevailing
    Assumptions
    Jeffers W. Chertok.......................... 17

2   Sociological Theory and the Differential
    Distribution of Impacts in Rural Resource
    Development Projects
    Richard P. Gale 37

3   Whose Ox Is Gored? A Sociocultural
    Model of Impact Distribution in
    Resource Development
    Raymond L. Hall 61

4   Assessing the Social Impacts of Rural
    Resource Developments: An Overview
    William R. Freudenburg 89

PART 2: THE CASE STUDIES

5   Work-Emergent Behaviors and Traits:
    The Segregation of Energy Workers
    in Boomtowns
    Kristen R. Yount 119

6   Ranchland: Impacts on Rural
    Communities
    Patrick C. Jobes 145

7   Women: Gemeinschaft in Boomtowns
    Elizabeth W. Moen 161

8   The Yupik Eskimos of St. Lawrence Island,
    Alaska: A Social Impact Assessment of
    Proposed Energy Development
    Ronald L. Little
    and Lynn A. Robbins 185

9   It Doesn't Have to Happen Again:
    Reflections on the Nuclear Atmosphere
    Simon J. Ortiz 221

10 Reflections on Resistance to Rural
    Industrialization: Newcomers' Culture
    of Environmentalism
    Allan Schnaiberg 229

PART 3: THE HEURISTIC DEVICE

11 Exploring Sociocultural Impacts:
    The Application of a Model
    Raymond L. Hall 261

12 Cultural Assessment of Rural Resource
    Impacts: An Addendum
    Pamela D. Elkind-Savatsky
    and Judith D. Kaufman...................... 283

Index.. 289

Contributors

Jeffers W. Chertok........Eastern Washington University

Pamela D. Elkind-Savatsky.Eastern Washington University

William R. Freudenburg.........University of Wisconsin, Madison

Richard P. Gale...................University of Oregon

Raymond L. Hall......................Dartmouth College

Patrick C. Jobes..............Montana State University

Judith D. Kaufman........Eastern Washington University

Ronald L. Little................Utah State University

Elizabeth W. Moen...............University of Colorado

Simon J. Ortiz........................Pueblo of Acoma

Lynn A. Robbins........................Huxley College, Western Washington University

Allan Schnaiberg...............Northwestern University

Kristen R. Yount................University of Kentucky

Series Editor's Preface

This book is about how different groups of people are differently affected by natural resource development in rural areas and in general. The groups considered are occupational (miners and ranchers), ethnic (Native Americans and Yupik Eskimos), age and gender (adolescents and women in western energy boomtowns). Their personal and social characteristics are bound up in a matrix of meanings and associations embodied and expressed in terms of culture and community. The consideration given them here varies among several intellectual and research traditions. One major axis of differentiation is that between the ethnographic (Little and Robbins, Freudenburg, Yount, Jobes, and Moen) and humanistic (Ortiz) on the one hand and that of political economy (Chertok, Gale, Schnaiberg) on the other. The degree of continuity and cohesion among these contributions is a tribute to the skill and persistence of authors and editors alike.

Traditional groups experiencing the impacts of rural resource development are often believed to suffer a common fate in the "destruction of community" (Erikson). The view advanced here rather emphasizes the distributive and differential impacts of rapid change. A dozen years ago I wrote that such impacts " . . . will be distributive in nature, the incidence of social benefits and detriments falling unevenly and unequally over various sectors and segments of the population, and . . . this will be more so the more highly differentiated the society becomes." This "dissociation" of social costs and benefits is a tenet and precept of social impact assessment (SIA). Indeed, the "bottom line" for SIA can be answered in terms of "Who are the winners and who are the losers?" Until now, this central interest of the field had not received focused study.

This central question is more than a little reminiscent of Harold Lasswell's classic definition of politics as the study of who gets what, where, when,

xiii

and how. From the political economy perspective, the distribution of social benefits and burdens accords exactly with differential (and preferential) access to the means of production and administration and, we may add, communication and legitimation. The notion of "stratification" indicates differential access to and control over social goods of every description, notably power, possessions, and prestige. From the standpoint of cultural analysis, however, the intersection between culture and power is not simply a "political economy explanation for subcultural differentiation." This fundamental proposition is posed but not resolved in Hall's conceptual framework. Indeed, it is not yet evident what is the most suitable method of characterizing and describing cultural systems, though recent life course and social network analyses seem to hold considerable promise.

Differential impacts may be analyzed along any line of social differentiation present in a society. The population and social characteristics of affected publics include: youth, aged, and handicapped; race, ethnicity, and gender; income, occupation, and education; place and length of residence; life cycle stage, marital status, and family composition. The cases reported in this volume sample many of these characteristics. Some axes of social differentiation are more emphasized in different times and places, reflecting in turn the distribution of social values. Their salience is an indicator of special impact significance. For example, "gender" has come to prominence in recent years, signalling a change towards greater equality in the status of women (though not so much as feminists would wish or claim as just).

How the cultural and group characteristics present in a particular impact situation correspond to general population and social characteristics, and how such distributions are likely to be altered by a proposed action, are fit topics for assessment. Some general relationships have been established in previous research, for example the distribution of environmental quality by income level. What is found is that poor people are exposed to greater environmental health risk; that in part is what it means to be poor in our society. Conversely, they stand to benefit disproportionately from efforts at environmental improvement such as air pollution control in inner cities. In most assessments, however, it is the absence of the stratification variable which is striking and distressing. Here as elsewhere, SIA affords an opportunity for active collaboration among many disciplines and professions, and for the unification of theory and practice.

In the present volume, the stratification variable is the central focus of attention inasmuch as differential impacts represent and evaluate differences in life conditions, chances, and outcomes altered by rural (or any) resource development. Although the authors focus mainly on western rural energy resource development, because that has been their and the region's experience over the last decade, clearly their analyses have much broader implications, for other types of resource development and for urban environments as well. By making the stratification variable explicit and focal, and joining it with the cultural variable in development analysis, the volume is an important step towards understanding the social dynamics of development processes. The authors, and especially the editors, deserve our gratitude for their sustained effort in advancing the field along this critical path.

C. P. Wolf
Series Editor

Acknowledgments

Generally, I find all of the "gratefuls" and other platitudes superfluous. I do wish to thank Dr. Judith D. Kaufman for her untiring editing of this volume. Until one has produced "camera-ready" copy, it is not possible to comprehend the number of details to which one must pay attention. Dr. Kaufman is an outstanding grammarian and editor without whom this volume would not exist.

Dr. William C. Hoekendorf, Dean of Eastern Washington University's College of Letters and Sciences, has extended a number of resources during this period. I thank Dr. Hoekendorf and his administrative assistant, Lillian Bilesky, for their assistance, as well as Elinor Best and Bette Colson-Tingley for typing the manuscript. Lastly, I greatly appreciate the patience and perseverance shown by the contributors during the long preparation period.

PDE

Introduction

Pamela D. Elkind-Savatsky

The cultural distribution of rural resource development impacts is the topic of this edited volume. Various dimensions of the distributive process are addressed, and important questions are raised: How are resource development decisions made? What are the political dynamics affecting impact distributions? Why are specific cultural populations and groups disproportionately impacted? What are the various dynamics of modernization and change that differentially affect cultural groups in rural areas? These issues are discussed from a variety of perspectives. In the midst of the discussion, a concept emerges and is tested. The concept, which is the beginning of a model, is not a cookbook for persons seeking an immediate answer, but rather a heuristic tool from which to consider the potential underlying inequities in specific resource distribution decisions. Such a device is likely to lead to meaningful assessments of social impacts.

The book should be read as a sequence of chapters rather than as a compilation of individual papers. Although each author approaches the subcultural distribution of rural resource development impacts from a different perspective, all the contributors share certain fundamental values which underlie the volume as a whole. These include a concern for equity in the distribution of impacts, an awareness of the cultural determinants of inequity, and an interest in the dynamic roles of the community and the state in the rural resource development process.

The social impact assessment literature has previously included little discussion of the structure of societal subpopulations or of the manner in which inequities in society help to determine the nature and degree of the impacts on particular groups within a community. Instead, the literature has considered each development project in terms of either advantaged and disadvantaged individual residents or isolated communities. The previous emphasis has been upon the potential microeconomic and demographic effects of a particular project on a particular region. The contributors to this volume have taken a more complex view, one that approaches the impacts of particular projects in terms of the projects' interactions with the whole of society and the societal system, one that predominantly considers the structure of inequality in society and the workings of the political economy (see also Schnaiberg et al. 1986).

THE CONCEPTS

The concepts of culture and subculture employed in this volume are, in most cases, similar to those articulated by Kai Erikson (1976). Erikson defines culture as "the moral space within which a people live, or, rather, the customary ways that develop within that space" (1976:81). These patterns make the culture distinctive. Culture comprises the attitudes, beliefs, norms, values, aesthetics, and lifestyles of a group and includes a number of variables related to the group's economic system, geography, history, language, and religion (see Raymond Hall, Chapter 3).

In the modern world, most societies of any size contain subpopulations, or subcultures, with special physical, environmental, historical, or attitudinal characteristics. Military expansion, immigration, and ecological migration are reasons for some diverse categories of people being within a single social system. Others share in a life cycle or in a generational or social history, setting them apart from the dominant group (Mannheim 1952). Erikson (1976:82) discusses subcultures in terms of the "axis of variation" within a culture. This axis cuts through the center of a culture's space, drawing attention to diversity, so that culture refers to methods not only of inducing conformity but also of organizing diversity. Unfortunately, in no society is this organization of diversity achieved without inequity.

> Inequality is found in all societies, . . . [in patterns] associated with the social positions people occupy. Positions such as occupation, gender, and race--or ethnicity--all influence the rewards that people earn. These rewards are grounded in the systems of values, beliefs, power and traditions of the society in which they occur (Rothman 1978:1-2).

The positions are defined by the politically and economically dominant culture, as is the distribution of rewards and sacrifices to these subcultural spaces.

Analyses of culture, and of subcultural inequalities, generally stress ethnicity and race. The contributors to this volume, while agreeing that ethnicity and race are the prime determinants of cultural diversity, believe that, in order to consider the "moral space" in which people live and their lifestyles, including behaviors, values, and attitudes, it is necessary to look at the occupational clusters in which they perform and at the very distinctive orientations towards life which they hold due to gender socialization. This volume thus defines occupational and gender-based subcultures, in addition to ethnic and racial ones. One might go even further and discuss, for example, age cohorts or regional groupings of persons as subcultures.

Occupations are highly differentiated in the present technological culture, allowing individuals to treat a narrow range of problems (Eisenstadt 1964). An implicit, and often an explicit, hierarchy of occupations is one basis for prestige and cultural inequality. Persons in an occupational grouping may share lifestyles, values, sets of meanings, and a general outlook which differentiate the group from the rest of society (Richard Hall 1975; Caplow 1954).

Differentiation based on gender is found in all human societies, along with behavioral expectations and generalized, idealized sex typing. One might take the Parsonian view that sex roles are necessary for the maintenance of marriage and society (Parsons 1955), or the Marxist notion that sexual domination is motivated by a desire for economic exploitation of female labor (Kaplan 1974), or the Freudian theory that it is an attempt to establish sexual rights over females as sexual property (Collins 1975). Yet, it is accepted that there are social differences in the rights and responsibilities of persons as determined by their gender. In addition, sexual definitions include gender-differentiated norms and values, and the members of each sex share a distinctive set of meanings and experiences. Thus, the two genders form two distinct subcultures, between which exists a history of inequity.

In considering rural resource developments in terms of cultural factors and the choices made by society based on subcultural differences, we are looking at forces that operate within the context of the political economy. A portion of this is, of course, reflected in the division within a community. In any community, some subcultural groups possess more political and economic power than others. But the development of rural resources also includes numerous factors beyond the structured inequalities that exist between community groups.

Rural resources are generally developed by non-resident industries, often with a national or multinational base. Permits for such development are issued by federal or state agencies with little more than professional interest in local populations. Often, informal coalitions among nonresident industry, dominant local business, and government insure the continued process of the externally directed development. Even citizen participation programs mandated by federal and state law prior to development have historically been directed by representatives of these coalitions and their powerful sympathizers. Thus, many times the interests of less powerful groups in the community or region are only peripherally represented in the development process. It all boils down to the political dynamics of the economic system. Powerful groups backed by the states and their vested interest in development put pressure on those elements not directly connected to the power base. This process is described in detail by Richard Gale in Chapter 2.

The overall community may benefit from much of the resulting growth and development. But certain subcultural groups within the community may experience negative impacts, as will be illustrated in Chapters 4 through 9 of this volume.

THE CHAPTERS: PART 1

The impacts on particular groups within a community can only be understood from a very broad perspective of the national, and perhaps world, political economy which determines the distribution of advantages and disadvantages within our societal system. Reflecting this perspective, the volume begins with broad, theoretical treatments of the implications for resource development impacts of the economic, political, and cultural systems in the United States. Only after these systems have been considered do the contributors proceed to detailed discussions of the impacts of specific development projects on particular groups.

Jeffers Chertok opens the discussion by offering a macroeconomic analysis of the structure of "American" society. He sketches the history of economic production in the United States and discusses the implications of this history for resource developments, now and in the future. Chertok also argues that it is not possible to evaluate inequities in the distribution of resource development impacts without considering the structure of social inequality. He reviews three common approaches to analyzing the inequities in society: stratification theory, elitism, and class analysis. The position that Chertok finally adopts is based upon class analysis, but includes elements of the other two perspectives.

By using a combined perspective to analyze the social and economic structure of society and its implications for resource developments, Chertok makes an important theoretical statement for the volume as a whole. The three perspectives that he employs represent two fundamentally different theoretical orientations: Stratification theory presents a "functionalist" view of social inequities, whereas class analysis and elitism are two versions of "conflict" theory. In general, functionalists regard society as a whole, as an integrated system of parts operating to maintain the total social organization. Thus, functionalists might, for example, believe that inequality in impact distribution can only be understood by analyzing the interactions between groups and the dynamics of those interactions. Since the groups necessarily work together, the analysis must consider both the benefits and the costs to each group with respect to its ability to function within the system.

In the alternative camp are theorists sharing a conflict perspective. They also seek to understand social interaction and organization. However, conflict theorists view society as a dialectic, a contradiction of social relationships. In each historical epoch are the conflicting forces that engender the following epoch. The conflict theory of Karl Marx has greatly influenced much of today's social theory. For Marxist-oriented thinkers, economics and production

> determines the organization of the rest of society. The class structure and institutional arrangements, as well as cultural values, beliefs, religious dogmas and other idea systems are ultimately a reflection of the economic base of a society. . . . Inherent in the economic organization of any society . . . are forces inevitably generating revolutionary class conflict (Turner 1982:122).

Conflict-oriented thinkers perceive a polemic with respect to resource development impacts. They question social divisions and economic power relationships. They are interested in potential changes due to conflicts between actors in the resource development process.

Admittedly, the distinction between functionalist- and conflict-oriented theories is somewhat arbitrary. In fact, most social thinkers would put themselves in neither category but rather somewhere in between. Nonetheless, the terms help to identify some fundamental differences among the contributors to this volume. The reader will note that the volume deliberately includes thinkers from both theoretical camps. Several contributors offer some form of intermediary or combined perspective. I believe that these varying perspectives must be seen as complementary, that only by using a variety of approaches can we begin to comprehend a complex social issue such as rural resource development impact distribution.

Like Chertok, Richard Gale in Chapter 2 approaches rural resource developments from a combined perspective. In Gale's case, the major theoretical components are elitism and class analysis, with overtones of stratification theory. Gale's analysis is less abstract than Chertok's and centers upon the economic ramifications of rural resource development politics. Gale provides an empirical demonstration of the interactions among classes or strata within rural communities during the decision-making processes surrounding rural resource developments. In analyzing the political economics of developing rural communities, Gale uses two urban-based models, Harvey Molotch's "growth machine" and J. Allen Whitt's class power dialectic, and ultimately integrates them into his own analytical framework. His discussion articulates the distinctive character of rural community politics in comparison with the urban system.

Gale's framework moves the volume from a societally based theoretical conception to a focus on "community" dynamics. For Gale, terms are defined by their political dimension: Community is a politically determined geographic unit with specific boundaries fitting into the regional system--for example, a town or township.

Other contributors will employ the same terms to describe societal groupings. The use of the term "community" to refer to both a political and a cultural unit has a long history. In 1939, Dwight Sanderson defined the rural community geographically "as a rural area within which the people have a common center of interest, usually a village, and within which they have a sense of common obligations and responsibilities" (1939:6). After studying numerous definitions of community, George Hillery, Jr., asserted that there was "basic agreement that community consists of persons in social interaction within a geographic area and having one or more additional ties" (1955:111). Harold Kaufman (1959) in his review further specified three areas of consensus with respect to community definition: First, community is a social unit with a spatial component; second, community is a small place; and third, people act together for their common good, so community is an interactional field. To further complicate, or perhaps simplify, the issue, the U.S. Census Bureau defines a community as a geographical unit of a specific size (depending upon whether it is rural or urban, small or large, metropolitan or nonmetropolitan) and with specified boundaries. Researchers accept the census definition to facilitate data collection. Thus, community analysis and discussion for social researchers is likely to be at least partially guided by the dimensions set forth by the federal government, but employing the sociological definitions as well.

Among the contributors to this volume, Hall and Freudenburg allude to communities in much the same way as does Gale, whereas Jobes, Little and Robbins, and Ortiz use the term for a cohesive traditional cultural unit as well. For them, in Toennies's (1940) terms, a community is a gemeinschaft entity with direct, constant interactions, dependencies, and shared value systems and lifestyles, rather than a gesellschaft-style urban area characterized by bureaucratic structure and independence. Elizabeth Moen employs both meanings. She looks at Meeker, for example, as a community in the sense of a political unit. However, Moen also refers to the work of Jessie Bernard, who interprets Toennies's traditional or gemeinschaft system to encompass many caring or affective dimensions characterizing the female gender subculture. Thus, Moen also employs Toennies's community perspective in the sense of a shared traditional value orientation or female gender mindset.

Subculture as a community of spirit, exchange, or value orientation is substantially affected by development. As later demonstrated in the case studies found in Part 2, the specific effects which are consequences of the political and economic system thus ultimately impact the substance of community.

Gale's chapter demonstrates community change and adaptation as well as the changing role of the state in rural areas. He portrays subdivisions within the communities, mentioning such factors as land ownership, employment, and religious associations which cut across the economic class system. He suggests that these factors may produce "somewhat autonomous subcultures [which] may crosscut the prevailing dominant/subordinate class order" and that the "cultural attributes of rural subordinate groups are those most vulnerable to displacement." Subcultural factors, along with the power dynamics among community groups and between the community and the state, help determine which groups win and which groups lose in the distribution of positive or negative impacts.

The focus of Gale's chapter is the power dynamics in their economic dimension. The questions of whose culture is to be in control and how power is distributed among the various subcultures are beyond the scope of his chapter. These issues are addressed in Chapter 3 by Raymond Hall, who begins to develop a heuristic cultural model of impact distribution.

Hall, while agreeing that economic forces predominate in society's structuring of inequality, demonstrates how the cultural variables found in particular subgroups become the basis for the inequitable distribution of impacts. Beginning with a treatise on the components of ethnic culture, he asks which groups might be affected inequitably by resource developments and why. Through discussions of inequality in the modern state, he looks at the roles and responsibilities of the multiethnic state. For Hall, much as for Gale, the state maintains societal control; a leveling process takes place whereby the state brings cultures together, reinforcing specific elements of the dominant culture. These elements are incorporated into a state culture which reflects the dominant group status and excludes cultural aspects of subordinate groups. This is easily demonstrable in the notion of separation between church and state in the United States. Although there is denominational separation, our currency reads "In God We Trust," the pledge of allegiance includes "under God," and persons giving court testimony or accepting public office are sworn to truth and honesty on the King James edition of "the Bible." These and numerous other religious references by the state demonstrate the dominant religious culture of the state, which is also part of the religion held by the dominant culture. All persons in the United States, despite ethnic culture or religious preference, accept these aspects of the dominant culture as part of state culture.

Hall's leveling perspective is to some degree an application of Chertok's discussion of ideological hegemony in the state. Each author suggests that there is a movement by the dominant culture to institutionalize its values, ideas, etc.; minority values are thus in conflict.

Beyond ethnic cultures, Hall observes that a variety of subgroups or subcultures vie for resources. These include occupational groups, such as farmers and miners, as well as age groups and gender groups. These subgroups cut across the layers or strata of society. Because such group members have diverse cultures and resource needs and because they are often external to the state political-decision processes controlled by the dominant culture, they are generally more negatively affected by the development process than are members of the dominant group.

Hall defines the parameters which differentiate cultures and subcultures. These parameters, or components of culture, are the basis for a conceptual model of cultural impact assessment to be constructed and tested throughout the remainder of the volume. Religion, language, history, and geography appear to be the significant cultural elements which separate subcultures from one another and from the dominant group in the political and economic system. These elements are also the most likely foci for the negative impacts of the rural resource development process.

Unfortunately, as William Freudenburg documents in Chapter 4, social impact assessment researchers have documented very few subculturally based impacts, since analyses have either been based upon a total community or an aggregate of individuals. Freudenburg demonstrates the lack of cultural orientation in the literature. It is essential, as we see in Freudenburg's literature review and in his own research analysis, that we assess the subgroups in the development process. Freudenburg indicates, for example, that one age-related cohort in boomtown communities is particularly likely to be affected by negative development conditions. Young people of student age are in constant contact with newcomers who have diverse value systems and ways that appear alien. They must attend school and participate in sports and other community activities that are often stretched well beyond limits by the influxes of new workers' families. Interactions characteristically engender hostility and mistrust in place of the feelings of neighborliness generally experienced in rural communities. The students in Freudenburg's sample thus report worse conditions than the adults. They are less satisfied with their communities than youth in adjacent towns.

THE CHAPTERS: PARTS 2 AND 3

Freudenburg points to numerous inconsistencies between findings and to a paucity of information. The intent of this volume is to present a heuristic tool as well as potential categories of impacted subcultures in order that scientists may begin to gather conceptually significant and similar bodies of data to assess social impacts on dissimilar groups of people undergoing resource development. The case studies in Chapters 5 through 9 are designed to provide information and data so we may test the ability of Hall's conceptual model to explain the culturally inequitable allocation of resource development impacts. In these chapters, we are provided with examples of ethnic, occupational, and gender differentials in impact distribution.

Ronald Little and Lynn Robbins (Chapter 8) present the case of the Alaskan Yupik Eskimos and potential oil development in the Bering Sea. They discuss an ancient patriclan community system where dependence on the sea for food and barter resources means that the entire culture is at risk from offshore oil exploration and development.

In many ways, reinforcement for the predictions made by Little and Robbins with respect to cultural change may be seen in the evidence presented by Simon Ortiz (Chapter 9). He views the inequities experienced by the Pueblo peoples of New Mexico as the result of a history of mining by largely out-of-region corporations. Ortiz demonstrates negative cultural effects in situations where economic development on the Native American lands was supposed to have improved quality of life. Though there has been improvement in the economy of the region over these years, the Pueblo peoples have been negatively affected, as demonstrated by living conditions, expectations, and patterns of fear.

In both of these case studies, we observe a pervasive minority group. The community is comprised almost totally by the cultural group. Outside development and the powerful external corporations with the majority-group orientation cause impacts that are particularly harmful to the people of the community due to the cultural differences between Native Americans and communities oriented toward dominant American values.

In studies of ranching and mining, respectively, Patrick Jobes (Chapter 6) and Kristen Yount (Chapter 5) demonstrate two cases of occupational subcultures that are affected differentially by rural resource development. Whether due to ties with the land shared by neighbors in ranchland or to experiences of danger shared by miners, subcultures or communities of feeling tend to develop. The constraints and benefits of development affect persons in these occupational groupings differently from other persons due to the specific shared aspects of their occupations. These shared aspects engender a "community of spirit" in the ranch families and in the miners and their dependents.

Cutting across each layer of the society are two predominant subcultural orientations, male and female. Elizabeth Moen (Chapter 7) demonstrates differences between gender groups in energy development communities. Due to differences in aspirations and value orientations, as well as to inequities in employment and family orientations in society, the gender subcultures experience inequities in resource development impacts.

Each of the case study authors has demonstrated the interaction between a particular group and the total community system. Each has seen the economically determined consequences of development as primary for the particular subgroup. Each has, however, then demonstrated the consequences of inequitable distribution on a particular part of the community or population sharing specific cultural elements. Religious rituals and belief systems, or constraints from geographic locations, or particular historical events comprise the cultural traditions affected by development. It is essential that these elements be considered in the assessment of rural resource development projects.

In the chapters discussed thus far, the volume has proceeded from an abstract consideration of the construction of cultural inequality and the political system through particular cases of cultural impact. However, much of this approach suggests a fairly romanticized notion of the disruption of communities by in-migrants and by changes made through development. Allan Schnaiberg ends Part 2 with reflections on community change. He suggests that it may be those persons brought in via development who finally reverse the subcultural inequities of impact in rural development regions.

Schnaiberg reports that rural communities often appear to welcome development. He finds that a good deal of the industrialization in rural areas is due to their perceived lack of resistance. Development stimulates migration from urbanized areas. Schnaiberg looks at the migrating population, i.e., the construction and operation employees, their families, and the new residents resulting from secondary development. He suggests that new subcultures move into the communities and set up a variety of dynamics with the oldtimers. At times, these new residents have different cultural orientations. Often present are the wives, an urban-educated cohort of women who are unemployed or underemployed due to lack of opportunities. Many of these persons have activist orientations. They, supported by a fringe element, become the organizers against further development, and at times even the protectors of the old community. Thus, Schnaiberg suggests that there is a "partial replacement of a rural folk by an ersatz 'folk,' a form of rural gentrification." These persons are actionists, "country cousins of urban 'yuppies'" who value a tranquil village-like environment and will organize to protect their new environment.

Differing cultural patterns are imported into rural areas. They often conflict with the dominant patterns. However, these dominant patterns have previously fostered the industrial development and have often created inequity for the various minority subcultures. In setting up his dialectic, Schnaiberg demonstrates the possibility that from the problems caused by rural industrial expansion a solution could emerge. Migrants moving into the rural region may become the active protectors of subcultural rural community life. In other words, the economic forces which cause rural resource development impacts are often counterbalanced by social and cultural factors.

The third segment of the volume allows the reader to process the abstract information from Part 1 with the case study data in Part 2. Raymond Hall (Chapter 11) assesses the conceptual model he developed in Chapter 3. He first considers the need for such a heuristic device in the dynamic political processes of resource development. Hall then reviews the various dimensions and variables of his cultural model, demonstrating their appropriateness in impact assessment.

Finally, Hall employs the case study information and analysis found in Part 2 to demonstrate the operation of his heuristic model. He shows how language and history, for example, have rendered groups as diverse as American women and the Yupik Eskimos both powerless and vulnerable to resource development impacts. Hall's analysis suggests to the reader that only through an analysis of structured inequality are we able to comprehend the potential and actual reasons behind the cultural distribution of impacts. Such in-depth analyses appear essential in all social impact assessments. Thus, we have returned to the need for abstract theoretical analysis in order to accomplish the practical requirements of social impact assessment.

The outcome of this analysis should provide the reader with a comprehensive schema useful in social impact assessment application. Ultimately, the goal is to provide a means for considering and for mapping the inequitably distributed impacts of rural resource developments on ethnic, occupational, gender, and other subcultures in the environmental assessment process. The conceptual model should provide the reader not only with a means for considering the cultural differences in resource development areas, but also with a heuristic device for assessing project impacts with respect to particular cultural variables. It will enable the social impact assessor and the policymaker employing a political economy approach to define and project culturally based impacts and to explore their societally determined causes.

REFERENCES

Caplow, T. 1954. The Sociology of Work. Minneapolis: University of Minnesota Press.
Collins, R. 1975. Stratification by sex and age: Part 1: A theory of sexual stratification. In Conflict Sociology: Toward an Explanatory Science, 228-59. New York: Academic Press.
Eisenstadt, S. N. 1964. Institutionalization and change. American Sociological Review 19:49-59.
Erikson, K. T. 1976. Everything in Its Path: Destruction of Community in the Buffalo Creek Flood. New York: Simon and Schuster.
Hall, R[ichard]. 1975. Occupations and the Social Structure. 2d ed. Englewood Cliffs, N.J.: Prentice-Hall.
Hillery, G. A., Jr. 1955. Definitions of community: Areas of agreement. Rural Sociology 20:111-23.

Kaplan, T. 1974. A Marxist analysis of women and capitalism. In *Women in Politics*, ed. J. Jaquette, 257-65. New York: Wiley.

Kaufman, H. 1959. Toward an interactional conception of community. *Social Forces* 38:1-10.

Mannheim, K. 1952. The problem of generations. In *Essays on the Sociology of Knowledge*, 276-322. London: Routledge and Kegan Paul.

Parsons, T. 1955. The American family: Its relations to personality and to the social structure. In *Family, Socialization and Interaction Process*, ed. T. Parsons and R. F. Bales, 3-33. Glencoe, Ill.: Free Press.

Rothman, R. A. 1978. *Inequality and Stratification in the United States*. Englewood Cliffs, N.J.: Prentice-Hall.

Sanderson, D. 1939. Locating the rural community. *Cornell Extension Bulletin* #413. Ithaca: New York State College of Agriculture at Cornell University.

Schnaiberg, A., N. Watts, and K. Zimmermann. 1986. *Distributional Conflicts in Environmental--Resource Policy*. London: Gower.

Toennies, F. 1940. *Fundamental Concepts of Sociology*, trans. C. Loomis. New York: American Books.

Turner, J. H. 1982. *The Structure of Sociological Theory*. 3d ed. Homewood, Ill: Dorsey Press.

Part 1
The Concepts

1
The American Society/Environment Relationship: Challenging Prevailing Assumptions

Jeffers W. Chertok

CONCEPTIONS OF SOCIAL INEQUALITY

The whole question of resource development, or the societal/natural resource relationship generally, is, sociologically speaking, a problem of social stratification. Social stratification usually refers to the sociological examination of social inequality in human societies. Social inequality is generally conceived to include structured social relationships of privilege and disprivilege, domination and subordination, and worth and unworthiness. It would appear, therefore, that the question of resource development presupposes an understanding of social inequality in contemporary American society. (In this chapter, "America" and "American" refer, for the most part, to the United States of America.)

This would be relatively easy to do if there were substantial agreement among sociologists regarding the nature, origin, functioning, and consequences of social inequality. There are, however, no basic agreements. Once acknowledged though, recognition of the different problems, methods, and conclusions may become the basis of a synthetic reformulation of social inequality in contemporary American society. This chapter presents a framework within which to understand the transformation of social inequality and resource development in American society.

There are three dominant approaches to the phenomenon of social inequality in advanced capitalist society. Class analysis is a sociological theory of the structural change of societies characterized by a capitalist mode of production. Elitism, in both its classical and modern "ruling elite" versions, is the sociological analysis of elites, which seeks to identify the elite(s), examine its internal composition, and understand the mechanisms by which it maintains its privileged position. Social stratification is the sociological study of the causes, functioning, and consequences of the unequal distribution of various forms of wealth, power, and prestige. Obviously, each approach has its own substantive interests, analytical foci, and data ranges; perhaps not so obviously, each has its own strengths and limitations. In what follows, I shall attempt to explicate the distinctive character of each as the basis for an effort to develop a propositional inventory of the structural framework within which resource development will take place.

Class Analysis

Class analysis has as its intellectual origins the work of Karl Marx and represents the first systematic interest in social inequality (Dahrendorf 1959). Much of Marx's sociology was addressed to the systemic explanation of structural changes generated by the inner working of capitalist societies (Balbas 1971).

For Marx, the concept "social class" was inseparably linked to a dialectical theory of social change (Ollman 1968). "Social class," in Marxist theory, is not a category for describing how a particular capitalist society looked at any given time, i.e., the distribution of wealth, power, or prestige; rather, it is an analytical tool for explaining the sources and direction of structural change within societies characterized by a capitalist mode of production (Stolzman and Gamberg 1973).

The Marxist theory of social change of capitalist society normally employs a two-class model of society, i.e., the bourgeoisie and the proletariat, with allowances for classes in liquidation (peasants, petite bourgeoisie, etc.) and emergence (middle strata). However, the two fundamental classes represent the opposite sides of a fundamental contradiction which is understood to be the source of conflicts sufficiently important to produce significant change of the structure of whole capitalist societies. The two-class model--the categories of which are defined in dialectical opposition to each other--is the starting point for Marx's theory of social change and revolution.

Marx claimed to have discovered that the two fundamental classes were embedded in the fundamental relationships of capitalist production. Capitalist production is an economic system based on private capital and a market in wage labor. The class structure of a capitalist society is based on private ownership of productive property and a market in labor. The productive and distributive processes in a capitalist society depend on the relationship of the two classes spawned by the twin capitalist institutions of private ownership of the major means of production and the market in labor (Stolzman and Gamberg 1974).

Marx's conceptualization of class, class interest, class structure, class conflict, and social change was derived from an analysis of the productive process in capitalist society. In a capitalist society, workers sell their labor power, i.e., their ability to produce. They receive in return wages which are sufficient for (and tend toward) subsistence. From a systematic and systemic frame of reference, Marx held that wages reflect the full value of workers' labor, and the intellectual problem became the origin of the surplus by which the capitalist lives. Marx reasoned that only labor is able to confer value on things; that labor creates greater value than is needed to sustain itself; that what the laborer sells is "labor power," i.e., the worker's ability to produce during a stipulated time period; and that in the wage bargain the capitalist acquires a certain number of hours of control and disposition over the worker's productive activity and capitalizes on the worker's ability to create value, i.e., more value than the cost of the original labor power (prevailing wage rates). The difference between the value of labor power (wages) and the value labor produces is surplus value. As a historical phenomenon, Marx expected a developmental transition of capitalist societies from production based on the creation of absolute surplus value (through prolonging the work day, depressing wages, and seeking cheaper raw materials) to one based on relative surplus value (mechanization to increase productivity) (Nicolaus 1967).

Marx's class analysis of capitalism has several distinctive features. First, it makes surplus value and profit a natural outcome of capitalist social organization. Second, it makes class exploitation central to the normal operation of capitalism. Third, it makes class inequality a normal outcome of market relations in a capitalist society. And fourth, it sees capitalist industrialization creating two distinct and mutually contradictory classes, without denying the existence of other classes or the existence of nonclass forms of social inequality.

The phenomenon of class domination and opposition best typifies the level and range of research interests of classical Marxists. Class domination refers to the process through which an intermarrying class, which owns the major means of production, controls a disproportionate amount of wealth, and has privileged access to the dominant institutions, attempts to preserve its superior position in the face of continuous and ongoing opposition by those deprived of a voice in the productive process. As a process, class domination occurs in three ways. Economically, the dominant class owns the major means of production, controls the process, and appropriates the products. Politically, the dominant class functions through the state, by holding appointive and elective offices or by financing the campaigns of those who do, to implement domestic and foreign policies that support its long-term interests. Ideologically, the dominant class attempts to preserve its position through consecration and justification of existing property relationships to the means of production through the direct inculcation of values, the censorship of heterodox views, and the limiting of the parameters of legitimate debate. The social structure simultaneously generates oppositional forces along the same three dimensions. These then constitute an illustration of the level and range of research interests of classical Marxists (Wesolowski 1979).

An important development in classical class analysis is the theory of imperialism. In an important sense, this development reconceptualizes the phenomenon of social inequality as a world system of capitalist domination and opposition. Imperialism is seen as the expansion of the capital accumulation process to world proportions in the search for labor, raw materials, and markets for the products of production. From this perspective, resource utilization patterns are seen as a special instance of the more general process of class domination and opposition in the capitalist system (Gurley 1970). Moreover, resource developments of all types would reflect the scope and logic of the capital accumulation process.

Elitism

A second approach to the phenomenon of social inequalty is elite theory. Modern ruling elite theory has as its classical origins the works of Vilfredo Pareto (The Mind and Society, 1935), Gaetano Mosca (The Ruling Class, 1915 [1939 ed.]), and Robert Michels (Political Parties, 1915 [1962 ed.]). In general, elitism is characteristically a theory of political inertia, i.e., a statement of the tendency of "political power" to devolve into the hands of a small, cohesive, and relatively closed elite that controls all decisions of major importance and is virtually invulnerable to oppositon to its monopoly of power (Olsen 1970). As a school or system of thought, it takes the positions that elites are inevitable and that participatory democracy is impossible (Barkley 1955).

The central premise of elitism is the proposition that elites are a universal and necessary feature of human society. There is a terminological or conceptual similarity among all elitists: All distinguish between the ruling or "elite" class and those who constitute the ruled class, or "masses." All three major theorists define the elite in the same way--political power, i.e., the ability to make decisions of national or international consequence. This is a definition first offered by Machiavelli and one which reflects the view that political power is a basic ingredient in all social relations.

The elitists' conceptual emphasis on political power affected their work in three specific ways. First, it necessarily led to a two-class model of society. Second, it led to a virtual disregard of the social and economic bases of social inequality. Third, it led to a focus on the dominant political group--the elite--to the exclusion of all others. Furthermore, despite minor differences with regard to the causes of the division of society into classes, the elite are characterized by "traits" or "qualities" that are alleged as necessary to attain and maintain their position of political dominance (Dahrendorf 1959). Michels, it is true, added an organizational view of elites as less numerous and, hence, better organized.

To summarize, elitism operates with a political conception of class, a zero-sum definition of power, a two-class model of society, and a virtually exclusive focus on the elite. This being the case, the analytical problems that suggest themselves are those of the viability of the elite; the mass becomes the residual "class/category" of analysis. In addition, the elitists were less concerned with explaining social change than stability; i.e., the focus on the elite caused the problem of social change to become one of individual social mobility, notwithstanding Pareto's and Michels's notions of the "circulation" and "rejuvenation" of the elite.

In their research, ruling elite theorists tend to seek to establish the existence of an elite (or elites), analyze the bases of its internal composition, and identify the means by which it maintains its privileged position. This approach to the phenomenon of social inequality would be expected to focus on the existence of foundations, associations, and regulatory agencies concerned with the societal/natural resource relationship and resource utilization patterns. Furthermore, research in this tradition should be expected to focus on the sources of funding and staffing of these organizations, as well as the interests served by their policy directives, i.e., the extent to which such organizations advance policies that promote and stabilize resource utilization patterns favorable to prevailing elites (Domhoff 1967:107-8).

Social Stratification

Although it is the most recent of the three dominant approaches to the phenomenon of social inequality, social stratification analysis has roots in the classical sociology of Max Weber. In the hands of contemporary stratificationists, the concept "social class" is antithetical to a Marxist usage of the term; in fact, the term "strata" best typifies the object of their attention. Like ruling elite theorists, social stratificationists offer a static and descriptive picture of how a given society looks at any point in time rather than a theory of social change. Political power is a direct function of social class position, "class" being understood in terms of position within a system in which hierarchical gradations are based on wealth, occupation, education, "prestige," or some combination thereof.

Whereas for class analysis the criteria of class position are opposite attributes and opposing interests, for social stratificationists the criterion of class position and membership is the individual's/family's relative share of the same attribute. Classificatory schemes based on this gradation concept of social class are undertaken with a view to describing a given society along a particular dimension, i.e., wealth, power, prestige, or some combination thereof, and not with a view to developing a theory of structural conflict and societal change based on contradictory interests (Stolzman and Gamberg 1973). It should also be mentioned that the interests and foci of social stratificationists are not inconsistent with those of the ruling elite theorists; both approaches may tend to lead to an interest in the existence, composition, and interactions among elites in society (Balbas 1971).

As the sociological students of the unequal distribution of various forms of wealth, power, and prestige, social stratificationists are typically concerned with a delimited set of research problems. In general, they have raised the following sorts of questions regarding social inequality: (1) How many strata are there? (2) How can one best stratify communities/societies? (3) What are the social, economic, and political characteristics of the various strata? (4) How does strata position affect the way in which people think and act? In addition, stratificationists have asked whether social strata are statistical categories or social groups and have questioned the extent of stratum consciousness and segregation. In regard to the society/environment relation, social stratificationists would be expected to be interested in the relationships between strata position and access to and control over environmental resources and in interstratum relationships and use patterns.

This section has presented the three dominant sociological approaches to social inequality as well as their typical and distinctive research interests. These approaches will become the basis of an effort to discuss the social inegalitarian character of contemporary American society and the implications of this social structure for resource development.

SOCIAL INEQUALITY AND OPPOSITION IN AMERICA

This section attempts to synthesize elements of the class, elitist, and social stratification analyses of the phenomenon of social inequality. An effort will be made to develop a propositional inventory of the inegalitarian character of American society. It is hoped that such an inventory will provide a useful framework within which to understand resource development.

Proposition 1: America is a class-structured inegalitarian society.

Ideological pretensions notwithstanding, America was historically, and is with respect to other comparable societies, a highly unequal society. It is also a stratified society. Stratified societies are those in which inequalities are socially structured, i.e., patterned, stable, and legitimated (Ossowski 1963). To argue that America is a stratified inegalitarian society is to suggest that inequalities give rise to groups and that these groups possess unequal amounts of wealth, power, and prestige, which are hereditarily transmitted from one generation to the next.

Social stratification, then, refers generally to the economic/occupational nexus of patterned, stable, and intergenerational hierarchical groupings. On the one hand, the term "class" has always been used to refer to the distinctly economic aspects of social stratification; on the other, it has usually also denoted the existence of a degree of organization, boundedness, and collective consciousness among members within the stratum. Traditional studies of social stratification in America have typically attended to the bases and number of strata, the nature of interstratum relationships, and the extent of stratum consciousness.

Proposition 2: Classes are structured economically/occupationally.

A central concern for sociologists, concerned as they are with the structuralization and continuity of group inequalities, is the social origin of social inequality. Generally speaking, it is fair to say that sociologists have approached the question in two ways. For the purposes of this chapter, I will treat these two approaches as tentative and suggestive explanations of social inequality.

Class analysts argue that wealth, power, and prestige are largely structured by the nature of (and position in) the property system. Class analysts use the term "social class" in an analytical and relational fashion, as a heuristic device to explain the organizational change of societies characterized by a capitalist mode of production. Forced to "stratify" a particular society at a specific moment in time, class analysts identify the two fundamental classes embedded in the production process, with allowance for classes in liquidation and development, middle strata, and nonclass inegalitarian groupings (Braverman 1974). From the perspective of class analysis, the "class structure" of a particular society at a specified time emanates from the property system in production.

Social stratificationists, for the most part, deny the validity of class analysis and approach the phenomena of social inequality very differently. Social stratificationists argue that wealth, power, and prestige are largely structured by the division of labor in the production of goods and services in society and by the systemically given or socially derived value of these goods and services to societal members. Social stratificationists' use of the term "social class" is descriptive and distributive, as a heuristic device to explain the structure and function of the unequal distribution of material rewards and prestige (Rothman 1978). Furthermore, social stratificationists frequently argue that, with the transcendence of capitalist social relations and the rise of postindustrial society, occupation has become the single most important determinant of class structure and of people's positions therein.

I began by asserting that America is an inegalitarian and class-structured society possessed of stability and persistence. Next, I have suggested that classes in American society are structured economically/occupationally and that the stability and persistence of the class structure emanate from the economic organization of society and its occupational division of labor. My understanding of class structure then is both relational (in terms of property relationships to the major means of production) and distributive (in terms of occupational market position). Such a conception should facilitate our understanding of the dynamic character of American social structure.

Proposition 3: The class structuralization of American society has evolved over time locally, regionally, and nationally.

Evidence of the class structuralization of American society is incomplete, fragmentary, and inconsistent (in part because the incomplete knowledge comes from diverse theoretical origins). Nevertheless, what evidence we do have suggests at least three distinct periods linked together in a developmental process. Furthermore, evidence suggests that these three periods are related in an ongoing process of restructuralization.

The first period of American history is antebellum American society, which was stratified on a local and regional basis. Here the results of ruling elite research indicate that the stratificatory hierarchies of American society were local, i.e., emanated from older cities such as Boston, New York, and Philadelphia, and regional, i.e., rural (agrarian) versus urban (industrial manufacture). Evidence is largely restricted to the elite (Amory 1947, 1960; Baltzell 1966; Domhoff 1967; Kavaler 1960).

The second period of American history is roughly post-Civil War through the turn of the twentieth century. The dates of the second period are inexact, but the events that brought about the nationalization of the class structure are quite specific. The nationalization of the class structure was ushered in by the rise and legal recognition of the corporate enterprise (Gilbert and Kahl 1982). Neo-elite research suggests that the national consolidation of the corporate elite was facilitated by the simultaneous appearances of national communication and transportation networks and supportive institutional organizations: schools, debutante halls, and gentlemen's clubs (Domhoff 1967). Marxist research suggests that this period of American history witnessed the institutionalization of a corporate form of the capitalist system, which is to say that the corporation became the dominant form of business enterprise preventing older and alternative forms of business enterprise from functioning as significant components of the economy (Braverman 1974). Both traditions of research identify an economic system characterized by numerous small, highly restricted, privately owned, personally managed corporations, which operated through classical laissez-faire competitive mechanisms--all of which broke the local and regional world of a previous epoch (Baran and Sweezy 1966).

The third period of American history occurred after the First World War. This period is the result of two basic interacting forces. First, there is the transition from laissez-faire to monopoly corporate economic circumstances. Recent scholarship suggests that since World War I the American economy has been increasingly characterized by a smaller number of larger, less competitive, conglomerated, publicly owned, professionally managed corporations, which operate through the mechanics of need creation, planned obsolescence, and price leadership (Baran and Sweezy 1966). Second, there is the growing internationalization of the economy, which penetrates other societies in search of raw materials, new markets, and cheaper labor (Kolko 1969). American society is enmeshed in an international stratification network such that industries, corporations, classes, and occupations must now be understood in a world systemic context.

Proposition 4: American class structuralization has occurred within the context of four basic societal imperatives (profit, concentration, conglomeration, efficiency) which have created contradictions and opposition.

In what follows, I will outline the features common to all capitalist societies having made the transition from the laissez-faire to the monopoly corporate stages of development. These characteristics are intended to convey the coercive and dynamic framework within which the class structuralization process has taken place. This framework will be the basis for understanding the nature and probable range of future resource developments (Parenti 1978).

Profit. From a societal perspective, the American economy is without formal central coordination and planning. Rather, productive and distributive decisions are based on the criteria of corporate profitability (corporate profit structure). This is to say that the American economy is possessed of informal central coordination and planning, but that such planning is geared to corporate profitability. Structurally imperative profit maximization may well work against long-range economic planning and the conservation of resources (Dowd 1977).

Concentration. As mentioned in the preceding section, there has been a long-term transformation in the nature of the American economy. Initially, we have characterized the economy as composed of numerous small and competitive corporate enterprises. Competitive corporate enterprises guided by the logic of profitability have had the long-term effect of reducing the number of units in each sector of production. This competitive process has given way to a new economy composed of a smaller number of larger and less competitive corporate enterprises. It is argued by some that the majority of production in many areas of industry and manufacture is contributed by several "dominant" corporations (Baran and Sweezy 1966).

Conglomeration. The process of concentration has given rise to a second characteristic of the American economy. The concentration of economic units has given rise to conglomeration. Conglomeration refers to the process through which corporate investments are made across industrial sectors. Whereas at one point corporate activity is limited to one area of production, increasingly, corporate investment and production activities cross industrial sectors. The related processes of corporate concentration and conglomeration dictate that owners, executives, and managers come to have broad interests in the econmic system as a whole and in the larger social system.

Efficiency. In an important respect, corporate concentration and conglomeration, and the structural logic of profitability, are largely due to efficiency. Efficiency refers to the systematic application of science and technology to the productive process. In fact, efficiency in the procurement of materials, labor processes, marketing, etc., could be termed a system imperative. Such an imperative may, on specific occasions, outweigh consideration of possible negative consequences to producers, consumers, and the natural and human environment.

The nationalization of the class structure has occurred within the framework of an economic system which is increasingly organized around the imperatives of profit, concentration, conglomeration, and efficiency. The two occur as simultaneous aspects of the growth of a monopoly corporate conglomerate economy. The imperatives of such a system generate contradictions between the ranks of owners and workers, machine production and human needs, and the advantaged and disadvantaged within and between nations. Such contradictions may also extend to resource utilization patterns.

Proposition 5: The integration of America is achieved through the process of class domination and opposition, and ideological struggle is an important aspect of that process.

As one dimension of the process of class domination, ideological hegemony has its classical roots in Marx's class analysis in The German Ideology.

Marx suggests: "The ideas of the ruling class are in every epoch the ruling ideas: i.e. the class, which is the ruling material force of society, is at the same time its ruling intellectual force" (1947:39). The Italian theoretician Antonio Gramsci used the concept "ideological hegemony" to refer to the way in which "a certain way of life and thought is dominant, in which one concept of reality is diffused throughout society in all its institutional and private manifestations" (Cammett 1967:204, quoting Williams).

More recently, the concept of ideological hegemony has been taken out of a class and analytical framework and developed by non-Marxist scholars. David Sallach, for instance, conceptualizes ideological hegemony as a process in which

> a dominant class, which controls the economic and political institutions of a society, also possesses privileged access to the primary ideological institutions of that society (religion, culture, education, communications media). The dominant class uses its privileged access to ideological institutions to propagate values which reinforce its structural position. Such propagation involves not only the inculcation of its values and the censorship of heterodox views but also and especially the ability to <u>define</u> the parameters of legitimate discussion and debate over alternative beliefs, values and world views (1974:41, original emphasis).

Sallach argues that the aforementioned process has the effect of fragmenting true class consciousness for a time, although it is not without limits. As is characteristic of non-Marxist views, Sallach is unable to explain the simultaneous existence of contradictory beliefs, values, and worldviews.

As Sallach and others (see Coulson and Riddell 1980) have pointed out, censorship and the direct inculcation of values are extreme instances of the ideological hegemonic process and are often counter-productive. In Sallach's words, "The most effective aspect of hegemony is found in the suppression of alternative views through the establishment of parameters which define what is legitimate, reasonable, sane, practical, good, true, and beautiful" (1974:41). Sallach begins to outline some of the means by which the parameters through which the general population thinks are defined: political socialization, media setting of the limits (defining the terms) within which debate over controversial topics takes place, and network self-censorship. Finally, Coulson and Riddell (1980:102) remake the point that the closer a situation comes to approximating ideological hegemony, the less the need for coercion, i.e., physical forms of restraint.

Proposition 6: Constraint is subject to continuous processes of class and nonclass resistance and opposition.

Ideological hegemony represents a recent and sophisticated development of the class domination literature. It is the case, however, that these theoretical and empirical advances stem largely from the ruling elite approach to inequality.

A major problem with this most recent addition to the ideological hegemony literature is that its proponents seemingly fail to understand or anticipate the existence of oppositional systems of thought and behavior (see, for example, Mills 1956; Domhoff 1967; Sallach 1974). In large part, this limitation is due to the particularities of elitism as an approach to inequality, as outlined in a previous section of this chapter.

Consistent with the foregoing propositional inventory, this chapter employs the rudiments of a class analytic framework. Such a model provides the basis for anticipating and understanding domination and resistance, hegemony and opposition. The advantage of this framework is the focus on coercion and resistance, both of which are seen as engendered by an inegalitarian class structure.

To explain the existence of ideological hegemony and opposition in America as in other societies, one may begin from the example of a simple society composed of two groups of people. The first group lives off the labors and at the expense of the other. The second group lives to provide for the first, which is to say they provide the material basis for the first group. It is clear that the two groups live in a necessary and inegalitarian relationship to one another.

If one accepts for the moment the simplified and imaginary society, it is also clear that the two groups have specific, structured, and opposed interests. They have specific interests in the future of the society and their position therein. Their interests are structured by the hierarchical relationship of the groups. The interests are opposed in that the first group should want to preserve the society and maintain its group position, and the second group should want to destroy the society and change its group position.

Note carefully what we have accomplished here and its relatedness to that which precedes it. What we have accomplished is a social structural account of ideological hegemony and opposition. The account does not suggest that all members of a "class" see and think in terms of their interests or that there are only two possible views. This account does, however, expect and explain the existence of opposition views in societies structured, as is American society, on conflicts of group interest. Furthermore, in light of the limitations of the ideological hegemony literature, it is hoped that this argument will be illustrated by subsequent case studies of opposition environmental movements contained in this volume.

Marxist, elitist, and social stratification analyses have facilitated our understanding of the inegalitarian character of American society. Based on the foregoing propositional inventory, we turn our attention to the phenomenon of resource development. In what follows, an attempt will be made to explain the relationship between social stratification and resource development, and to anticipate its nature and direction.

1. We have characterized America as a class-structured society. For sociologists, this implies a determinate set of social, economic, and political relationships which persist over time. Furthermore, every determinate social structure rests on a historically specific pattern of resource development and distribution (e.g., productive relationships, level of technological development, distributive principles).

2. In addition, we have suggested that the integration of class-structured societies is achieved through the process of class domination and opposition. As traditionally defined, this process occurs simultaneously along three related dimensions: economic, political, and ideological. Struggles over the development and distribution of resources should also be expected to be contested along all three of these dimensions.

3. It has been a major effort of this section of the chapter to argue that the American class structure has undergone a fundamental historical transformation. On the one hand, we have differentiated the laissez-faire from the monopoly corporate and conglomerate periods of development, while, on the other, we have discussed the nationalization of the class structure.

4. Now it would seem to follow that the transformation of American social structure has involved changing patterns of class domination and opposition. Not only might the dimensions along which the struggles are contested vary, but the content of issues may change. As well, the sites of struggle may be local, regional, national, or worldwide.

5. Implicit to the argument presented in this chapter is the view that the class structuralization process has rested on an expanding pattern of resource development, i.e., the nationalization of the class structure, which began locally/regionally, became

national in scope, and ultimately led to a dependence on international resources. This evolving pattern of resource developments has provided the framework within which various dimensions and issues of class domination and opposition (including resource development and distribution) have occurred.

6. This expansionist pattern of resource development has reached its geographic and political limits--having penetrated the globe and facing mounting opposition from indigenous peoples.

7. The expansionist pattern having reached such limits, it would appear that preservation and maintenance of the existing national class structure presuppose a limited set of future options: new international sources of resources, heightened efforts to stabilize international sources of "essential" resources, and increasing efforts at domestic resource developments. These represent probable future avenues of resource development. None appear demonstrably more probable than others in the near future, and all three may occur simultaneously.

8. However, to the extent that dominant class interests become increasingly dependent on domestic resource development, we should expect increasing efforts at economic, political, and ideological class domination and opposition.

IMPLICATIONS FOR RESOURCE DEVELOPMENT

This chapter begins with the assumption that the phenomenon of resource development, the societal/natural resource relationship, is a problem of social stratification. The effort to trace out that relationship in a historically specific context led to a discussion of the stratification of American society. The nationalization of the class structure, it was argued, has depended on an expansionist resource development pattern, which has reached geographic and political limitations. In light of this, it is suggested that one probable response to this will be the intensification of efforts at domestic resource development, which predictably would carry in its wake growing domestic opposition, i.e., heightened domestic class domination and opposition over the utilization.

The direction of the societal/natural resource relationship is based on the following reasoning. Class structures stand in a determinate relationship to resource development patterns. They are also dynamic systems characterized by processes of domination and opposition. In the American case, the nationalization of the class structure has depended on a geographically expansionist resource development pattern which has reached worldwide proportions. This is to say that the class structuralization process has been based on changing sites and patterns of efforts at the domination of and opposition to resource development. In some part, domestic opposition to inequalities and resource development has been abated by the internationalization of resource development. However, this expansion has engendered its own resistance. This situation imposes a limited set of alternatives for the maintenance of American class structure. We anticipate intensified efforts at domestic resource development in the near future.

It is the major expectation of this chapter that the intensification of domestic resource development will lead to increasingly antagonistic relations of class domination and opposition, one face of which will be resource development patterns and the environment. As a specific aspect of the more general process of class domination and opposition, one element of the ideological struggle should focus on the societal/ natural resource relationship. Ideologically, the relationship should be contested within the framework suggested by the domestic social structure: the questions of private ownership of resources; resource development for private profit in an efficient fashion; and national policies for resource development, distribution, conservation, and replenishment. Growing awareness of an environmental contradiction might be cast in terms of private benefit at the expense of public cost.

Simply stated, the general implication of this chapter is that the expansionist resource development pattern which facilitated the nationalization of the class structure in American society has reached geographic and political limitations beyond which it cannot go and which leave its dominant interests limited, more costly, and less predictable access to world resources--and increasingly problematic domestic resources.

CHALLENGING PREVAILING ASSUMPTIONS

To demonstrate the distinctiveness of this stratificational approach to resource development, I will compare it to a recent theoretical treatment of environmental sociology. In formulating the outer area of environmental sociology, Catton and Dunlap (1978) have argued that a changed American society/environment relationship has called forth a new approach to understanding the relationship itself.

In their path-breaking essay, Catton and Dunlap called for supplanting the so-called "Human Exceptionalism Paradigm" with the "New Environmental Paradigm." In a society which had been characterized by high rates of hierarchical social mobility, material comfort, prosperity, and progress, American sociologists employed what is termed the Human Exceptionalism Paradigm. This paradigm is composed of the following propositions: (1) humans are culture bearers; (2) culture is variable and changes faster than biology; (3) human differences may be altered; and (4) thus, progress is possible, and problems are solvable (1978:42-43). However, in a society which has become increasingly characterized by growing environmental problems and constraints, American sociologists are expected to increasingly employ the New Environmental Paradigm. This paradigm is composed of the following propositions: (1) all species coexist in a state of interdependence; (2) human actions affect everything else; and (3) the world is finite and limited (1978:43,45).

While I remain unconvinced of the general argument of their paper that the shift of paradigms facilitates our understanding of stratification in contemporary American society, Catton and Dunlap have clearly made sociologists more conscious of the perspectival underpinnings of their work. However, in an important respect the argument presented in this chapter takes an opposing position, i.e., that the society/environment relationship must be placed in a historically specific stratificational context. The results of the position taken in this chapter also contribute to the clarification of sociologists' understanding of the society/environment relationship by challenging others among their prevailing assumptions.

The results of the tack taken in this chapter challenge several assumptions made by sociologists about the relationship between American society and its environmental context. Many American sociologists (of all stripes and suasions) adopt what I will facetiously term the "American Exceptionalism Paradigm." Proponents of American Exceptionalism adopt the view at varying levels of explicitness that America is best understood as a unique advanced industrial society. Many of these sociologists argue that this is the result of its having been geographically isolated, comparatively underpopulated, and endowed with an abundance of natural resources (Dowd 1977:49-52; Eitzen 1985:65-91). It is my view that adherents to both the Human Exceptionalism and the New Environmental paradigms may be wedded by their common adoption of the American Exceptionalism view.

The results of the foregoing analysis complicate the exceptionalist views on at least three specific counts. They do so by placing the American society/environment relationship in a world-historic context and making it problematic and consequential. In the first place, how did geographic isolation, size, and abundance of resources make a contribution to the structural and cultural uniqueness of American society? Second, even if we grant their finite character, can it be demonstrated that the sole or even most important issue surrounding resources is their diminution? And third, is systematic governmental planning and regulation of resource development a probable, if significant, response to the present situation?

In contrast to the exceptionalist view, the results of the analysis presented in this chapter suggest that: (1) the class structure of contemporary American society owes less to national geography, population, and resources and more to an expansionist pattern of global resource development; (2) the issue may be less the diminution of domestic resources and more international "class" domination and opposition to global resource development; and (3) growing geopolitical limitations will in all likelihood heighten awareness that domestic resource development has not been the result of systemic planning and regulation.

In conclusion, this chapter has attempted to establish the systemic character of resource development as a social problem. The approach has suggested that such developments may be seen as rooted in systemic inequality. Systemic inequality, the process of class structuralization, creates forces for both control and resistance. Furthermore, these forces are the framework within which resources are developed. It is hoped, then, that this chapter has provided a structural interpretation of the dynamics of resource development in contemporary American society, one that presupposes a systemic conception of social inequality and that leads to the problem areas posed in other chapters of this volume, i.e., the distribution of resource developments occupationally, racially, ethnically, and in terms of gender.

REFERENCES

Amory, C. 1947. *The Proper Bostonians*. New York: E. P. Dutton.
———. 1960. *Who Killed Society?* New York: Harper and Brothers.
Balbas, I. 1971. Modern capitalism and the state. *Monthly Review* 23(May):36-46.
Baltzell, E. D. 1966. *The Protestant Establishment: Aristocracy and Caste in America*. New York: Vintage Books.
Baran, P., and P. M. Sweezy. 1966. *Monopoly Capital*. New York: Monthly Review Press.

Barkley, R. 1955. The theory of the elite and the mythology of power. *Science and Society* 19:97-106.
Braverman, H. 1974. *Labor and Monopoly Capital: The Degradation of Work in the Twentieth Century*. New York: Monthly Review Press.
Cammett, J. 1967. *Antonio Gramsci and the Origins of Italian Communism*. Stanford, Calif.: Stanford University Press.
Catton, W. R., and R. E. Dunlap. 1978. Environmental sociology: A new paradigm. *The American Sociologist* 13:41-49.
Coulson, M., and C. Riddell. 1980. *Approaching Sociology*. 2d ed. London: Routledge and Kegan Paul.
Dahrendorf, R. 1959. *Class and Class Conflict in Industrial Society*. Stanford, Calif.: Stanford University Press.
Domhoff, G. W. 1967. *Who Rules America?* Englewood Cliffs, N.J.: Prentice-Hall.
Dowd, D. 1977. *The Twisted Dream: Capitalist Development in the United States since 1776*. 2d ed. Cambridge, Mass.: Winthrop Publishers.
Eitzen, D. S. 1985. *In Conflict and Order: Understanding Society*. Boston: Allyn and Bacon.
Gilbert, D., and J. A. Kahl. 1982. *The American Class Structure*. Homewood, Ill.: The Dorsey Press.
Gurley, J. 1970. Capitalism: The root of the problem. In *Up Against the American Myth*, comp. T. Christoffel, D. Finkelhor, D. Gilbarg, 48-55. New York: Holt, Rinehart and Winston.
Kavaler, L. 1960. *The Private World of High Society*. New York: Douglas McKay.
Kolko, G. 1969. *The Roots of American Foreign Policy*. Boston: Beacon Press.
Marx, K., and F. Engels. 1947. *The German Ideology*, ed. R. Pascal. New York: International Publishers.
Michels, R. 1962. *Political Parties: A Sociological Study of the Oligarchical Tendencies of Modern Democracy*, trans. E. and C. Paul. New York: Free Press.
Mills, C. W. 1956. *The Power Elite*. New York: Oxford University Press.
Mosca, G. 1939. *The Ruling Class*, trans. H. D. Kahn. New York: McGraw-Hill.
Nicolaus, M. 1967. Hegelian choreography and the capitalist dialectic. *Studies on the Left* 7:22-49.
Ollman, B. 1968. Marx's use of class. *American Journal of Sociology* 73:573-80.
Olsen, M., ed. 1970. *Power in Societies*. New York: Macmillan.
Ossowski, S. 1963. *Class Structure in the Social Consciousness*, trans. S. Patterson. New York: Free Press.
Parenti, M. 1978. *Power and the Powerless*. New York: St. Martin's Press.

Pareto, V. 1935. The Mind and Society, trans. A. Bongiorno and A. Livingston. 4 vols. New York: Harcourt, Brace.

Rothman, R. A. 1978. Inequality and Stratification in the United States. Englewood Cliffs, N.J.: Prentice-Hall.

Sallach, D. 1974. Class domination and ideological hegemony. Sociological Quarterly 15:38-50.

Stolzman, J., and H. Gamberg. 1973. Marxist class analysis versus stratification analysis as general approaches to social inequality. Mimeograph.

──────. 1974. Some misconceptions regarding the scientific status of Marxism. Mimeograph.

Wesolowski, W. 1979. Marx's theory of class domination. In Classes, Strata and Power, trans. G. Kolankiewicz, 9-77. London: Routledge and Kegan Paul.

2
Sociological Theory and the Differential Distribution of Impacts in Rural Resource Development Projects

Richard P. Gale

INTRODUCTION

The central focus of this chapter is the differential, hierarchical distribution of impacts of rural resource development projects (RRDPs). Many environmental issues have evolved to the point where they increasingly impact nonmetropolitan areas. Megaprojects devoted to mineral extraction, nuclear and fossil fuel power generation, and toxic and radioactive waste storage all have consequences for rural areas. This chapter presents an analytical perspective which emphasizes the effects of such projects on community power structures.

Preoccupation with the theoretical relevance of rural sociology has accelerated during recent years (Newby and Buttel 1980). In a recent attempt to remedy "a conspicuous absence" of theory "pertaining to structural linkages impinging upon nonmetropolitan social and economic change," Lovejoy and Krannich (1982:475) employ concepts such as dependency and neocolonialism, which are more often applied to Third World nations, "to delineate a more adequate theoretical approach to rural industrialization and other phenomena accompanying development and social change in nonmetropolitan sectors of advanced industrial societies" (1982:476). In a review essay titled "Resource Allocation and the State," Havens (1982) provides a broader theoretical framework for many of the issues discussed by Lovejoy and Krannich. One of Havens's major concerns is the failure of rural sociologists to include an analysis of the state as a key part of research on agrarian social change.

This chapter attempts to respond to some of these concerns by using the work of two urban-oriented conflict sociologists, Molotch (1976) and Whitt (1979), as the basis for an analysis of the distributional consequences of RRDPs. Molotch's "growth machine" illustrations refer primarily to urban land-use conflicts, and Whitt's "class-dialectical" power model is illustrated with examples drawn from a study of the San Francisco-area BART system and efforts to develop mass transit in Los Angeles. Because the roles of internal and external power structures have typically been important in how rural communities respond to resource development projects, applications of the concepts of Molotch and Whitt suggested in this chapter may facilitate a more complex analysis of the hierarchical consequences of change.

Most current project-specific community research, such as that employed in impact assessment studies, appears to adopt a functionalist framework. The approach presented here, in contrast, employs a conflict perspective.[1] The first two sections discuss central concepts from Molotch and Whitt, applied to rural resource developments. The third section presents a detailed theory of the distributional effects of rural resource development projects which integrates and extends the work of those authors. While the intent of this chapter is primarily theoretical, it will occasionally draw on the author's observations of conflict surrounding a large recreational and residential development in the McKenzie River Valley of Oregon.

MOLOTCH AND THE CITY AS A GROWTH MACHINE

Molotch's "growth machine" (GM) is a notion which combines ecological conceptions of land development with sociological assumptions of locality-based power and class hierarchy (for studies that use the GM concept, see Krannich and Humphrey 1983; Lyon et al. 1981). Although he argues "that the very essence of a locality is its operation as a growth machine," Molotch (1976:310) presents no formal definition. However, a definition which summarizes its key components is that a growth machine is a system of community-based politics which is based on the shared interests of land-owning elites in promoting community growth. One of Molotch's major emphases is the conceptualization of land (and natural resources) as a vehicle for profit. For Molotch, increased density of development is the key to profit. Thus, transforming a single-family parcel into one usable for multiple-family dwellings typically yields a substantial profit to the landowner, as does the conversion of fringe areas to residential, commercial, or industrial uses. Conceptualizing increased density as the key to land-based profits is perhaps even more appropriate to rural areas than to urban environments where the density or type of existing development may constrain or limit permissible options. Subdividing rural tracts, developing mining or recreational facilities in otherwise "unused" land, and increasing farmland productivity through irrigation are all examples of profit-yielding increases in development density. Nearly all RRDPs involve some increase in density. In contrast, some urban projects may involve a shift in populations, but relatively little change (or even a reduction) in the density of development. For example, urban gentrification may include a reduction in density where central city apartments are converted into condominiums.

Molotch then argues that many land-use conflicts within communities involve disputes over where development (and increased densities) shall occur. These disputes occur within the context of more general agreement (among landowners and others who may profit from density increases) that growth is desirable. "Each unit of a community strives, at the expense of the others, to enhance the land-use potential of the parcels with which it is associated" (1976:311). This generalization also applies to rural areas, but in a more complex way. Conflict over rural development projects may focus on both the location and the timing of projects. That is, although it may not be accurate to assume (as is implicit in this discussion) that nearly all rural landowners have some vested interest in growth and development, rural landowner opposition that appears to be focused on the location of projects ("not on my land") may instead attempt to delay current development to enhance future options. While this also occurs in urban areas, options for delay may be fewer where urban areas feel they must respond to pressing demands for housing and industrial land.

Intra-area disputes over rural project siting may also be conditioned by the multiple roles played by land-controlling or land-owning government agencies, such as the Corps of Engineers, the U.S. Forest Service, and the Bureau of Land Management. In some instances, these agencies may be active participants, behaving like private GMs in attempting to insure that developments occur on their land at the expense of other agencies and private landowners. They may also strive to limit development on lands under their jurisdiction. In other cases, they may act as "brokers," negotiating conflicts between other landowners. In this latter case, they may assume an "objective," independent posture regarding project siting, while continuing to support general progrowth goals which assure that the project will be located somewhere within their sphere of influence and that development will assist agency interests such as personnel and budget expansion and generation of constituency support (Johnson 1982).

Another concept central to the growth machine model is obtaining financing to create infrastructure systems which are among the preconditions of growth. In an attempt "to achieve a common land-enhancement scheme,"

> ... an attempt is made to use government to gain those resources which will enhance the growth potential of the area unit in question. Often, the governmental level where action is needed is at least one level higher than the community from which the activism springs (Molotch 1976:311-12).

Molotch views government as "the arena in which land-use interest groups compete for public money and attempt to mold those decisions which will determine the land-use outcomes" (1976:312). How these preconditions of growth are distributed may significantly alter access to potentially developable resources, as well as affect attractiveness of the area to external developers, who are members of extracommunal, regional GMs.

Issues concerning infrastructure development and the governmental level (or corporate unit) most appropriate, or most likely, to provide financing are central to rural development projects. One strategy for obtaining payment of large-scale "front end" costs is to seek funding from extralocal governmental units such as counties, states, or the federal government. Another is to require new industries to make advance tax payments to finance infrastructure improvements.

Rural areas are also likely to have relatively primitive infrastructure systems. Where constructing these preconditions of growth requires substantial public investment, a GM may seek financing to bring such systems to a level of development that will both satisfy requirements of the project and attract additional growth. Providing these preconditions may also have direct impacts on rural capitalists. To the extent that project-related infrastructure improvements improve rural area access, the areas may become suitable for additional externally generated development. However, at some point, these developments, and their associated infrastructure costs, may result in a decline of power for rural capitalists and the replacement of a locally based GM with one that is regional, national, or even international.

Molotch notes that an additional component of the preconditions of growth is the "business climate," including "reasonable" taxes, "good" labor relations, and minimal overt social conflict (1976:312). Control over, or manipulation of, the development ideology is a key development feature in rural areas. In contrast to the more unified or homogeneous progrowth ideology of small city GMs, rural areas may reflect substantially more diversity. For example, growth ideologies appropriate to existing development, such as agriculture and

forestry, may not be transferable to those supporting a new project, such as a destination ski resort.
Molotch also draws on Edelman (1964) in distinguishing between two kinds of community issues.

First there is the "symbolic" politics which comprises the "big issues" of public morality and the symbolic reforms featured in the headlines and editorials of the daily press. The other politics is the process through which goods and services actually come to be distributed in the society. (Molotch 1976:313)

It is this latter "welfare" politics that relates to growth and to the distribution of its costs and benefits. In rural areas, greater cultural homogeneity may reinforce commitment to symbolic issues which override localized disagreement over the location of new projects. One consequence of this cultural commitment is that symbolic issues may surface in conflicts over rural projects. Indeed, perceived urban/rural cultural differences may be among the reasons why rural capitalists oppose new projects.
To the extent that rural areas are more likely to favor a laissez-faire regulatory system, and reflect a lower "density" of government, information about project costs and benefits is likely to be unequally distributed within rural areas. One function of government in community controversies is to encourage public discussion of issues. Governments and local newspapers, however, may be highly selective in the information they choose to share publicly (Molotch 1979). Further, statistical information on economic issues may be less available in rural areas. Thus, subordinate groups wishing to influence new projects face two obstacles--inexperience in using governmental resources to pursue interests and inadequate information about both existing and potential economic issues relevant to the area.
There may also be variability in the types of economic issues relevant to RRDPs. Some, such as employment, stimulation of economic activity, and higher incomes, may be consciously used to elicit project support. These positive impacts may be portrayed by dominant-class representatives as accruing disproportionately to the subordinate class. Other economic impacts, such as profits from land development and new commercial ventures, may be more positively distributed, and, as in urban areas, these may receive less public discussion. However, where rural capitalists are uncertain or divided concerning the distribution of economic impacts, these issues may receive more public perusal. (This may be especially likely where projects are novel to the area, imply a substantial increase in

governmental involvement, or are sponsored by external dominant interests.)

Although Molotch focuses on conflicts among members of the local GM, he also notes that several groups are less likely to become involved in intralocality debates, preferring instead to remain above these disputes, while continuing to favor aggregate growth of a locality (1976:315). Metropolitan newspapers and leaders of public or quasi-public agencies, such as universities, are examples.

In rural areas, these institutions may play a somewhat different role. For example, metropolitan newspapers from distant urban areas oppose rural projects that threaten recreational areas or downstream or downwind water or air quality. Local newspapers may take on the pro-aggregate growth stance more typical of metropolitan newspapers, choosing not to endorse a project location or to comment on other details likely to provoke conflict within the local GM. Rural representatives of universities, such as the Agricultural Extension Service, may favor aggregate growth, or they may become involved in GM intra-area disputes over the location of new projects. Other groups which may choose not to become involved in locational disputes, or may even oppose projects, include owners of recreational property and managers employed by corporations headquartered elsewhere (who are also less likely to manifest much interest in local growth in urban environments [Molotch 1976:317]). The stance taken by personnel employed by public agencies is problematic and depends on the extent to which they reflect agency interests or more personal interests as local residents. Typically, they are not members of the local GM, unless they, too, are local property owners and investors.

WHITT'S CLASS-DIALECTIC MODEL

The first major feature of the class-dialectic model is the conceptualization of the class system as composed of two competing groups--dominant and subordinate. In contrast to the power elite model, the class-dialectic model points to divergence and conflict within the dominant class. Another important component of the power structure, although not explicitly treated as such by Whitt, is the state. While the state is typically viewed as serving dominant-class interests, Whitt (1979:83) also notes that the state requires a degree of autonomy from segments of the dominant class and consequently avoids embroilment in intraclass conflicts.

This perspective undergoes several modifications when applied to rural areas. First, somewhat autonomous subcultures may crosscut the prevailing dominant/subordinate class order. Rural and small town residence, agricultural employment or ownership of agricultural (or other natural resource) lands, and a range of urban/rural differences have the potential for subdividing the class system. Thus, dominant/subordinate relationships among small town residents, or among rural landowners, may be distinct from those among urban dwellers.

It is also possible that the basis for class assignment, which Whitt does not deal with, may differ in rural, small town, and urban environments. Within different environments, individuals or family units may find themselves considered as part of the dominant or subordinate class. Further, class assignment may be altered by rapid change in rural areas. Immigrants from urban environments may provoke a major modification of dominant/subordinate relationships or even the imposition of a new urban-based dominant class on top of the existing rural or small town dominant class. Local elites thus find themselves pushed downward, into an expanding subordinate class.

The dominant/subordinate distinction is also the basis for an understanding of the distribution of impacts of RRDPs. An initial analytical question is the extent to which the distribution of impacts is in accord with the existing class system. Does the dominant class obtain the bulk of the benefits, while the subordinate class suffers most of the costs? Are impacts distributed, either inadvertently or by design, so as to alter dominant and subordinate class composition? Do impacts emerge as major criteria in an altered rural class system? Do impacts affect the relevance of subcultural designations which have previously cut across class lines? Does class become more important as a consequence of the project?[2]

A second major feature of the class-dialectic model is the need of the dominant class for legitimacy and issue-specific responses from the subordinate class.

> This need, from the standpoint of dominant classes, for a certain level of acquiescence on the part of subordinate classes leads to the institution of various methods aimed at attaining social control, mass persuasion (cf. Schiller, 1969), and the maintenance of the legitimacy (Miliband, 1969) of present institutional structures upon which class hegemony is based. . . . the class-dialectic model . . . points to the seeking of legitimacy as a further restriction on the actions of the dominant class (Whitt 1979:96-97).

A key determinant of potential subordinate-class power is the amount of cooperation from subordinate classes needed to maintain dominant-class legitimacy, or, at least, to continue the acquiescence of the subordinate class in a rapidly changing environment.[3] In RRDPs, the role available to subordinate groups may vary. For example, externally "imposed" projects may require little in addition to minimal acquiescence from rural subordinate groups, as well as from rural dominant-class interests. Conversely, where controversy requires local dominant groups to seek local support, the ability to withhold legitimacy may be a key vehicle for the temporary gaining of power by a segment of the rural subordinate class. (Obviously, a strategy for rural subordinate groups wishing to capitalize on a project to further their own interests is to link project approval to the basis for continuing legitimacy of the local dominant class.)

The existing basis of interclass legitimacy may be tied to systems for local natural resource allocation decisions. Examples include the purchase of timber from national forests (Colfer and Colfer 1978) and rural land-use and zoning regulations. Where a new project is of the type or magnitude to require a major alteration of this system, the project may have a significant impact on interclass legitimacy. For example, local dominant-class interests in a rural Oregon area, faced with a proposal for a large riverfront recreational and housing development to be constructed by a large, multinational timber company, found existing zoning regulations useless in fighting the projects and instead based their fight against the project on statewide land-use goals which they had previously opposed.

The antiproject campaign of the dominant group affected interclass relations in two ways. First, their traditional allies, local working- and middle-class residents, employed by the company or in closely related woods products industries, were reluctant to attack the company. This reluctance reduced the legitimacy of local dominants as antiproject spokesmen; indeed, project opponents were surprised, and dismayed, when a local proproject group suddenly appeared at a public hearing. Second, the opposition campaign attracted surprisingly little attention from nearby middle-class urban environmentalists, despite their long-standing struggles with the company about air and water pollution from its mill and their efforts to preserve riverfront access. Thus, a major land-use shift, from timber management to residential development, split apart the traditional alliance of dominant and subdominant locals, threatening the legitimacy and power of the once-dominant group. New projects that do not use traditional resource systems may, therefore, threaten the existing basis for rural class relationships.

Potential local subordinate-class divisions surrounding likely project impacts also influence dominant-group legitimacy. Subordinate-class divisions may disengage a segment of the local subordinate class from the dominant class, making them, in effect, "up for grabs" from the perspective of external dominant classes seeking a measure of locally based legitimacy. One possibility is capture by external dominant-class project sponsors or proponents. Another is an attempt by urban environmentalists (who may be marginal members of an urban dominant class) to gain assistance from local, disengaged subordinate groups in opposing the project. In summary, RRDPs have the potential to alter the existing basis for legitimacy of local dominant groups. From the perspective of these groups, "delegitimation" is a potential project outcome and, in fact, may be one basis for their opposition to a project.

Whitt (1979:97-98) also explores several "contradictions which the dominant class must face," and presents these as dichotomous choices which can divide dominant classes, thereby permitting the exercise of limited power by a segment of the subordinate class. The first describes the extent to which a market economy is to prevail, in contrast to the need for a degree of economic planning. Rural areas are often characterized by a highly segmented economy, involving some linkages to an urban, regional economic system, local bartering and exchange, and the intrusion of external market adjustment and price alteration systems, such as federal timber sales and dairy price supports. These features complicate disputes over the need for economic planning or some other modification of a free-market system. RRDPs often signal an important economic change, stimulating a market economy response (land is subdivided and sold; speculation in housing increases), while simultaneously provoking a retreat from a market economy approach to the provision of local services (water, sewage. transportation). New development may also link the economy to a different external market system. All of these factors suggest that new projects may stimulate intercapitalist conflict over the preferred economic system.

Other features of rural economies might be summarized as "cooperation within the context of capitalism." For example, arrangements for the marketing of crops and the purchase of farm supplies have often included the formation of a cooperative. Extended barter systems may also be seen as informal cooperatives. However, these organizations typically operate as unified capitalist organizations when dealing with external, corporate units. New projects may disrupt existing formal and informal cooperatives. Some participants may decide to join new, externally linked economic units. The potential for disruption is also increased because existing cooperatives are unlikely to be organizationally capable of responding to new external organizational units, such as large, urban-oriented bureaucracies and multinational corporations.

A second contradiction deals with how public services are to be supplied, and whether they are to be sold as private goods or provided as public services (Whitt 1979:97). A key characteristic of the provision of services is local control. While Molotch (1976:312) suggests that public financing will always be sought, existing, preproject conditions in rural areas may involve the private provision of services, or supply through some limited market mechanism, such as a cooperative. Thus, major projects are likely to impact the existing provision of services and to generate a search for ways to minimize costs for local dominant classes.

A third issue or contradiction mentioned by Whitt (1979:97) is "the competition among cities and among capitalists for growth-generating development vs. coherent structure and regularity in urban development." As with the previous issue, a major factor is the differing levels of existing system development in urban and rural areas. That is, to the extent that zoning and land-use planning have the potential for creating a minimal level of "coherent structure and regularity," the existence and effectiveness of these systems may be limited by usual rural-based opposition. And, where conscious efforts to secure rural development projects are new, rural capitalists are likely to be inexperienced in competing with other rural areas and towns for development.

A related issue is the level at which such intercapitalist conflict will occur and its impact on local dominant classes. For example, rural groups will have little influence where conflict to secure projects is at the regional level. Local interests concerned about a project sponsored by the Bonneville Power Administration would probably channel their comments through regional trade associations composed of public utility districts or rural electric cooperatives. Conflict at the county level, in contrast, may more directly involve local dominant-class groups and may, in fact, reflect a tradition of intercounty competition. Conflict between locally based capitalists is more likely to occur within counties, paralleling the intracity conflicts over the location of development that are the focus of Molotch. As the conflict moves "upward," and beyond the borders of the local community, conflict or disunity among local capitalists becomes increasingly dysfunctional.

Another issue is who benefits from "coherent structure and regularity . . . in development" (Whitt 1979: 97). From one perspective, it is in the best interests of small-scale local capitalists to oppose such structures as complex zoning and land-use regulations because of increased expansion costs for local enterprises. On a statewide or regional basis, such regulations may benefit large corporations seeking large areas for development. A final point concerns the impact of local traditions with respect to minimally regulated growth-oriented conflict and procedures which assure coherence and regularity. One impact of new projects may be to alter or disrupt existing allocative mechanisms. From the perspective of local capitalists, then, the challenge is to seize control of the "new regularity" associated with the project.

A DISTRIBUTIONAL FRAMEWORK FOR RURAL
DEVELOPMENT IMPACTS

This section applies a conflict-oriented perspective to rural development impacts in a way that attempts to integrate and extend the work of Molotch and Whitt discussed above. The framework focuses on social conditions surrounding RRDPs from immediately prior to the transformation of the area as a consequence of major project impacts.

System Assumptions

Multiple Growth Machines and Emergent Rural Conflict. The general framework posits the existence of multiple, layered growth machines, which compete both within themselves and between each other. RRDPs may thus elicit involvement by regional, urban, small city, town, and rural- area growth machines. Their linkages to the geographical area directly affected by the project are diverse and are not limited to direct economic ties, such as resource ownership.

The complexity of these multiple growth machines is such that the consensus regarding the desirability of growth suggested by Molotch (1976:310) may, at times, be significantly reduced by the intercapitalist conflicts outlined by Whitt (1979:97-98). In relatively undeveloped rural areas, issues such as prepayment of infrastructure costs and the extensiveness of planning are sufficiently close to fundamental questions regarding growth that their potentially divisive impact on GMs is higher than in urban areas.

The fragility of the basis of legitimacy of rural growth machines results from the changes in a variety of social relationships. That is, rural growth machine legitimacy may rely on factors such as family ties and paternalistic employment relationships which are no longer appropriate to rural areas with extracommunal linkages. An additional consideration is variation in the bases and relative strength of legitimacy among the different GM layers.

These two fundamental characteristics of the several growth machines--fragility of legitimacy (especially in rural areas) and varying bases of legitimacy--set the stage for several different types of conflict, some of which are discussed by Whitt. One useful distinction is between inter- and intra-growth machine conflict. Some of the conflicts described by Whitt may emerge between GMs, especially where different GM layers (rural locality, adjacent urban area) disagree over the optimum rate of growth and development. Conflict may also occur within a GM layer over issues such as government intervention and infrastructure financing (Whitt 1979:97-98).

It is also likely that the existence or involvement of different GMs will influence conflict over the location of development. An urban-based GM may side with one faction in a locational dispute among members of a predominantly rural GM. In this instance, some of the intraclass divisions suggested by Whitt may become the focus of disputes over the location of RRDPs.

Equilibrium "Pockets" and Equilibrium as a Rural Ideology. This framework suggests the possibility of subsystems within which relative equilibrium prevails. Although rejecting functionalist equilibrium assumptions, the framework does allow for geographical or cultural areas that approximate a state of relative equilibrium, particularly when contrasted with urban areas.

For several reasons, an understanding of these equilibrium pockets or enclaves is important for an analysis of rural project impacts. These areas are often those most likely to undergo significant change. In some instances, it is the appearance at least of equilibrium that attracts recreational and residential developments designed for urbanites. Further, the basis for the existing equilibrium may be unfamiliar or unknown to outsiders. Projects that inadvertently disturb the basis for this equilibrium may provoke unexpected opposition by local publics or by nonlocal interests seeking a community-based rationale for project opposition. In addition, characteristics of these equilibrium pockets, such as history, location, appearance, and local use, may have important symbolic value during periods of rapid change.

In situations where equilibrium is being threatened (or describes an environment that has disappeared), "equilibrium" may emerge as an important rural ideology. Paradoxically, it may encourage support for rural- or locality-based GMs. In addition to the commercial and public relations value of rural equilibrium themes which lure urban investors and part-time residents, there are several possible functions for an equilibrium ideology as a rural-based false consciousness. First, it directs attention away from obvious, urbanizing impacts. This may calm locals worried about adverse impacts of change. It is also a partial rural adaptation of the favorable "business climate" maintained by urban GMs (Molotch 1976:312-13). That is, an image of rural equilibrium may fit with the image sought by urban-based developers. Second, an emphasis on equilibrium by local, rural GMs may provide a vehicle by which these interests can convince concerned locals that these local interests are not allied with urban project sponsors or proponents. Local GMs may thus seek to "defend" rural equilibrium against distant urban forces (while simultaneously preparing to take maximum advantage of project impacts). Third, an equilibrium ideology may provide a strategy whereby rural GMs can retain some control over services or sectors of the economy which will, with project development, be increasingly controlled by extracommunal forces. For example, maintenance of an equilibrium ideology may minimize awareness by local publics of those impending changes that, if realized, would stimulate project opposition or efforts to transfer privately held infrastructure services to the public sector (at some loss to the local GM).

Response to Change

Reduced Boundary Maintenance Capability and Altered Subsystem Relationships. Boundary maintenance systems are those which distinguish rural areas from one another and from adjacent urban areas. Political boundaries, geographical features, economic marketing areas, and transportation routes are examples. Nearly all of the changes associated with major rural projects challenge, strain, or otherwise impact existing rural boundary maintenance systems and control over such systems. An initial response may be to channel resources into boundary defense and preservation. Indeed, several aspects of the intracapitalist conflicts noted by Whitt (and reviewed earlier in this chapter) can be understood in terms of boundary maintenance issues, especially when placed in a rural context. Thus RRDPs that require a lengthy and complex, government-controlled planning process commit rural dominant classes to time frames beyond their control. Rural capitalists who follow their urban counterparts in what Molotch terms "asking the next level up" must similarly deal with the loss of autonomy that accompanies this external involvement. This loss includes the reduced ability of rural growth machines to control or manipulate system boundaries. Conflict over projects may include disagreement on the extent to which area resources should be used to maintain (or alter) system boundaries.

The Relative Influence of Internally and Externally Generated Change. Internally generated change is initiated in the local community. Externally generated change is initiated elsewhere. A characteristic impact of RRDPs is significant alteration in the balance of internally and externally generated change. Multiple effects include increased strain on system abilities to manage internally generated change and the need to develop mechanisms for handling vastly increased amounts of externally generated change. In addition, RRDPs affect local systems by enlarging the group from which internally generated change emanates, particularly where change increases the power of previously suppressed groups. The new participation of these groups is especially likely where they become allied with external forces or where, as Whitt suggests, segments of the power structure seek their direct support in promoting or resisting change.

Exponential Rate of Change. The likely rate of change in areas soon to be impacted by rural projects may encompass a relatively long period (even including the initial project phases) during which the rate of change differs little from that to which the area has been accustomed. This period may be followed by a time of rapid, cumulative change, resulting in irreversible community impacts. Once this time of rapid change has begun, it may be too late for the community to alter the trajectory of change.

The rate of change affects the ability of local GMs to adapt to, and hopefully influence, community change. A basic GM position is likely to be "we agree on the desirability of that rate of growth which will not unduly alter existing intramachine relationships." A long-lead explosive growth pattern, of course, will eventually exceed these limits, provoking major changes in local GMs.

It is also likely that the position of each relevant growth machine on the intercapitalist issues outlined by Whitt is specific to a targeted rate of growth. For example, under locally agreed-upon conditions of relatively stable rural growth, members may favor private provision of infrastructure services and minimal formalized planning, while their growth machine counterparts in adjacent cities may favor the opposite. Under conditions of more rapid growth, rural interests may opt for public infrastructure financing and a formal planning process that would at least stabilize preproject land uses.

Externally Imposed Procedures for Responding to Change. RRDPs usually mean highly formalized, bureaucratized, technically sophisticated planning and impact analysis procedures. Typically (but not exclusively, as in the case of large corporate ventures), these are somehow linked to state involvement in the project. Government-assisted financing, state provision of infrastructure services, and analysis of impacts (as in environmental impact statements) are, together with provisions for data collection and monitoring, parts of the package which may accompany state involvement. Further, these procedures are not confined to project design and impact analysis, but extend as well to efforts to mitigate adverse impacts. Provisions for project employee housing, transportation and other services, especially for projects located in isolated rural areas, and systems required for mitigation of other environmental impacts all typically involve intrusion of systems controlled by forces external to the community.

Second, RRDPs often produce alterations in how to think about change. Such projects immediately connect rural areas to larger regional, national, and even international populations. Project development is often in the interests of distant consumers with little understanding of localized effects associated with product manufacture. Numerically, and politically, the interests of local groups may pale in comparison to those of a state or region. Analyses of project benefits and costs--what might be labeled as equity or distributional effects--may be cast in terms of regional, instead of local, impacts and "tradeoffs" and project contributions to international trade.

Third, it may be difficult for local rural growth machines to uniformly define their stance to the project and to present these views via externally generated and controlled channels. Their posture may be more complex than simply that local GMs always favor growth; they are likely to prefer projects that promise relatively direct economic benefits. Large, externally generated projects may thus compete with the aspirations of local developers, particularly when locally generated small-scale projects are constrained by land-use regulations and planning policies not applicable to relatively self-contained outside projects. In Oregon, rural landowners found it difficult to endorse a large recreational and residential project proposed for their area by a multinational corporation when their own subdivision plans were severely limited by county regulations and state land-use goals. The impact of these restrictions on the proposed development was minimized because, unlike local projects, this plan incorporated its own sewer, water, and security systems. Further complicating the posture of local GMs are instances where project developers are corporations that have previously engaged in resource development activities strongly supported by local GMs. In the Oregon example, Weyerhaeuser Corporation, the project proponent, had long enjoyed strong community support as the area's primary industrial employer in its timberland, sawmill, and papermaking operations. People were reluctant to attack Weyerhaeuser directly in public hearings and generally confined their protests to lawn signs gently admonishing the company to "grow trees, not houses."

Distribution of Impacts

Invasion of New, Culturally Distinct Impacts. A fundamental characteristic of change attributable to RRDPs is the arrival of new, distinct cultural traits, such as consumer goods, interaction patterns, and leisure activities. A variety of frameworks have been used to summarize these changes, and most rely on the fundamental insights of classical theorists such as Durkheim and Toennies. These frameworks typically posit a series of changes in the direction of increased complexity and impersonality. A somewhat more conflict-oriented perspective would conceive rural lifestyles as unequally layered subcultures, each of which is in some ways either linked to, or parallel with, an urban counterpart. Rural dominant classes may be linked to their urban counterparts through contributions to the financial infrastructure (banking and taxation), while rural subordinate groups and their urban peers may share perspectives relating to work organization. Placing issues of cultural change in this context, then, directs attention to issues such as whose culture is to be imported, what differential economic benefits attach to new cultural patterns, and to what extent will new patterns integrate with, or displace, existing patterns.

The issue of whose culture penetrates rural areas has several facets. First is control over the cultural transmission system. Media are the most obvious carriers, and one can expect major loss of power for rural-based media, with a consequent, parallel loss of local GM ability to define relevant "issues" (Molotch). Retail stores and other services offered by regional, national, and multinational entities are additional entrants into the rural environment.

Issues concerning the relative mesh or compatibility between existing rural culture and that imposed by RRDPs must, given the perspective of this chapter, be viewed in terms of power relationships. Thus, cultural attributes of rural subordinate groups are those most vulnerable to displacement. Although this displacement is most likely to occur via the invasion of urban-based marketing systems, when local GMs favor cultural change among subordinate groups, they may compete with urban interests to supply these people with new cultural traits.

In addition, the cultural attributes of local GMs themselves may be displaced. Instrumental to this change may be exposure to systems such as local and regional governments which are directly linked to RRDPs. Recreational and other social contacts between urban and rural GMs may induce cultural change, particularly where RRDPs include relocation of urban GM representatives into rural areas.

Finally, it is not possible a priori to predict which cultural traits will best resist external challenges. Attributes central to the identity of both dominant and subordinate rural classes may be particularly strong. A good example is moral-value-based conflict over construction of large ski resorts in traditional Mormon communities in Utah. A second category of change-resistant traits includes those instrumental in preserving legitimacy and control of rural GMs and dominant classes. Basic rural values and behaviors which reinforce locality-based social control may be defended by local GMs who regard these "symbolic," moral, and normative values as central to their control of local populations. Thus, when seen as threatening to local GM interests, even "symbolic" issues are defined in "welfare," distributional terms. For example, local GMs may react to the housing of project workers in their community on the basis of moral behavioral issues, such as drinking, as well as in terms of their fears that new, possibly competitive, businesses will also be drawn to the community.

Dominant-Class Involvement in Marketing of Previously Nonmarketed Goods. A key feature of preproject rural social systems is the distribution of a variety of nonmarketed goods, from agricultural products to outdoor recreation opportunities, through informal barter of local welfare systems. Existing nonmarket arrangements reflect a variety of factors, including investment decisions by local dominant classes, potentially higher costs for marketed goods and services, a subordinate class with limited economic resources, and a relatively small potential clientele for such goods and services.

RRDPs are likely to affect these systems in two ways: encouragement of the marketing of previously nonmarketed goods and increases in the availability of nonmarketed public services. With regard to population-generated increases in demand, the interests of both local and external groups in profiting from the provision of previously nonmarketed goods and the demands of newly relocated urban residents for more sophisticated goods and services may all contribute to a major change in the way in which many goods (often those identified as central to rural lifestyles) are provided. Informal fishing and camping sites become available for fees, campgrounds are upgraded and their fees increased, and the handy neighbor down the road incorporates as "Bill's Electric."

The second change along a market/nonmarket dimension is an increase in the availability of typically nonmarketed public services. In addition to the increased provision of user-paid infrastructure services (sewer, water, public transportation), other services offered without charge or financed by (also increasing) taxes become available. Libraries, adult education, physical and mental health services, and even tools and implements may be provided by public agencies and, in some instances, be used as inducements to local subordinate classes for support of GM-favored RRDPs.

Decline or Collapse of Preproject Support Systems. Preproject support systems include local infrastructures (roads, public utilities, schools), existing economic relationships, and local units of extracommunal systems (corporations, government agencies--such as the U.S. Forest Service and the Bureau of Land Management) which support locally based GMs and existing dominant/subordinate class relationships The powers of the dominant class include allocation of these services, and it can be assumed that, in part, the allocation also reflects the results of competition within the local GM concerning the location and distribution of services within the local area. To extend Molotch's analogy, these are the systems that fuel and sustain the operation of local GMs. RRDPs are likely to significantly strain the operation of these systems. Indeed, documentation of socioeconomic impacts often focuses on the consequences of change for these organized systems.

Especially notable may be the impact of major rural projects on the ability of natural resource bureaucracies to continue active support of local GM interests. In general, major RRDPs reduce the ability of local governments (and locality-based natural resource bureaucracies) to support existing local dominant-class and GM relationships. When existing agencies are project sponsors, the likely outcome is substantial increase in agency resources combined with possible reduction in the autonomy of local units because decision-making and even data-collection responsibilities are moved to regional offices. In addition, projects sponsored by others may displace agency responsibilities or reduce agency influence when the magnitude of the new projects dwarfs existing agency programs, thus further eroding support of the local GM.

Dramatic Change in Role of Government. Dispersed throughout the above discussion are many references to the changing role of the state which accompanies the evolution of RRDPs. This section discusses four key dimensions. These are (1) reduction in the traditional distributional roles of rural government; (2) imposition of policies of larger governments on rural areas; (3) local government monitoring of external impact; and (4) creation of RRDP quasi-governmental units.

While the traditional roles of rural government obviously vary, an appropriate characterization, in contrast to urban governments, includes lower density, extensive informal ties to local GMs, and freedom to provide benefits to these groups. The combined impact of changes associated with RRDPs may severely curtail the ability of traditional rural governments to retain this benign, distributional posture. Limited local government resources are, as noted above, likely to be strained by new infrastructure requirements, and deliberations on growth-related issues may force these governments into a more open, pluralistic arena. Groups other than those traditionally involved may claim their share of local government resources, whether as newcomers to the area or as existing subordinate-class groups struggling to deal with project impacts on their lives. These and other pressures may force rural governments into mediating between competing groups.

RRDPs almost always involve the imposition of larger, previously external governments. County governments may increase involvement in areas such as land-use policy, rural zoning, coordination of development in unincorporated areas, and sponsorship of new communities through the creation of "new development centers." State government involvement may take diverse forms, ranging from state financing and construction of major infrastructure improvements, such as highways, to application of statewide land-use goals and policies to evaluate proposed RRDPs. Regional and national governments may become involved as direct project sponsors, e.g., the nuclear power plant of the Washington Public Power Supply System and the hydroelectric projects of the Corps of Engineers; as coordinating agencies, e.g., the U.S. Forest Service role in the development of ski areas; and as reviewers of projects and impacts through the preparation or review of environmental impact statements. The consequence of these new invasions of government is the presence of multiple, potentially competing governmental layers, which increasingly intrude upon the daily lives of rural people.

As mentioned previously, Molotch emphasizes efforts by local GMs to locate a different level of government to finance growth-facilitating infrastructure improvements. This search for alternative funding accelerates with RRDPs, and, as noted elsewhere in this chapter, this new money guarantees increased governmental involvement. Concurrent with this involvement is the increased necessity for local governments to be sensitive to matters of intergovernmental relationships. Relations with the next state layer (or another unit of infrastructure financing) are particularly crucial if the money is to be secured. Thus, rural governments may devote substantial time and dollars to relationships with counties and intracounty units (such as councils of government). Rural governments may also journey to state capitals and to Washington to lobby for project construction and impact mitigation monies.

Finally, there are several ways in which RRDPs can directly influence the proliferation of governmental agencies. Most typical is project-related population change that results in the creation of new governmental units. Such units may appear as special districts for services such as sewage, water, fire protection, and cable television, or as newly incorporated communities. New community formation can occur with the establishment of "project city" communities, the development of new towns (such as ski resorts), and the utilization of previously unincorporated communities which encompass little more than project boundaries, thus avoiding taxes which would occur if the project was annexed to a nearby community. Most recently, Alaska logging camps have been incorporating to obtain revenue-sharing and taxation benefits.

A distributional effects perspective incorporates the ideas of Molotch and Whitt into all of these aspects of the changing role of the state. All of the four changes have impacts on the relative power of different GMs. All have, as well, consequences for the ability of the state to distribute costs and benefits of RRDPs. Most fundamentally, all suggest an increased role for government in the lives of rural residents.

CONCLUSION

A major implication of the concept presented here is that analyses of RRDPs which give only minimal attention to class-based impacts are likely to neglect a key dynamic underlying project impacts and community response. Further, such analyses are likely to overlook conflicts that emerge between local and external elites struggling to direct project-related growth in ways favorable to their own interests. In many ways, of course, this emphasis is hardly novel; a systematic effort to predict impacts in terms of subcultures could well lead to an approximation of the class-based approach suggested here. However, this approach provides a strategy for examining more than the layering of subcultures: The focus is also on the interaction within and between social strata.

In addition to the suggestion that cultural analyses should pay more attention to subcultural layering, the framework presented here has a further implication related to life within the layers. The political economy emphasis of Molotch, Whitt, and others focuses on the structure of interclass relationships without portraying much of the internal texture of life within each layer. We know what GMs fight for, but we know little of the lives of those within locality-based GMs. Applying a cultural approach to the political and economic structure outlined in this chapter might yield a more effective enthnography of local growth impacts.

In summary, the framework presented here uses two recent contributions to conflict theory to develop a schema for the analysis of rural resource development projects. The underlying assumptions posit a stratified rural preproject political structure within which system equilibrium serves as an ideology which helps maintain rural dominant-class legitimacy. This system undergoes a dramatic change with the emergence of major resource development projects. The framework outlines an approach to the analysis of these changes which emphasizes class-based responses to the benefits and costs of such projects, facilitating more detailed social analysis of rural resource development projects.

Finally, field application of the framework presented in this chapter may increase opportunities for the participation of subordinate groups in the process of social change. A fundamental message of both Molotch and Whitt is that growth generates conflict within community-based dominant groups. This conflict may provide access for the interests of subordinate groups, particularly where community autonomy is threatened by large-scale, externally generated change. As recipients of these changes, local communities typically struggle to integrate these changes into existing lifestyles and power structures. The purpose of this chapter has been to develop an understanding of resource-dependent communities which would increase the probability that the distribution of benefits of RRDPs would improve the quality of life for those asked to bear the most direct impacts, while preserving the range of lifestyles within nonmetropolitan America.

NOTES

1. The implicit referent for this discussion is a preproject rural social system. While it is unlikely that any area would actually manifest the features predicted by either ideal/typical characteristic, the opposing functionalist and conflict theories are relevant to this chapter and form a baseline for it. Further, they are reflected in existing approaches to the analysis of rural areas. For example, classic community study sociology and most approaches to social impact

assessment which are applied to projects in such areas draw heavily on the functionalist perspective (see Gale 1984). While the conflict perspective is relatively new to analyses of either rural conditions or social impacts, there are some recent examples (Lovejoy and Krannich 1982).

2. Project impacts may include the obliteration of traditional subcultural distinctions within rural areas. With distinctions such as small town merchant, farm owner, and farm or rural company employee no longer relevant, class relationships may become defined almost exclusively in terms of urban-based economic relationships. It is the latter which may form the basis of a more general dominant/subordinate class order.

3. Whitt (1979:84) does suggest that "power is potentially available to the subordinate classes if they become sufficiently class-conscious and politically organized to wrest control or to challenge the control of the means of production," but this is seldom a likely alternative.

REFERENCES

Colfer, C., and A. M. Colfer. 1978. Inside Bushler Bay: Lifeways in counterpoint. *Rural Sociology* 43:204-20.

Edelman, M. 1964. *The Symbolic Uses of Politics*. Urbana: University of Illinois Press.

Gale, R. P. 1984. The evolution of social impact: A post-functionalist view. *Impact Assessment Bulletin* 3(2):27-35.

Havens, A. E. 1982. Resource allocation and the state. *Rural Sociology* 47:561-67.

Johnson, R. N. 1982. The budget maximization hypothesis and the USDA Forest Service. *Renewable Resources Journal* 1(2,3):16-18.

Krannich, R. S., and C. R. Humphrey. 1983. Local mobilization and community growth: Toward an assessment of the "growth machine" hypothesis. *Rural Sociology* 48:60-81.

Lovejoy, S. B., and R. S. Krannich. 1982. Rural industrial development and domestic dependency relations: Toward an integrated perspective. *Rural Sociology* 47:475-95.

Lyon, L., L. G. Felice, M. R. Perryman, and E. S. Parker. 1981. Community power and population increase: An empirical test of the growth machine model. *American Journal of Sociology* 86:1387-1400.

Miliband, R. 1969. *The State in Capitalist Society*. New York: Basic Books.

Molotch, H. 1976. The city as a growth machine: Toward a political economy of place. *American Journal of Sociology* 82:309-32.

———. 1979. Media and movements. In *The Dynamics of Social Movements*, ed. M. N. Zald and J. D. McCarthy, 71-93. Cambridge, Mass.: Winthrop Publishers, Inc.

Newby, H., and F. H. Buttel. 1980. Toward a critical rural sociology. In *The Rural Sociology of the Advanced Societies: Critical Perspectives*, ed. F. H. Buttel and H. Newby, 1-35. Montclair, N.J.: Allanheld, Osmun & Co.

Schiller, H. 1969. *Mass Communications and American Empire*. Boston: Beacon Press.

Whitt, J. A. 1979. Toward a class-dialectical model of power: An empirical assessment of three competing models of political power. *American Sociological Review* 44:81-99.

3
Whose Ox Is Gored? A Sociocultural Model of Impact Distribution in Resource Development

Raymond L. Hall

INTRODUCTION

Natural resource exploration and development is a continuing process in modern technological societies. The search for and development of natural resources, especially oil, gas, uranium, and other relatively scarce natural resources, has increased dramatically in the United States in recent years. Escalation of this natural resource quest stems in large measure from the 1973 oil embargo, along with the ever-present need for such resources to provide energy for an expanding technological society. Consequently, natural resource exploration has become a nationwide activity, with large as well as small companies leaving no stone unturned, so to speak, in search of one kind of natural resource or another. Individuals, groups, and communities throughout the nation, especially in the West, often are faced with questions and issues involving the impact of resource development on their everyday lives.

It is highly unlikely that those who reside in areas where resource development takes place can escape all the consequences of the resource development process. That is not to say, however, that development consequences will cluster necessarily around any one set of negative or positive impacts or that they will be unidirectional. Almost every impact that negatively affects X may positively affect Y. For example, development of an oil field on a specific piece of land might be good for a community in general, but what if all or part of the land happened to be the ancestral burial grounds for a specific group in the community? In another case, suppose noise and/or dust pollution posed a problem for those residing in the vicinity of a development project, but the project itself promised to ease the tax burden of the community in general—including those experiencing the problem?

Since one kind of impact, direct or indirect, positive or negative, will be felt by everyone residing in the development arena, two important questions arise: (1) Which groups are likely to benefit from development impacts?[1] (2) Which groups are likely to bear the brunt of development impacts?

In answering these questions, we must consider the social status of those affected, as well as the cultural variables that determine the social structure of the environment where resource development takes place. The importance of sociocultural variables in assessing differential impact distributions in natural resource development, although not totally absent, has not been a priority of the environmental impact literature. My purpose in this chapter is to provide a framework for discussion of this vitally important topic.

INEQUALITIES IN THE MODERN STATE

Social inequality of all sorts is a continuing problem characterizing all modern states. One of the inequalities that stands out most prominently in all multiethnic states--which constitute all but a handful in the international system--is that of ethnic and racial inequality (see Said and Simmons 1976). Following the tenets of democratic theory, the state's central role is to regulate its constituent parts with a view towards providing a shared social environment where, differences aside, all groups receive equal treatment and protection under the law. However, no multiethnic state has yet solved the problem, except in theory, of ensuring that social justice and equal protection are equitably distributed, quantitatively or qualitatively, among all groups in its domain.

While the principles of equal justice and protection in the multiethnic state are envisioned as means of neutralizing ethnic diversity, or making it inconsequential as a social fact, their practical application is quite difficult. The difficulty arises because each ethnic group in the state's shared environment possesses, in lesser or greater degree, a different culture. The state's laws and enforcement patterns may be taken by one ethnic (cultural) group as an infringement on some aspect of its culture. The same may be true for a number of other ethnic (cultural) groups in the multiethnic social environment. Hence, the state's attempts to enhance social justice (equal protection) may be perceived differently by each ethnic group in its jurisdiction.

Thus, the state faces the perennial difficulty of enforcing equal protection under the law to meet the approval of each ethnic group. This difficulty becomes exacerbated when two (or more) ethnic groups perceive their respective cultures as fundamentally incompatible, and perhaps irreconcilable. In this case, the state must continually engage in the management of latent or manifest ethnic conflict in order to keep peace in the shared social environment. And when an ethnic group believes that it is superior to all others and seeks to make its culture the dominant one within the state, the possibility of open ethnic conflict is heightened (see Hall 1979; Snyder 1982:13).

The usual mode of state management of ethnic diversity is to intertwine ethnic group rights into the fabric of democratic pluralism. That is, ideally the state is comprised of a composite set of cultures from all the different ethnic groups within its territory. Thus, a generalized basis for "national" identity with, and loyalty to, the state is established, and each group retains important features of its ethnic culture without violating state-defined values common to all groups. In this way, national politics embodies acceptable proportions of each group's interests, and all groups participate proactively and positively, rather than reactively and negatively, within the political system. The process used to achieve positive participation involves a number of interesting variables: ethnic and "state" cultures, power and control.

Ethnic Culture

Culture is the basis of ethnic identification and loyalty because it contains a code that only cultural insiders can fully understand. (I would prefer to use the term "verstehen.")[2] An ethnic culture is comprised of and describes the collective values, norms, attitudes, and worldview of a particular group over time, and each ethnic culture is specifically different from all others, although general similarities do exist among a number of ethnic cultures. For example, Americans of English, German, Italian, Irish, Swedish, Polish, and other European national/ethnic descent share European cultural features. Taken together in the American context, I refer to them as affinity cultures because they share a number of similar phylogenetic traits and factors, such as skin color, as well as one or more common values, beliefs, or attitudes in reference to the supernatural, aesthetic preference, or form of social organization. The Apache, Arapaho, Sioux, Comanche, Modoc, and others share a Native American culture. These, too, are affinity cultures.

Although affinity cultures possess certain general features in common, each individual culture within such a group is specifically different from all others. German and Irish cultures, for example, are distinctively different; so are those of Apaches and Modocs.

One way that differences as well as similarities among cultures can be highlighted is to isolate specific cultural components. More could be used, but I choose to limit my examples to four: geography, history, language, and religion. In addition, economic factors constitute a latent element to be considered (see Table 3.1).

Since ethnic culture is the product of in-group experiences, definitions, and worldviews, each ethnic group in the state's shared environment defines and explains the components differently from every other group. And that is precisely why these cultural components promote ethnic solidarity and identity: Out of this common cultural sharing come language, religion, and history; ethnic groups tend to be located in or identify with a particular geographic location within the state; and they tend to voluntarily or involuntarily engage in particular kinds of economic pursuits which may be associated with the geographic location or with a specific kind of expertise.[3]

State Culture

Every state that has existed over a relatively long period of time develops a "culture." State culture is not the same as ethnic culture except in some instances, as, for example, when the state is monoethnic (as in Iceland) or when one ethnic group forces its cultural will on all other groups (as in the Republic of South Africa). While in theory the state is a neutral and objective "honest broker" operating in the best interest of all groups in its domain, it is, to be sure, more than that. The state is, in fact, a construct conceived of and managed by individuals and groups who use it in their own best interest. The state is people, the sum total of the human groups and individuals who operate it, and its culture, ideally, is the sum total of all the cultures of the diverse groups of which it is comprised.[4] Hence, "state culture" is comprised of the same variables as "ethnic culture," only now with state instead of ethnic definitions (see Table 3.2).

The economy, of course, is the most important element under state control. Whether the economy is laissez-faire, "mixed," or socialist-oriented, the state is, to varying degrees, involved in its operation. Geography, or territory, an internationally recognized geopolitical boundary, is the specific space in which the state exists and carries out its domestic and foreign policy. The recognition of language is important because whether a particular language is "official" or "unofficial" depends on the politics and ethnic composition of the state. The state's attitude

Table 3.1
Generalized definitions of variables comprising ethnic culture

---

ETHNIC CULTURE

CULTURE: Attitudes, beliefs, norms, values, aesthetics, and lifestyles of a group; its knowledge, actions, and material objects.

ECONOMY: Systematic organization, production, management, and distribution of material and status values.

GEOGRAPHY: Territory and boundary identified with or designated to specific ethnic/cultural or "national" groups.

HISTORY: The construction or reconstruction of a group's past from an ethnic perspective; the differences among ethnic groups' pasts in relationship to a national history, especially between superordinate and subordinate groups.

LANGUAGE: Oral/written communication of a group's systematized values, beliefs, norms, and knowledge among its members.

RELIGION: Attitudes and behavior of a group's belief regarding its relationship with the supernatural.

Table 3.2
Generalized definitions of variables comprising state culture

---

STATE CULTURE

CULTURE: Attitudes, beliefs, norms, values, aesthetics, and lifestyles of a state; its knowledge, actions, and material objects.

PATTERNS OF
DOMINATION: Legitimate and illegitimate superordination; techniques and mechanisms of gaining and perpetuating superordination; exercise of transcendent authority in a state social system.

ECONOMY: Systematic organization, production, management, distribution, and consumption of material and status values.

GENDER/
ETHNICITY: Characteristics of internally and externally defined groups who behave and are regarded as distinctive social entities.

GEOGRAPHY: Space comprising the internal territory and specific boundaries of a state; territory comprising a state's geopolitical boundaries.

HISTORY: The construction or reconstruction of a state's past from the state's perspective.

LANGUAGE: Oral/written communication of a state's systematized values, beliefs, norms, and knowledge.

RELIGION: Attitudes and behavior of a state's belief regarding its relationship with the supernatural.

---

toward religion, in many instances, is similar to that toward language. The state's construction of history depends upon the particular regime in control of the state power apparatus at the time. Thus, for a variety of reasons, the state's "official" history may not be acceptable to particular groups. The state's attitudes toward language, religion, and history suggest the importance of an additional underlying variable labeled patterns of domination (political impact) which, together with the economic variable, aids in the explanation of potential sociocultural development impacts. Consideration of this variable leads to a discussion of the notions and basis of power within the state. Gender/ethnicity is also included in the table and will be explained later in the discussion.

Power: State and Ethnic

Power in the democratic multiethnic state is best conceptualized as a set of exchange relationships which are almost always part of intergroup relations, both among ethnic groups themselves and in state management of interethnic relations, including conflict. That is not to deny that power is ultimately based on physical coercion--A getting B to do X. But it is to say that the state's modal use of power in the multiethnic democratic state involves influence (real or imagined), persuasion, incentives, rewards, and other factors that deter, hinder, dissuade, discourage, or otherwise prevent the use of physical coercion (see Blau 1964; Oberschall 1973; Baldwin 1978). By conceptualizing power and its use in this way, we can focus on the primary means of conflict management in the multiethnic state.

Although the state's role, theoretically, is to organize, regulate, and mediate in the public interest, it often defines public interest as "in the interest of the state." The state thus possesses superordinate veto power over the sum total of its parts. Ideally, the state should use this power to insure that each ethnic group is free to pursue its own goals and those of the state, at best without strife and at worst with a minimum conflict of interest.

However, the state's use of power may not affect all groups equally. (Here I am treating the state as a monolith in its dealings with a number of different groups.) For example, when and if the state distributes power among "power centers," some groups may receive more benefits than do others. Some groups may receive none, meaning either that the state is merely responding to the fact that some groups possess more power than do others or that the state is operating on the basis of the monopoly of power by one group.

Since the state and the most powerful group(s) in its domain tend to be two sides of the same coin, rarely do more than two or three ethnic groups in a multiethnic society possess binding decision-making power. As Burkey (1978:32) observes, "because of the overwhelming importance of the state, the group that controls it has dominance." Where the state favors particular powerful groups, less powerful groups, depending on the nature of their powerlessness, may engage in conflict with the state itself, the most powerful group(s) in the state, or both.

Other, nonconflictive alternatives may be chosen. One may be a decision to withdraw from state-controlled competition for resources with other groups, especially more powerful ones, and instead to construct internal parallel opportunity structures (see Light 1972). In this instance, the ethnic group may continue to occupy its territory (e.g., Amish and Hutterites in the United States); migrate elsewhere in the state's geopolitical territory (e.g., Mormons, Hutterites); or emigrate to its traditional "homeland" (which may pose a problem for another state). Such action is inconsequential to the state in cases where the group poses no threat to state power (because of size, for example) and has a radically different cultural orientation from that of the mainstream.

Patterns of Control

In general, the state utilizes the components of ethnic culture (history, language, religion, geography, and economics) as instruments of control. The state may use ethnic cultural variables in order to favor certain powerful groups and to place other, less powerful groups in disadvantageous positions. For example, the state may impose restrictions on the use of a particular ethnic language, while distinguishing another language as the dominant or "official" means of communicating; or the state may facilitate the relocation of what it considers powerless or noninstrumental groups to less favorable geographic locations. The devaluation of a less powerful group's history and the placement of the group in a position of economic inequality are always used as controls. Some American examples include: religion--the ban on the Mormon practice of polygamy; language--the controversy over the status of Spanish; race and ethnicity--the conflict between minority groups--Mexican Americans, blacks, Native Americans--and the white majority; geography--the isolation of blacks in central cities, Native Americans on reservations, and Hispanics in ghettos. In summary, I have attempted to demonstrate how the multiethnic state seeks to subordinate ethnically diverse cultures to a state civic culture. In this way, as we shall soon see, the state can establish "national" unity and carry out domestic and foreign policy.

Given the power of ethnic cultural bonds, this is no easy task. Ties that bind one group together are responsible for separating that group from another with a different set of ties. One could conclude from the foregoing that I am arguing that cultural differences between groups in themselves are the primary causes of ethnic superordination and subordination. Such a conclusion would be wrong. I argue that ethnic power asymmetry results if and when the state places greater value on, and grants power to, a particular ethnic group (or groups) at the expense of others. Ethnic differences in themselves are neutral realities until the state--reflecting the will of the powerful group(s)--utilizes specific components of ethnic culture(s) to create, maintain, or support one group over another. When the state assumes such a posture, powerless ethnic groups may activate their own sociopolitical definitions, having lost faith in the integrity of the state to act on their behalf. Given that the state has the power to manipulate group options and life chances, tenuous stability quite often characterizes the relationship between ethnicity and state civic culture. Thus, ethnicity itself is a component of state culture, as is gender (see below).

ETHNICITY IN THE UNITED STATES

America has always been a land of diversity--in ethnicity, race, language, and religion. However, the initial dominant power groups did not reflect this diversity. In fact, much of the diversity was consciously and deliberately excluded from the various conventions assembled to design and shape the nation (Beard 1913; Kolko 1962; Jordan 1968). What the Founding Fathers did, in short, was to use White Anglo-Saxon Protestant (WASP) values--along with the ideas of Enlightenment "Latins" such as Montesquieu, Rousseau, and "the Philosophes"--as the foundation upon which the nation would build (see Gordon 1964). Apparently, they believed that this combination of free enterprise and restricted political democracy would produce a social structure and political economy where all but a few would believe that opportunity and mobility were unrestricted, unlimited, and even inevitable; that in America everyone would have the opportunity to pursue the American Dream; and that the achievement of the dream was determined only by one's imagination and willingness to work hard, to sacrifice, and to defer gratification in order to reap future benefits.

How did such an ideology become politically embedded into the American character? The Founding Fathers were able to use democratic pluralism to deal with diverse white ethnic groups within the state because the dominant American value and cultural complex was essentially the sum total of the diverse ethnic groups of European origin (Anderson 1970). Most of the "old" immigrants before the late nineteenth century were of northern and western European origins. Animosity, and sometimes conflict, occurred among these immigrants. In the final analysis, the English emerged as the dominant social, political, and economic group in American society. Therefore, Anglo-conformity set the value and normative patterns around which evolved the process of Americanization (see Cole and Cole 1954; Gordon 1964). Consequently, the "new" immigrants (most of whom were of southern and eastern European origin) were "Americanized" to fit the Anglo mold.

In sum, the American political and economic system operated, then and now, in the best interest of the Anglo majority. Although ethnic groups of European origins tend to regard assimilation as the fusion of their different cultures into an American culture, Native Americans, Afro-Americans, Hispanics, and some Asian groups are still seeking adequate adaptation of their cultures, of their race and ethnicity, into American society. These groups in particular still face discrimination, racism, and other forms of exclusionary pressures that militate against equality. I shall briefly highlight important aspects of the relations between these groups and the dominant white American of European descent.

Black Americans

White racism has promoted and maintained black inequality from the time blacks disembarked from slave ships until the present time. Much of the history of the interaction between Afro-Americans and white Americans includes blacks attempting to become part of the American mainstream--by individual efforts and group demands. In general, black demands have not required major structural changes in American society. Integrationists tend to operate from one of the following points of view: (1) although blacks may possess a different cultural base from that of whites, the long period of interaction beween them has significantly modified, if not totally erased, any previously incompatible differences; or (2) because their African cultural heritage has been erased from their cultural "memories" over time, and they have operated for almost four centuries in Euro-American culture, the question of African culture is at best irrelevant, if not nonexistent. According to this second line of reasoning, blacks are merely "ethnic" Americans, nothing more, nothing less.

But there is another idea about the black condition that would require major changes in black/white sociopolitical and cultural arrangements--black separatism. This idea is predicated on the notion that Afro-Americans possess a culture that is separate and different from that of Euro-Americans and that the price of integration into the dominant culture is not worth the possible loss of black cultural identity. The essence of this ideology suggests that what blacks want may differ from, and in some cases oppose, the sociocultural and political arrangements of the status quo (see Hall 1978).

What may loosely be called the black liberation movement of the 1960s included both integrationist and separatist ideology, with the militant wing of the civil rights movement calling into question the wisdom of the demands of the old-line, integration-oriented civil rights organizations--"Integrate into what?" asked Malcolm X--as well as the basic premises upon which the call for integration was built. Further, the black rebellion of the 1960s prompted other ethnic groups, e.g., Native Americans, Mexican Americans, white ethnics, and some Asians, to question the conventional wisdom of plunging blindly into the melting pot.

Native Americans

When Europeans "discovered" the New World, they also became aware of indigenous populations with cultures and modes of social organization that in many ways differed from their own: Seminole, Apache, Ute, Arapahoe, Sioux, Shoshona, Onondaga, Chippewa, Shinecook, Modoc, Comanche, Navajo, to name only a few. As Europeans settled, spread, and expanded, their initial contacts with these groups were mostly peaceful and harmonious. In fact, Native Americans initially aided the newly arrived Europeans by providing them with food, land, and other means of survival. The Thanksgiving holiday commemorates native generosity.

Peace and harmony were not permanent fixtures in native/European relations, however. Eventually, European expansion, and native resistance to the attempt to impose European culture on them, resulted in the decimation of the native population. In the precontact period, the indigenous population numbered somewhere in the neighborhood of seven to ten million. Today they number fewer than half a million. The subordination of the native population resulted in the expropriation of their land, followed by the unsuccessful attempt to enslave them. Their refusal to become slaves was followed by their relegation to reservations on the most unproductive, desolate, and undesirable lands. In addition, the buffalo--the natives' basic source of food, clothing, and shelter, and a large part of the locus of native culture--was destroyed.

Hence, any basic comprehension of the present mood, action, and purpose of Native Americans requires a knowledge of and sensitivity to their perspectives on the historical dynamics regulating native and European (white) relations in America. Part of what I mean by that is succinctly and uncompromisingly put by Dorris (1979), himself a Native American:

> From the beginning, [whites] have consistently assumed that their particular brands of social organization, religion, language, and life-style would prove so compelling, so magnetic, that all indigenous alternatives would, almost as an act of nature, give way. . . . This belief, engendered by millenia of European isolation from the rest of the world, and reenforced by apparent competitive success, was grounded in two basic--and short-sighted--hypotheses: (1) all inhabitants of the New World constituted in fact but a single ethnic community; and (2) human culture was universally and teleologically evolutionary, with Western Civilization forever holding "most advanced" status (1979:66).

> However, in the final analysis, Native American cultures have never viewed themselves as submerged in, or even a subset of, the Euro-American world. They are not, singly or collectively, "separatist" for they have never been a part of a larger multi-ethnic matrix. They did not join and then renege; they simply never joined. Even when deprived of every outward badge and banner of cultural autonomy, they have steadfastly hung on to that one reality which no amount of pressure or punishment could dislodge: their right to be distinct, to be plural, to be un-American (1979:81-82, original emphasis).

In sum, Native Americans have never given up their cultures, have never been slaves, have never lost their dignity or cultural pride. Now they want their land back. Accommodation of this demand would clearly require a major change in the American sociocultural structure.

Mexican Americans (Chicanos)

Chicano ethnicity is complex. The complexity stems from the fact that it is a composite of racial, cultural, and linguistic factors. A mixture of native groups of pre-Columbian Mexico led to the Aztecs, whose blood was then mixed with that of their Spanish conquerors. Finally, as Mexicans emigrated to North America, they mixed with various northern European groups. The Chicano may be a recent Mexican immigrant or a descendant of sixteenth-century settlers; he may or may not speak Spanish; in either case, he usually speaks English. Although most Chicanos feel that they belong in the United States, they also feel some ties to Mexico (Kleitz 1979)

The Chicano movement in the United States is primarily concerned with forging a common Chicano identity in order to eliminate intragroup conflict and confront the larger society with certain demands. These demands include recognition of Spanish as an official language on a par with English and social, political, and economic control of their communities. Already, the more militant elements of the Chicano movement label the states of Texas, New Mexico, Arizona, and California as Aztlan, the name of the old Aztec empire.

If what might loosely be labeled the Hispanic movement (Puerto Ricans, Cubans, etc.) is added to the Chicano movement, together and separately they are calling for more than mere inclusion into the American mainstream. They envision nothing less than a redirection of the cultural flow, a cultural emphasis different from WASP conformity. Like Native Americans, Hispanics possess clear cultural (linguistic, religious, and so forth) differences from the dominant group. Accommodation of these differences would require major structural changes in social arrangements.

Other Ethnic Groups

Blacks, Native Americans, and Chicanos are the quintessential ethnic groups still struggling for equality and justice in American society. That is not, of course, to suggest that other ethnic groups are free from victimization because of their ethnicity. In fact, a rather long list of ethnic groups who qualify as victims because of their ethnicity could be drawn up. Two points justify my decision not to do so: (1) white ethnic groups work out their grievances within the system; (2) despite past and present problems experienced by Asian Americans, they, like white ethnics, have not engaged in large-scale, extra-institutional social movement activity to elevate their ethnic status.

Even in California, where the largest number of Asian Americans reside (Tachiki et al. 1971; Hsu 1971), Asian protest activity is at a much lower level than that of Chicanos, blacks, and Native Americans. Reasons for this stem from (1) the tendency of Japanese and Chinese (and other Asians) to construct parallel opportunity structures in their own communities (see Light 1972) which effectively tend to minimize the need for resource competition with the dominant group; (2) the fact that the educational level of Chinese and Japanese Americans is equal to that of whites; (3) the tendency of these groups to pursue technical and professional activities where--because of the need for such expertise--competition with the dominant group is not a major factor; and (4) the strong emphasis on community which lessens the need for other than work-related "integration" into the larger society. Some social scientists (Kitano 1976; Daniels and Kitano 1970; Lyman 1974) have maintained that the close value proximity of Japanese and Chinese cultures to the dominant Anglo-Saxon culture contributes to compatibility within the dominant social structure (see Schaefer 1979:341-62).

ETHNIC GROUP STATUS: A SUMMARY

The task of constructing precise causes and explanations of group status, an often difficult and imprecise undertaking in any society, is more difficult still in the American context because of the individualist ideology undergirding the social mobility process. However, given that social inequality is a reality in all social systems, a fruitful place to begin digging for its roots is in the way the dominant social structure--the state--interacts with and relates to different groups in its domain (see Hall forthcoming). The degree of support the state's activities receive from each group is closely related to the degree of cultural affinity existing between the state and the group: The closer the cultural affinity, the more likely it is that the state's activities will be in congruence with and therefore receive support from affinity groups; the more distant the cultural affinity, the more likely it is that hostility at worst, and nonsupport or neutrality at best, will characterize the state's relationship to groups outside its "sphere of affinity."

Hence, high group status in the United States is closely related to whether or not the group is of European origins. These groups possess a virtual monopoly on American social power. For groups that are not of European origin, status is dependent upon their cultural proximity and instrumental use-value to the

American political economy. Asian groups, particularly Japanese and Chinese, tend to fall at a middle point in the status system because of the nature of their communities and their value proximity to the dominant (European) cultural system.

In general, group status, like that of an individual, is subject to the ebb and flow of a variety of social, political, and economic currents; it is possible that domestic and/or international developments could bolster a group's status or have a deleterious effect. For example, developments in Japan, Israel, South Africa, and Latin America can have important ramifications for American ethnic or racial groups whose origins, symbolic or real, are located in these geographical areas. A group may also engage in domestic political activity geared to bring about favorable state actions that could alter its status vis-a-vis other groups in the social system. Viewed from the perspective of the competing groups themselves, and perhaps from a wider lens as well, the process of exerting pressure on the state in order to improve a group's position in the state's power arrangement may be called "resource competition" (Despres 1975). The resource may be either symbolic or material.

The way the state responds to a group's attempt to influence its attitude and action is often a telling indicator of the group's status and power. As the foregoing discussion has demonstrated, ethnicity is a major determinant of group status. In addition, in the process of competing for resources, a hierarchy of subgroups within the dominant white male/ethnic culture becomes apparent. Women constitute one such group that falls into the lower status category.

WOMEN AS A STATUS GROUP

The last two decades have witnessed a renewed and reinvigorated women's movement confronting both the larger society and government to redress their grievances. Basing their arguments and appeal on the fact that their exclusion from social, political, and economic pursuits effectively insures their inability to attain equality with men, women have confronted the total spectrum of psychological, legal, and bureaucratic barriers obstructing their path to freedom, dignity, and equality.

Whereas in the past women fought merely for "equal opportunity" in the political and economic arenas, their recent thrust for equality has employed a different set of arguments, a new approach to the use of empirical data, and a "reconstruction" of history based on a "deconstruction" of mythical and stereotypical sociohistorical constructs. Most importantly, women are paying close attention not to the male (and some female) apologists for their position and status, but to those who speak of women as having a distinct "culture," a different frame of reference, a different worldview. Carol Gilligan (1982), for example, writes about the virtual omission from the social psychological literature--especially that of developmental psychology--of data, interpretations, and theories inclusive of the female experience: "I began to notice the recurrent problems in interpreting women's development and to connect these problems to the repeated exclusion of women from the critical theory-building studies of psychological research" (1982:1). She cites the influential and popular work by Daniel Levinson (1978), The Seasons of a Man's Life, as an example in which a man "sets out on the basis of an all-male study 'to create an overarching conception of development that could encompass the diverse biological, psychological and social changes occurring in adult life' (p. 8)" (Gilligan 1982:151-52).

Gilligan believes, correctly, that an "overarching conception of development" is not possible unless the female experience is also included; in her teaching, research, and observation of men and women, she hears from women a voice that is different from that of men. She therefore sets out to record "different modes of thinking about relationships and the association of these modes with male and female voices in psychological and literary texts and in the data of [her] research" (1982:1).

As is clear in Moen's chapter in this volume, women, even where they exist in the same setting as men--in this case in the arena of resource development --tend to encounter experiences and impacts different from those of men. The validity of this observation is corroborated in a study by Moen et al. (1981) entitled Women and the Social Costs of Economic Development.

The question such an observation raises, however, is whether or not women's "different voice" is different enough to be categorized as a culture separate from that of men. I am not suggesting that men and women of the same ethnic/national origins may possess and adhere to different cultures, for ethnic culture is an overarching, pervasive, and mutually inclusive social reality for both men and women. The question I am raising, however, is to what degree must differential perceptions and interpretations of the primary culture, stemming from unique experiences, diverge, in this case between men and women, in order to "qualify" as a separate or different subculture? I shall argue that, at least in the context of resource development, women do possess their own "culture." In fact, many occupational groups, such as miners, construction workers, and ranchers, also share perceptions and interpretations leading to a mutually inclusive reality which would further suggest a number of occupational subcultures.

I next move to the construction of a model of impact distribution based on and extending the discussion above.

A MODEL OF SOCIOCULTURAL IMPACT DISTRIBUTION

At the beginning of this chapter, I stated that it was very unlikely that anyone residing in the arena of natural resource development could escape, unscathed, all its attendant impacts. Given the asymmetrical distribution of power in communities in the United States, two telling statements or hypotheses about negative impact distributions can be made. First, these differential impacts are more likely to negatively affect the poor section(s) of a particular community than those well off. Second, these kinds of impacts are more likely to affect the minority-group section(s) of the community than the majority-group section(s).

The well-off part of the community is likely to escape most or all negative impacts because of "impact elitism," to use a term coined by Dunlap and Morrison (1980) in a slightly different way. Because of their educational and occupational attainments, the prosperous in the community are more likely to have more information in advance of resource development--largely because they have initiated or participated intimately in every stage of the decision-making processes. Therefore, these community elites are in a position either to dull the edges of negative development impacts or to shift the impact(s) to other less-powerful sections through the use of political, legal, and economic mechanisms easily available to them, i.e., zoning.

For example, low-income families suffering from airborne dust, sand, or smoke from a construction or mining operation have little choice but to remain where they are. They may cover openings, close windows, and stay inside, thus altering their leisure activities, work habits, and patterns of social interaction. The affluent, on the other hand, can either move out of the reach of the airborne particles or invest in "home improvements"--air conditioners, vacations--to minimize or neutralize their effects. They can go inside these adjusted home environments and carry on their normal, routine activities. Another example may involve forcing a plant to install scrubbers to insure air quality, where the added cost of the installation would affect the poor more dramatically than it would the well-to-do. That is, the price of the product is raised, i.e., passed on to the consumer, to pay for the newly installed scrubbers.

I do not want to leave the impression that the community elite are only concerned with shifting negative impacts to other sections of the community. In reality, they may be more keen on attracting positive benefits to their section of the community. Historically, for example, it was no accident that the elite initially resided in the city center near factories and businesses, only to abandon the city to the poor once adequate transportation made it possible for them to commute from their suburbs. And it is no accident today that the suburbs, where the well-off generally reside, are the location of the high-tech industry. Unlike the large, often dirty, labor-intensive factories found in or near the city core with workers who would be unacceptable in the tree-lined, affluent suburbs, the clean high-tech plants require well-trained, skilled individuals to operate them. These workers are, in fact, themselves suburbanites, occupying a relatively safe middle ground between negative resource impacts in the center city and those inherent in energy resource development in rural areas.

The "literature" regarding the impact of rural energy resource development has only in the last twelve to fifteen years focused on questions of equity and distributive justice in rural America. From this new focus has emerged a near consensus among social scientists concerned with such questions: Social impacts of resource and energy projects affect groups located in resource development arenas differently (Schnaiberg 1975; Humphrey and Buttel 1982; Dunlap and Morrison 1980). However, cost-benefit analyses that generate propositions such as "the quality of environment available is proportional to socio-economic status" (Krieger 1970) tend to ignore sociocultural factors.

It is true that all attempts to integrate poor and well-off income groups and individuals into the same residential neighborhood have failed miserably in the United States. This is not so with minority groups, however. It is in fact not uncommon even today to find minority individuals with high and low incomes residing in the same neighborhood, whether because of cultural affinity or external force, e.g., the unavailability of housing outside their own community. This class/income/ethnic/racial residential patterning usually results in three types of locational groups: "elite" and well-off dominant-group neighborhoods, not-so-well-off dominant-group (blue-collar) neighborhoods, and neighborhoods where minority-group members reside. In the latter case, Chicanos, blacks, and Chinese, as examples, tend to live in separate, distinct neighborhoods. (Because the level of racial integration in most communities is so low, here I discount individual minorities living in dominant-group neighborhoods).

In this residential configuration, negative distributional impacts from natural resource development will be related to class; i.e., elites and the well-to-do will be less negatively affected than poor minority-group neighborhoods, with the blue-collar dominant groups somewhere in the middle. Moreover, when the elite must garner community support for an impact decision, they are more likely to appeal to (and receive support from) the blue-collar dominant-group members. The most devastating impacts on the nonelite groups may thus involve cultural, rather than economic variables. Take a piece of sacred land, for example: What if the dominant group(s) decide that a minority group's cemetery occupies a space a developer believes possesses vast oil resources?

Furthermore, I contend that distributional effects are not confined to lower socioeconomic status groups. The affluent who do not belong to a low status group may also be negatively affected by environmental impacts. What of nonpoor farmers and ranchers? Is it possible for them to pick up and move or merely go inside when a negative environmental impact is introduced into their community? Some might, but the vast majority may not--even if they can economically afford to do so. Thus, socioeconomic status notwithstanding, farmers and ranchers, because of their special and unique spatial location and the way their location inhibits interaction with "outsiders," develop "insider" values, norms, attitudes, and behavior. In short, they and other occupational groups, like ethnic and racial groups and women, may be said to have a distinct subculture. Farmers and ranchers, as examples, have little or no sustained contact with other groups, and thus they construct their social reality from the "givens" and imperatives of their own rural farm- and ranch-oriented cultural milieu.

I wish to continue pursuing the notion of culture. I have argued that some American ethnic and racial groups possess cultures that are distinctive subcultures. Similar arguments are made in this volume by Elizabeth Moen for women and by Patrick Jobes and Kristen Yount for occupational groups--farmers, ranchers, and miners (see Chapters 5-7). Resource development impacts negatively not only on groups, but also on the cultures of those groups. While other contributors to this volume address specific cultural impacts, it is my task to provide a theoretical overview in which to assess a variety of cultural impacts. I shall apply the model in Chapter 11.

This task requires an inclusive definition of culture, especially as it relates to the resource development arena. Fortunately, of the many thousand definitions and discussions of culture in the sociological and anthropological literature, one of the most insightful and useful has been provided by Erikson (1976). His definition emerged from his research on the psychosocial impact of the flood that devastated the Appalachian community of Buffalo Creek, West Virginia. To begin with, he regards culture in general as the way of life of people who "share a distinctive style of life and thought":

> . . . those modes of thinking and knowing and doing that a people learn to regard as natural, those beliefs and attitudes that help shape a people's way of looking at themselves and the rest of the universe, those ideas and symbols that a people employ to make sense of their own everyday experience as members of a society (1976:79).

Because cultural malleability or plasticity is one of the more prominent features of the human animal, Erikson believes that the range of values, norms, attitudes, and behaviors is without limit. But in order for civil society and the individuals comprising it to exist, culture defines certain limits. Culture is responsible for societal continuity. Erikson puts it this way:

> In one sense, then, cultures can be said to set *moral* limits on the behavior of human beings to compensate for the fact that biology has failed to set many *natural* limits. Every people stake out a *particular* territory on the broad plain of human potentialities, drawing boundaries around that sphere of activity or thought and declaring it to be uniquely their own. Culture, then, is the moral space within which a people live, or, rather, the customary ways that develop within that space and make it distinctive (1976:81, original emphasis).

Erikson's discussion of culture both incorporates and extends my own previous treatment of ethnic, racial, and gender culture. Moreover, it corroborates the argument that occupations, too, can possess a culture.

However, Erikson's treatment of culture has still more utility for our purpose in that he goes on to add an unusual dimension to the notion of culture. Not only should the concept of culture include "those forces that promote uniformity of thought and action," but it should include also those cultural forms that

> help determine what a people will *imagine*. And it is one of the persisting curiosities of human life that people are apt to imagine the complete contrary of the ideas and attitudes that figure

most significantly in their view of the world. The mind that imagines a cultural form also imagines (which is to say "creates") its reverse, and to that extent, at least, a good measure of diversity and contrast is built into the very text of a culture (1976:81, original emphasis).

What calls attention to the diversities is what Erikson labels an "axis of variation," an axis being "a line passing through a body or system around which the parts are symmetrically arranged" as well as "the principal line along which anything may extend, grow, or move" (1976:82):

> . . . the identifying motifs of a culture are not just the <u>core values</u> to which people pay homage but also the <u>lines of point and counterpoint</u> along which they diverge. That is, the term "culture" refers not only to the customary ways in which a people induce conformity in behavior and outlook but the customary ways in which they organize diversity (1976:82, original emphasis).

Social differentiation, then, is the phenomenon that manifests cultural diversity and contrast. Hence, within any culture may be found a number of widely varying subcultures, each pursuing "lines of point and counterpoint" that reflect and contravene the larger culture. It is in this regard, therefore, that ranchers, miners, farmers, women, and perhaps other groups as well, because of the plasticity of the human organism, may evolve a culture that is "peculiar to itself." However, in the instance of miners, farmers, and ranchers, and to a large extent women, I would argue that theirs is a subculture because they belong to the larger dominant Euro-American culture. Therefore, whatever contrasts emerge in their case are only a variation of and a counterpoint to the larger culture. Native Americans, blacks, and to a certain degree Mexican Americans may, in fact, have a culture that is different from, i.e., not a subculture of, the dominant Euro-American culture.

The model of cultural impact distributions (see Figure 3.1) that I shall suggest is only one such heuristic device to indicate various ways that the development of natural resources may affect the "way of life" of individuals and groups residing within the development arena. Unlike the usual mode of studies focusing on such impacts, the main purpose of this model is to explicate some of the noneconomic, sociocultural impacts, although I am aware that it is difficult, at best, to separate out economic impacts from purely social ones. Following my previous argument, I wish to reiterate that distributional

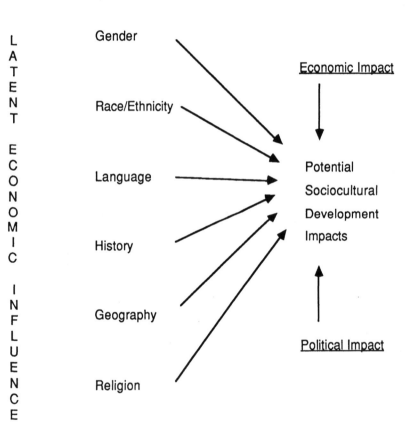

Figure 3.1 Schematic Diagram of Potential Sociocultural Impacts

impacts are always asymmetrical. The groups least likely to be negatively affected would include white nonfarmer/nonrancher males, well-off white males and females, and minority group individuals/families residing in predominantly white nonfarmer/nonrancher communities. Those most likely to be negatively affected would include poor minority groups (e.g., Native Americans and Mexican Americans), white women in poor or middle-income families, and white men whose occupations tie them to a particular location.

The reason for placing white nonfarm males at the top of the list of those least likely to be affected stems from their close relationship with the state. Consider the following: It is reasonable to assume that those companies engaging in resource development are either large corporations (even multinationals) or other smaller operations that possess or have access to large amounts of capital. How likely is it that women or minorities would either possess or have access to such large resources? Now, since the American state is the dominant white or Euro-American groups comprising it, it is also reasonable to assume that the state and the dominant white males--not women--would have a cozy relationship.

That is not to suggest that all white males have equal access to power and privilege in American society, not to mention native, black, Asian, and Mexican-American (Chicano) males. For similar reasons and in the same way that the American state reflects Euro-American culture, the state is rather selective when it comes to which groups of males within the Euro-American culture complex have more access to economic opportunities than others. Take, as example, the chief executive officers and board chairmen of the Fortune 500. Not one native, black or Mexican-American male occupies either position. (A handful of Asian males may be included, and these--except for the Wang Corporation --are closely connected with companies based in Japan or elsewhere in Asia. I am not aware of any women occupying these positions; if so, they are rare and very recently arrived). This select group of individuals--CEOs and board chairmen--belong to ethnic groups of northern and western European heritage (see Levine 1985:App. B). Few, if any, are Turkish, Jewish, Armenian, and so forth. The point of this example is that when it comes to wielding power in the American economic system, and the Fortune 500 wield an astounding amount of it, ethnic belonging makes a great deal of difference.

By analogy, I would make the same argument when it comes to energy resource exploration and development. Those enterprises, large and small, that engage in the business of supplying energy, upon close scrutiny, would be operated by individual males belonging to the

American majority power groups. Engaging in a critical and lucrative enterprise such as energy resource development is not an undertaking that minority-group members and women are encouraged to pursue. Thus, those prominently found in such ventures tend to be white males characteristic of those found in the large corporate sector. It is therefore reasonable to conclude that when white males exercise their power to facilitate natural resource development, they believe that such development is unrelated to cultural--and especially subcultural--considerations. In short, the mode of thinking that guides resource development tends to ignore development impacts that do not directly benefit dominant community elites. The dominant elements regard resource development as being good for all concerned, for the society as a whole. This is an excellent example of "impact stratification" and how skewed distributions of impacts get lost for both social analysts and policymakers.

Those on the other side, those most adversely affected by the development process, take a different view. They argue that culture, race, ethnicity, occupation, and gender should be considered in development decisions. The exclusion of these constituents from the matrix of development decisions, they argue, is prima facie evidence that dominance and insensitivity work hand in hand.

As a preview of the possibilities offered by a cultural model in looking at such issues of dominance in resource development, consider the following examples: Religion--It is not unusual that physical structures used in the development process are constructed on land considered sacred by a certain group. Geography--Natural resource development projects have been located in the midst of "natural areas" and have thus led to the virtual destruction of traditional communities. When development communities emerge in the midst of a traditional "natural community," legal and criminal codes tend to emerge that reflect the dominant group's culture. These may be at variance with indigenous notions, and the possibility of open conflict is heightened. History--The commemoration of "national" holidays, the conducting of certain ceremonies, and the holding of certain historical reenactments--all based upon the dominant group's view of history and culture--are examples of insensitivity, or even worse, arrogance.

In Chapter 11 of this volume, I will analyze a variety of cultural phenomena in the natural resource development arena with respect to rural resource development impacts. The case study materials preceding Chapter 11 will serve as data to demonstrate the applicability of the cultural model outlined in this chapter.

NOTES

1. Benefit in this context is not limited to pecuniary or material well-being alone. It also includes nonmaterial benefits such as minimum environmental impacts stemming from natural resource development. For example, in an economically heterogeneous community, dust or air pollution does not discriminate, in terms of its areal distribution, against community members based on their socioeconomic status. However, socioeconomic differences play a large role in the ability to minimize real and potential pollution effects.

2. The German word "verstehen" better conveys the meaning of "understanding" used by Merton. It refers not merely to a mentated comprehension or cognitive understanding, but to these as well as the process of value and norm internalization through initial socialization into the culture.

3. Clearly, there is a problem of multicolinearity: e.g., history has an economic component; economy has a historical element; language may be associated with geography and vice versa; religion may contain historical, linguistic, geographic, and economic features; economics may be the product of all of these elements ad infinitum. Nevertheless, one of the benefits of disaggregating ethnic culture is that it affords the opportunity of thinking more specifically about the relationship among the variables. And it is precisely because of the close association among the components of ethnic culture that it is important to zero in on the phenomenological definitions of the particular ethnic culture involved.

4. Others, notably conflict theorists, for instance, argue that the state, to be sure, is more than that. These theorists take it that the state is in fact no more than a construct conceived of, used, and controlled by groups constituting the superstructure exclusively in their own interest. In other words, the state is merely a group of people using it as a means toward their personal ends.

REFERENCES

Anderson, C. H. 1970. *White Protestant Americans: From National Origins to Religious Group*. Englewood Cliffs, N.J.: Prentice-Hall.

Baldwin, D. A. 1978. Power and social exchange. *American Political Science Review* 72:1229-42.

Beard, C. 1913. *An Economic Interpretation of the Constitution of the United States.* New York: Macmillan.

Blau, P. 1964. *Exchange and Power in Social Life.* New York: John Wiley.

Burkey, R. M. 1978. *Ethnic and Racial Groups: The Dynamics of Dominance.* Menlo Park, Calif.: Cummings.

Cole, S. G., and M. W. Cole. 1954. *Minorities and the American Promise: The Conflict of Principle and Practice.* New York: Harper and Brothers.

Daniels, R., and H. Kitano. 1970. *American Racism: Exploration of the Nature of Prejudice.* Englewood Cliffs, N.J.: Prentice-Hall.

Despres, L., ed. 1975. *Ethnicity and Resource Competition in Plural Societies.* The Hague: Mouton.

Dorris, M. 1979. Twentieth-century Indians: The return of the natives. In *Ethnic Autonomy--Comparative Dynamics: The Americas, Europe and the Developing World*, ed. R. L. Hall, 66-84. New York: Pergamon Press.

Dunlap, R., and D. Morrison. 1980. Elitism, equity and environmentalism. Presented at the annual meeting of the American Sociological Association, New York.

Erikson, K. T. 1976. *Everything in its Path: Destruction of Community in the Buffalo Creek Flood.* New York: Simon and Schuster.

Gilligan, C. 1982. *In a Different Voice: Psychological Theory and Women's Development.* Cambridge, Mass.: Harvard University Press.

Gordon, M. M. 1964. *Assimilation in American Life: The Role of Race, Religion, and National Origins.* New York: Oxford University Press.

Hall, R. L. 1978. *Black Separatism in the United States.* Hanover, N.H.: University Press of New England.

_____, ed. 1979. *Ethnic Autonomy--Comparative Dynamics: The Americas, Europe and the Developing World.* New York: Pergamon Press.

_____. Forthcoming. *A State of Fear: Ethnicity in the Modern World.*

Hsu, F. L. K. 1971. *The Challenge of the American Dream: The Chinese in the United States.* Belmont, Calif.: Wadsworth.

Humphrey, C. R., and F. R. Buttel. 1982. *Environment, Energy and Society.* Belmont, Calif.: Wadsworth.

Jordan, W. D. 1968. *White over Black: American Attitudes Toward the Negro, 1550-1812.* Baltimore: Penguin Books.

Kitano, H. 1976. *Japanese Americans: The Evolution of a Subculture.* 2d ed. Englewood Cliffs, N.J.: Prentice-Hall.

Kleitz, M. 1979. Chicano identity: A tree growing from many roots. In *Ethnic Autonomy--Comparative Dynamics: The Americas, Europe and the Developing World*, ed. R. L. Hall, 85-101. New York: Pergamon Press.

Kolko, G. 1962. *Wealth and Power in America: An Analysis of Social Class and Income Distribution*. New York: Praeger.

Krieger, M. H. 1970. Six propositions on the poor and pollution. *Policy Sciences* 1:311-24.

Levine, J. H. 1985. *Levine's Atlas of Corporate Interlocks*. Vol. 1. Hanover, N.H.: Worldnet.

Levinson, D. J., with C. N. Darrow, E. B. Klein, M. H. Levinson, and B. McKee. 1978. *The Seasons of a Man's Life*. New York: Alfred A. Knopf.

Light, I. H. 1972. *Ethnic Enterprise in America: Business and Welfare Among Chinese, Japanese and Blacks*. Berkeley: University of California Press.

Lyman, S. 1974. *Chinese Americans*. New York: Random House.

Moen, E., E. Boulding, J. Lillydahl, and R. Palm. 1981. *Women and the Social Costs of Economic Development: Two Colorado Case Studies*. Boulder: Westview Press.

Oberschall, A. 1973. *Social Conflict and Social Movements*. Englewood Cliffs, N.J.: Prentice-Hall.

Said, A. A., and L. R. Simmons, eds. 1976. *Ethnicity in an International Context*. New Brunswick, N.J.: Transaction Books.

Schaefer, R. T. 1979. *Racial and Ethnic Groups*. Boston: Little, Brown.

Schnaiberg, A. 1975. Social synthesis of the societal-environmental dialectic: The role of distributional impacts. *Social Science Quarterly* 56:5-20.

Snyder, L. L. 1982. *Global Mini-Nationalisms: Autonomy or Independence*. Westport, Conn.: Greenwood Press.

Tachiki, A., E. Wong, F. Odo, with B. Wong, eds. 1971. *Roots: An Asian American Reader*. Los Angeles: Asian American Studies Center, University of California at Los Angeles.

4
Assessing the Social Impacts of Rural Resource Developments: An Overview

William R. Freudenburg

INTRODUCTION

As is apparent from the preceding chapters, one of the reasons for a book on differential impact assessment is that the considerations highlighted here have often been overlooked in past work. The present chapter[1] will elaborate on this point, beginning with a brief conceptual overview meant to include my own approach to the topic and then turning to a relatively detailed review of a body of work where attention to differential impacts would appear to be particularly appropriate--studies of "energy boomtowns" of the western United States.

Turning first to the broader conceptual issues, it is quite common in the United States to hear references to a "good" or "bad" community, to "community improvements," and so forth. At least at a general level, most people seem to have a moderate level of agreement about what these terms mean. Discussions of "the good community" even show up in sociology textbooks (e.g., Warren 1977). Upon closer examination, many such discussions seem to reflect a kind of medical metaphor: Just as a living body is more than the sum of the individual cells that make it up, so that we may speak of the "health" of the body as a whole, a "living" human community is more than just a collection of isolated individuals, so that we may speak in meaningful terms of the well-being of the community as a whole.

The argument is plausible, and indeed it often makes more sense to focus on the whole instead of on the parts, or the individuals, that make up that larger entity. Yet, in the area of social impact assessment, as this entire volume suggests, such a seemingly plausible approach actually carries some very important risks--risks that are conceptual, ethical, and pragmatic.

The conceptual risks include an unnecessarily high likelihood for confusion. "Well-being," I submit, cannot be meaningfully experienced by humans except at an individual level. Communities are abstractions in a way that an individual human's body is not. A "community" cannot laugh, cry, bleed, hope, or feel boredom, even though most of the individuals in a given community are capable of these plus many other experiences. It is meaningless to speak of an "improved quality of life in the community" unless we mean by that statement that the individuals in the community, on average, are better off now than they were earlier. Even then, as will be noted below, to be truly meaningful, the statement would need to include further details--e.g., whether this meant that everyone in the community was a bit better off, or that some groups were better off while others were less well off, and if so, which group was which.

Consider the ethical limitations of the medical metaphor. If an otherwise healthy body should come to contain a malignant or cancerous tumor, most physicians and most of the lay public would consider it only sensible to preserve the health of the body by attacking the cancerous cells through various medical technologies or by removing them from the body entirely. The situation is far less clear if the "body" is a human community. Even if it were possible to demonstrate by some criterion that an otherwise "healthy community" were somehow threatened by the presence of a "dangerous element" of persons, it is not at all clear that it is always or even generally defensible in ethical terms to "treat" or "remove" the offending individuals in the interest of preserving the well-being of the larger community. If those individuals happened to be dangerous criminals, for example, or enemy spies during a time of war, most observers would find their removal appropriate, and the medical metaphor would hold. But by far the more common examples of such "dangerous elements" seem to be minority groups, persons with unpopular opinions, dissidents, and so forth--and the determination of the "danger" presented by such groups to the "health" of the larger collectivity is most frequently made by totalitarian regimes. In ethical terms, it is not entirely clear that the "health" of the larger group is indeed protected by an attempt to isolate or exclude dissenting voices, and it is highly unlikely that the infringements upon human rights for the individual so identified could actually be justified through such logic.

The pragmatic limitations are easiest to illustrate by means of an example: Assume a community of 1,000 persons, where each person in the community has an annual income of exactly $10,000. The total income of the community would therefore be $10,000,000. Add one new person to the community--make him a king, someone who can divert $2,000 out of the next year's salary of every person in the community, thus gaining himself a regal salary of $2,000,000. Assume further that this allows him to pull in a "matching salary" of another $2,000,000 from outside. In that case, even if there were no other changes in the income of the community, there would be a total community income of $12,000,000 for that next year. Overall, this would lead to a significantly higher mean or "average income for the community" than existed in the previous year-- $11,988.01 per capita, to be exact, up almost 20 percent from the year before. If we were allowed to speak only of "the good of the entire community" in undifferentiated terms, or if we simply accepted the data on mean incomes without inquiring more deeply, we would probably conclude that the "average" income had improved. The only reasonable conclusion to be drawn from more careful analysis of actual individual experiences would be that approximately 99.9 percent of the people in the community had experienced a significant decline in their financial well-being.

These two examples should be sufficient to illustrate the general conceptual importance of disaggregating community findings, particularly when they are seen in the context of the rest of this volume. Accordingly, the remainder of this chapter will be devoted to a literature review intended to show the importance of differential impact analysis in a specific area of empirical research--the work on the "energy boomtowns" of the western United States.

DISAGGREGATING THE GLOBAL ASSERTION:
THE CASE OF ENERGY BOOMTOWNS

In the aftermath of the 1973-1974 oil embargo by the Organization of Petroleum-Exporting Countries, or OPEC, the Nixon administration crafted "Project Independence"--a program designed to lessen the dependence of the United States upon international sources of fossil fuels. One of the key elements of that program, and of all U.S. energy policy since that time, was a greatly increased reliance on domestic coal supplies, with a particular emphasis on the fuel reserves of the Rocky Mountain region. One of the consequences of this emphasis was the phenomenon of the "energy boomtown"--a small community experiencing very rapid growth, often on the order of a 100 percent increase in population within a period of two to three years, due to the effects of large-scale projects to develop the energy resources.

The growth of these communities was soon followed by the growth of a "boomtown literature"--a body of research and analysis that has been singled out both for praise (see especially Finsterbusch 1980:28) and for criticism.

Probably the most important single exchange on the boomtown research has been a special issue of the Pacific Sociological Review (July 1982, Vol. 25, No. 3) devoted to the "boomtown debate." Kenneth Wilkinson and his colleagues (1982) published a highly critical review of previous work in this area; their review was, in turn, followed by a series of highly critical responses (Albrecht 1982; Finsterbusch 1982; Freudenburg 1982b; Gale 1982; Gold 1982; Murdock and Leistritz 1982). Wilkinson and his colleagues criticized authors whom they felt to have exaggerated the presumably negative consequences of rapid community growth; several of the responses criticized Wilkinson and his colleagues--as well as a number of other authors--for accepting uncritically a number of assertions about the presumed benefits of rapid community growth. In fact, it appears that there is validity in both points of view: Both the presumed benefits and the presumed drawbacks of rapid growth have often been accepted uncritically, albeit by different persons. At least as important, however--and this is the central argument of this chapter--is that we must resist the temptation to view "pathology" or "benefit" in undifferentiated terms. As in the example of "average" community income noted above, if we wish to come to a better understanding of what development actually means for the individuals who experience well-being in a community, we need to move beyond vague or global assertions about the "overall" improvement or deterioration in the quality of life. We must begin to ask how different groups of people may differ in their experiences and to examine both our concepts and the communities to which we apply them a bit more closely. This is the task to which the remainder of this chapter will be devoted. The chapter will first review the accumulated research on different groups of "newcomers" in energy boomtowns and will then move on to findings about the long-term residents of the same communities.

Newcomers

Construction Workers. In general, researchers have not directly addressed the question of the construction workers' well-being, but most writers seem to feel that, for this group, the advantages of growth outweigh the disadvantages for two reasons. The first reason is economic: In the case of communities that grow because of large construction projects, the employment and income benefits tend to go to persons coming in from outside the community (Summers et al. 1976). For such construction workers, a job in an energy boomtown may be a highly desirable alternative to unemployment. The second reason is a matter of "free choice": Unlike the longtime resident (who, as Cortese and Jones [1977:86] have noted, often "wakes up one morning in his own bed in a different town," having had very little choice in the matter), the construction worker has the opportunity to choose whether or not to come to a new community. His very presence is thus an expression of choice (see Susskind and O'Hare 1977, for further discussion on this point).

Yet a construction worker's position is not always an enviable one. Indeed, the simple fact that a construction worker often needs to choose between unemployment and moving ("again") may indicate that the choice is not entirely a free one. Additionally, as pointed out by Massey (1977), construction workers tend to have a relatively high "dropout rate": For men who do not climb into management positions after several years, the job may begin to feel like a dead end. For persons who sometimes face extended periods of unemployment between high-paying jobs, and particularly for those who are also forced to move frequently to stay employed, savings fail to accumulate despite high paychecks. For the workers who are married and have children, "the desire to live a more settled life is hardly unusual, especially when the children enter school (Massey 1977:37-47; quotation from p.44). On balance, the construction workers appear to be helped more than they are hurt by the construction-related growth, but the balance may not be as strongly favorable as is sometimes assumed.

<u>Construction Workers' Wives</u>. The experiences of the workers' wives, by contrast, may be somewhat more bad than good. It is important to stress that very little quantitative information about this group is available, but existing literature on boomtowns generally reflects the viewpoint that rapid growth (and the "construction-worker lifestyle") have negative consequences for local women generally, and for the construction workers' wives in particular (see, for example, Albrecht 1978; Denver Research Institute 1975; Gilmore and Duff 1975; Gold 1974; Ives and Schulze 1976; Johnson and Weil 1977; Lillydahl and Moen 1979; Little 1977; Moen et al. 1979; Susskind and O'Hare 1977; Trigg 1976; Uhlmann 1978; U.S. Department of Housing and Urban Development 1976; for related findings from the literature on rural industrialization more generally, see Clemente and Summers 1973; Clemente 1973). The arguments are reasonably plausible: A construction worker's wife is generally not able to make friends or to gain a sense of personal worth from work, for her family may not

stay in a community long enough to make it worth her while to search for a job. The wife generally reports that she does not have as much influence or free choice as her husband in deciding whether or not to move to a new community, and she may also be bothered more than her husband by inadequacies in housing, recreation, and educational opportunities, or by problems of isolation that result from living in a "fringe" trailer settlement.

The few quantitative data that are available, however, appear to provide only mixed support for the predominant hypotheses: Gilmore and Duff (1975:92, 116) report that the women in their Rock Springs/Sweetwater County, Wyoming, sample were less satisfied with life in the area and had a higher level of alienation than the men in the same sample. Lantz and McKeown (1979:46) note that a greater portion of the increased caseload at the Craig, Colorado, Mental Health Center between 1973 and 1976 was due to women rather than men. These authors note, however, that the Center had an unusually high proportion of male clients in the preboom period. In addition, neither the Gilmore and Duff study nor that of Lantz and McKeown provides information specifically on the responses of construction workers' wives.[2] A study providing more detailed information (Freudenburg 1981) found only limited evidence that the newcomer housewives had any greater level of problems than the newcomer housewives in three slow-growth or no-growth comparison communities, while the highest levels of "alienation" existed not among women who were newcomers but among men who were longtime residents of the boomtown.[3] Due to the limited extant data, the hypotheses about the difficulties of construction workers' wives should be treated as reasonable, but clearly not as proven, until further research is completed. Elizabeth Moen will present an analysis of the difficulties faced by these women newcomers in Chapter 7.

"Permanent" Newcomers. As was noted earlier, not all newcomers are construction workers, and many of the nonconstruction newcomers tend to have a very different set of experiences. Researchers and local officials have tended to ignore most of the nonconstruction newcomers, and have particularly tended to ignore the higher-status newcomers associated with growth-inducing developments--the managers and supervisors, the highly skilled operatives of a "permanent workforce," or the retirees and other "urban refugees." The oversight is somewhat ironic, for the nonconstruction newcomers may indeed be somewhat more likely than the locals (or the construction workers) to have "urban values"; they may also tend to come from higher-status socioeconomic backgrounds.[4]

Probably the major reason for the lack of attention, however, is the fact that persons in this higher-status group tend to have fewer visible problems in coping with or being accepted by their new communities. They tend to want to "put roots down," to become established and esteemed members of the communities they enter. They also tend to experience different reactions from the host communities. In particular, the long-term new residents tend to be "joiners" and volunteer "workers," often becoming leaders of community clubs, churches, and business and voluntary associations; they tend to be seen as "positive," "community-building" people; their children often become leaders in the local school system, as well. Hogg and Smith (1970) report that newcomers in Sweet Home, Oregon (who were mainly former suburbanites from the Portland and Salem areas, drawn to Sweet Home for its recreational potential) soon became "influential members" of the community--city manager, superintendent of schools, newspaper editor, president of the Chamber of Commerce, and so on. "Long-term" newcomers of four Colorado study communities showed a similar pattern, with some of their children becoming cheerleaders, scholastic leaders, athletic stars, and even homecoming queens (Freudenburg 1979a). Clearly, a significant number of newcomers who have decided to make the effort have been able to be accepted quite well into their new communities, although most of them report they continue to be seen as "newcomers" for a very long time. Kristen Yount will present a case study of miners as newcomers in Chapter 5.

One more thing needs to be said about the difference between "temporary" newcomers and "permanent" newcomers before we move on to long-term residents: The "temporary" newcomers often turn into permanent residents, and they do so more often than most observers realize. The construction workers who "drop out" of the migratory lifestyle, by definition, have to drop out someplace, and a certain proportion of them will decide to settle in the communities that have grown because of their presence. This is further evidence that even the "modern-day nomads" are not greatly different from the locals in their values; when the newcomers decide to settle down, moreover, they become even more difficult for an outsider to distinguish from the long-term locals: Little (1977:418) reports that many of the very "oldtimers" in Page, Arizona, who complained about the "undesirable elements" brought to their community by a boom had actually been "boomers" themselves on earlier projects.

Longtime Residents

Local Government Officials. Among the first of the locals to feel the impacts of rapid growth are the persons who work in the local public sector. Unfortunately, while most of the major environmental impact statements to date have discussed the effects of rapid growth on local governments (see, e.g., U.S. Geological Survey and Montana Department of State Lands 1979:II: 83; U.S. Bureau of Land Management 1978b; see also the overview guidebooks such as U.S. Department of Housing and Urban Development 1976; U.S. Energy Research and Development Administration 1977; U.S. Environmental Protection Agency 1978), virtually no research has been done on the impacts on local governmental officials. Part of the problem, at least in terms of collecting systematic data, is the fact that there tend to be so few officials in any given community: Even if "every single mayor in town" is severely affected by rapid growth, for example, it is difficult to know how much that tells us about "mayors" and how much it tells us about the unique characteristics of a given person who happens to be mayor of a given town. At least in qualitative terms, however, some preliminary "findings" are beginning to emerge, although they should be treated as tentative for the time being. On the positive side, for those officials who have wished to see their communities grow, or who have successfully managed to channel or plan the growth in desired directions, substantial benefits may come in the form of feelings of personal accomplishment or the satisfaction of a job well done. Additionally, some officials have been able to "benefit" from growth in a very direct, financial way.

On the other hand, Cortese and Jones (1977) have succinctly pointed out two ways in which rapid growth can tend to make life less than pleasant for local officials. The simpler of the two is that the officials are often asked or required to do more of something: They need to provide more police protection, treat more sewage, maintain more roads, and so on. But the second set of changes tends to be more troublesome, because it comprises "impacts upon the local government [that are] qualitative in nature," changes that require a governing body "to do something it had not done before, such as planning and zoning, conducting new and complicated intergovernmental or government-industry relations, devising new taxation schemes, or seeking federal or state funds" (Cortese and Jones 1977:80).

The officials' difficulties are often made worse, moreover, by the very "impact researchers" who are supposed to be helping out. On many occasions, some of the difficulties are caused by genuine value differences between local officials and impact researchers--

for example, on the merits or drawbacks of "informality" in governmental procedures--but the more serious problems generally have to do with the accuracy of projections. The overall projections, in turn, depend on the accuracy of the companies' own figures. Errors of 50 to 100 percent in company projections are not at all uncommon, and the figures sometimes seem to change almost on a weekly basis (for an excellent discussion, see Moen 1984). Projects that are "absolutely definite" one week are "economically infeasible" the next; projects that are expected to require five hundred new workers wind up bringing in more than a thousand. As one researcher put it privately:

> Those workforce projections are absolutely vital. They're the starting point for every computation we make. They're the most critical stage of the whole process--and they're nothing but papier-mache . . . if the project manager can move something up, and get it done sooner, he's going to do it. . . .
>
> The locals really like those nice, pat numbers--but they don't work. . . . And something they don't usually understand is that I have about as much say over _actual_ project manning as [the local priest] has over the selection of the pope.

The local governmental officials, however--not the impact researchers, and not generally even the companies whose developments cause the impacts--are the persons who will be held responsible for whatever "preparing" the communities actually do. Given the degree of uncertainty that usually exists--in addition to problems of inequities and imbalances, the fact that facilities are often needed before tax revenues become available, and the fact that the problems of rapid growth often require a set of skills very different from those required in a stable situation--the officials are almost guaranteed of either "overpreparing" or "underpreparing." They can also be sure that they will get blamed, no matter what happens. My own observations suggest, to oversimplify only slightly, that virtually none of the officials who are in office the year before rapid growth begins are likely to be in the same office a half dozen years later, although they may be at least as likely to leave through resignation or retirement as through election-day defeats. Some of the happiest boomtown residents I've met are persons who completed their terms in office just before a boom began.

In addition to the officials who fill local elected posts, there are persons who work in the public sector in a salaried capacity--the professionals who staff law enforcement agencies, mental health centers, hospitals, etc. The literature has only recently begun to include research on these public servants (see, e.g., Weisz 1980 or Guillaume and Wenston 1980:90-95), and the group appears to deserve much closer attention in the future.

Businessmen. The one group of longtime residents most often expected to benefit from rapid growth is the local business community. Indeed, perhaps the only persons who are expected to benefit more than business owners in general are persons who are subsets of that group, such as real estate agents or landlords. The advantages can be summarized quite simply: If there are more people and more dollars in town, there will generally be more business as well (for further discussions, see Shields et al. 1979; Johnson and Weil 1977).

Available data indicate that rapid-growth communities generally do experience substantial increases in total sales volume; considerably less is known, however, about the distribution of the increased sales or about the actual implications of the changes for the personal well-being of local businessmen. According to Thompson et al. (1979:15), "it appears that during the early stages of construction, sales increases accrue mainly to existing businesses, as opposed to new trade and service establishments. However, this pattern may change as construction at each site proceeds." By contrast, Vander Muellen and Paananen (1977), using figures from the Department of Commerce on the Rock Springs area of Wyoming, actually found:

a decrease in nonfarm proprietors' incomes in Sweetwater County between 1970 and 1974 of 14 percent in constant dollar (1970) prices. We question the accuracy of this estimate, but on reflection it is not clear that small businessmen enjoy the large gains from impact that we originally thought. We have noted the private service sector in Sweetwater County expanded rapidly in response to growth. This growth often means the entry of new businesses rather than expansion of older firms. Some of the newcomers are large, efficient, and incorporated which means their income does not show up as proprietors' income.

Older businesses may find themselves facing large, efficient competitors rather than more customers. . . . The likelihood that some small businessmen are inefficient and unable to adapt . . . is not a plea for compensation, but a recognition that high incomes to original businesses may be exaggerated and are almost certainly temporary (1977:312-13).

While local businessmen may tend to overestimate the level of financial benefit that they will gain from growth, a limited amount of information seems to indicate that they may underestimate the degree of change likely to take place in other areas. In particular, many business owners have found that growth requires them to change their ways of doing business--using new advertising techniques, discontinuing specialized services, learning that they "can't afford the time" to chat with customers, and so on (Cortese and Jones 1977:80-81; Little 1975). Even if the businessmen make numerous changes, it appears that they will often discover to their chagrin that many of the newcomers still choose to shop elsewhere, so that much of the community's anticipated wealth "trickles out" to other areas, rather than strengthening the local business sector (Summers 1978; Murdock et al. 1984). Moreover, in a free-enterprise economy, the increased numbers of real consumer dollars that do stay in the community will usually attract an increased number of real competitors as well--and, at least in the communities I have studied, the new competitors include national chains. All in all, it appears that growth will generally lead to greater increases in revenues than in expenses, but the margin may not always be so great as businessmen and others expect it will be.

Perhaps the bottom line here is that rapid growth is often accompanied by a rapid rate of turnover in business ownership. The preboom owners, faced with numerous changes in their community and clientele, but offered very attractive prices for their businesses, often just decide to sell out. The turnover is by no means all bad, leading as it often does to "new blood" and to a more aggressive approach to merchandising, as well as often creating sizable profits for those who sell. The turnover often does mean, however, that businesses are taken over by persons with less familiarity with the area and sometimes by persons with less of a reputation to protect as well. If the new business owners go deeply into debt to buy the businesses, they may find themselves unable to meet their commitments, and if their situation becomes desperate, they may take desperate measures. In particular, pregrowth communities that do not have the capacity to investigate arson cases may wish to develop just such a capacity.

It may be, indeed, that the greatest advantages of rapid growth for the local business sector occur not in owner profits, but in the selection and prices of the economically purchasable goods and services that become available. Despite numerous references to the "soaring cost of living" in boomtowns, the best available data indicate that, except for the critical area of housing, "prices for goods and services in [impact] counties differ only slightly from those in [nongrowth] control counties" (Watts et al. 1977:15). My own firsthand impressions generally support the quantitative findings of Watts and his colleagues.

In other words, while the cost of living does seem to rise substantially in the area of housing--with the sudden presence of new people causing the laws of supply and demand to work with a particular vengeance in that area--the other costs of living may rise no faster in rapid-growth communities than they do on a national average. In fact, this author's admittedly subjective impression is that--outside of the important area of housing--the ratio between the quality of goods and services available for purchase, on the one hand, and the prices charged for those services and goods, on the other, may actually improve slightly as a community grows. The national chains, whatever their disadvantages, are often able to sell toothpaste more cheaply than the local mom-and-pop drugstore. The mom-and-pop drugstore has other advantages and may provide other services (such as personalized attention, a longer-term commitment to customers, community-specific credit policies, specialized delivery services, and so on) that a K-Mart does not provide, and we would be foolish to disregard those services simply because they do not result in lower price-tag totals. It is similarly important to recognize, however, that the price tags on the toothpaste may actually reflect slightly lower costs, and that the range of choice available is quite likely to expand, when the number of retail outlets in the community and the competition among retailers increase. Despite the presumed increases in the economic cost of living in boomtowns, in other words, it may be that business customers face a somewhat improved situation after growth occurs.

Ranchers and Farmers. Persons in the local agricultural sector, by contrast, tend not to be affected in a positive way by rapid growth. The only consistent exceptions appear to be those landowners who are nearing retirement, or who for other reasons wish to sell their property, and who can do so at inflated rates because of the growth of a community.

One study (Bradley et al. 1979) interviewed 252 ranchers and farmers in northeastern Wyoming's Powder River Basin and found that agriculturalists who expected to sell or lease land for development within the next ten years favored development (51.4 percent versus 28.6 percent, with 20 percent undecided), while those who did not expect to sell or lease land generally opposed development (16.3 percent in favor, and 63.3 percent opposed, with 20.4 percent undecided). These findings, however, need to be interpreted with considerable caution. The response rate in this survey was somewhat low (only 130 of 252 agriculturalists, or approximately 51.6 percent, actually responded to the survey), and even the 252 clearly would not have been a representative sample of agriculturalists in the area. A criterion for inclusion in the survey was that the agriculturalists "own surface land overlying potentially developable coal" (Bradley et al. 1979:17). In other words, while the survey respondents were 9 percent of the operators in the area, their responses might not be representative of those that might have been obtained from ranchers and farmers whose lands did not lie above potentially strippable coal. To make a more reliable comparison between ranchers who plan to sell or lease and those who do not, it would be desirable to compare all of the respondents from this sample to the very ranchers and farmers in the area who were excluded from the sample at the outset. Moreover, because this study apparently identified the agriculturalists who were likely to benefit from development by asking survey respondents whether or not they "expected to sell or lease land for development within the next ten years" (Bradley et al. 1979:36), the study encountered some difficulties with what researchers call "confounded causality": While it is logical to expect that persons who sell their land will benefit, it is similarly logical to expect that ranchers favoring energy development would be more likely than opponents to report that they "expect" to benefit, and that the ranchers opposing development would be more likely to report that they "expect not to sell or lease" their land--strictly because of the attitudes toward development that they hold. In short, while the findings of Bradley and his colleagues are quite plausible, and are based on the largest sample of its kind available today, the findings should be seen as merely suggestive until more definitive research has been completed.

All researchers appear to be in clear agreement with Bradley and his colleagues on one point: For agriculturalists who do not hope or plan to sell their land, rapid growth commonly creates a situation that they wish would go away.

Again here, the best documentation comes from studies of energy development in the West, starting with the early studies of Raymond Gold and his associates at the University of Montana in the early 1970s (Gold 1974). One important reason for agriculturalists' problems can be stated quite simply: Ranchers are likely to be in competition with the new developments (and with the people attracted to the area by the new developments) for water, for workers, and sometimes even for land. The significance of the competition for water in the arid West should be self-evident; the competition for workers--a situation I have come to call the "hired hand problem" (Freudenburg

1979a)--can be explained almost as quickly. Most ranchers will tell you that they simply do not receive enough income from their ranches to be able to "compete with the wages that they're paying out at the plant." While many hired hands and other persons who work in agriculture may have very little interest in what they disdainfully call a "nine-to-five job," the lure of higher wages is still quite attractive to many of them. Competition for land becomes salient to ranchers who feel a need to expand their operations in order to remain competitive, yet who are similarly unable to compete with the high prices that developers can pay for land. On the other hand, if the new developments offer part-time employment to the ranchers and farmers themselves, the developments can provide significant assistance in helping otherwise marginal agriculturalists to keep their operations solvent. This is particularly true if the development can offer "part-time" work on a seasonal basis. To date, however, most major construction projects have shown little inclination to "bend" union or company rules or to hire large numbers of locals on a part-time basis.

More generally, agricultural pursuits do not always coexist very comfortably with high or increasing population densities. If there are more people in the area, there will also be more cars on the roads--and off the roads--hitting livestock by accident or sometimes just chasing them around for the "sport" of it. Paved roads can make things just a bit easier for rustlers, while increased traffic on the same roads can make it harder to use the roads for moving livestock from summer to winter range. A population increase means there can be more vandals around, shooting up signs and buildings or even simply "making a lot of noise and scaring the livestock." In general, the presence of more people also means that there will be more gates left open on the ranch and more dogs roaming around nearby, and it may even mean that ranchers and farmers will be forced to pay higher tax bills, although quantitative data to test this last suggestion have been quite limited to date. All of these changes, however, can perhaps be seen most accurately as relatively minor irritants rather than as major problems.

Perhaps equally important are the changes that very few of the ranchers or farmers have talked about--changes in their local status, changes in the ways in which persons in agriculture are treated in a growing community. At least in most rural sections of the West, persons in agriculture have traditionally been the "backbone of the local economy," and they have tended to exercise a good deal of influence in local affairs. With the new people (and the new sources of income) flooding into the area, the ranchers' symbolic position has been affected at least as much as their "objective" position has been. Existing studies (see, for example, Blevins et al. 1974:34-43; Montana 1974:111-831; Gold 1974, 1976; Freudenburg et al. 1977) have consistently found that ranchers and other persons in agriculture are among the most vocal opponents of growth before it occurs, and my Colorado study found substantial unhappiness among ranchers after growth had begun. In fact, the growth appeared to have affected the boomtown-area ranchers quite deeply.

Among most adults, my study found very few differences between the boomtown and the three nonboom communities; adults in all four communities were generally similar in their attitudes toward growth, in their feelings about existing or future changes in their communities, and in their assessments of the overall quality of their lives. Among the ranchers, by contrast, there were clear and consistent differences. When compared with the ranchers in three nonboom communities, the boomtown ranchers were significantly more likely to say that their community had grown "worse" in the three or four years before the survey, to say that the recent rate of change had been "too fast," and to assess the quality of their own lives in a very negative way. They were significantly less happy, significantly more likely to describe their lives as "disappointing" (rather than "rewarding") and as "discouraging" (rather than "hopeful"); they were even more likely to have experienced a number of stress-related physical symptoms (Freudenburg 1979a).

Clearly, because these are strictly comparisons of boomtown ranchers against the ranchers of the other three communities, we would not expect to find such differences if the boomtown-area ranchers had not been substantially affected by the growth, or if they were merely upset by the same kinds of high costs and low prices that were affecting ranching operations in general. It is similarly clear that these data cannot be explained by a malaise that is limited to newcomers, for the ranchers in all areas were highly likely to be longtime residents of their regions. These data are merely suggestive, coming as they do from a single study; but what they suggest is that the ranchers may have been so deeply affected by the growth that the changes may have altered their views, not only of the community, but of life itself. Further discussions on ranchers and farmers will be found in Patrick Jobes's chapter (see Chapter 6).

Other Local Workers. The remaining "workers" who live in a community before growth occurs can generally be divided into two groups, and those two groups will experience growth in very different ways. They are, to put it simply, the persons who get better-paid new employment because of the growth and those who do not.

In general, at least in the economic literature on growth, the entire group of local workers is felt to benefit from growth because of the higher average income that is often reported for the group after growth occurs (see, e.g., U.S. Bureau of Land Management 1978a; for a critical review, see Summers et al. 1976).

The example of the king at the beginning of this chapter, however, should teach us to be wary of such assumptions. For persons who take new, growth-related jobs, the effects of growth would generally seem to be quite positive. The rancher may not be very happy about losing his hired hand--nor might the local business owners or local governmental officials, who often lose their "hired hands" as well--but by an economist's definition, persons who take new and more highly paid jobs at a new facility were underemployed before the growth took place, and they will have benefited directly from the growth. Some of them, in turn, might be replaced in their old (but less highly paid) jobs by other local residents who were not previously in the workforce,[5] and most observers would agree that the persons in this second group of workers will have received a direct financial benefit from the growth as well.

Before we conclude that growth is positive for the entire category of "pregrowth local workers," however, it is important to consider as well the experience of the people who do not take new, growth-related employment--the ranch hands, teachers, policemen, mechanics, plumbers, and other local workers who keep on doing whatever they had been doing before the growth occurred. Again here, in other words, it is useful to remember that aggregate-level data may not adequately reflect the experiences of all (or even most) members of a given group or subgroup (Summers et al. 1976:3). Moreover, it is useful to divide the workers who do not take new jobs into two smaller groups: those who rent their homes and those who own them.

As was mentioned earlier, while the general (economic) cost of living may not increase greatly in a growth community, the cost of housing often does rise substantially. In energy boomtowns, it is not uncommon to see rent and house prices double or even triple within a period of two to three years. Obviously, most persons who own homes will have few objections to an increased value of real estate unless their taxes rise substantially, but persons who rent their residences-- and who remain in their pregrowth jobs, with salaries that rarely come close to doubling or tripling--are likely to be rather dismayed by the changes (Gilmore and Duff 1975:10; Dixon 1978:224; Little and Lovejoy 1977). This, too, is an area that needs further research, but it is probable that local workers (particularly in the service sector) would be among the least likely of all local residents to own their own homes before development occurs, often simply because their relatively low wages do not permit them to own homes. It goes almost without saying that low wages are equally ill-suited to paying dramatically increased rents. For the relatively substantial subgroup of local workers who remain in their pregrowth jobs and who did not own their own homes prior to the growth, the "average" increase in economic well-being for the entire category may provide relatively little consolation, although for homeowners and for persons whose employment status improves, our common wisdom about the beneficial effects of local growth for local workers may be generally accurate.

Elderly Persons. Of all the propositions and findings which exist in the literature on rapid community growth, one of the most frequent is the hypothesis that elderly persons are among the most negatively affected of all local groups (see, for example, Albrecht 1978:87; Weisz 1979:34-36; Davidson 1979:21; Gold 1978:22; Little 1977:411; see also the regional environmental impact statements such as U.S. Department of the Interior and U.S. Geological Survey 1978; U.S. Bureau of Land Management 1978b; North Dakota and U.S. Department of the Interior 1978). The usual argument is as follows: First, the local elderly populations are highly likely to be living on fixed incomes and would therefore be negatively affected by a presumed increase in the cost of living. Second, elderly persons are among the least likely of all locals to get jobs from new, growth-inducing developments. Third, according to some authors, elderly persons are also less flexible or adaptable than are young people (see the review in Freudenburg 1976).

But while these arguments seem reasonable enough, it appears that they have never been backed up with quantitative evidence; recent evidence, moreover, raises serious questions about the accuracy of the proposition. In one of my own studies, which compared the responses of the elderly residents in a boomtown with those of elderly residents in three control communities, I was unable to find any evidence that the elderly persons in the boom community felt significantly worse about the quality of their lives than did the elderly persons in the three nonboom communities. Indeed, if any differences existed, they may have run in the other direction--the elderly persons in the boomtown may have felt slightly better about life than did the elderly persons in the other three communities --although the differences were always so small that they were not statistically significant (Freudenburg 1979a:224-31). A more recent study, which examined stress levels in Gillette, Wyoming, found that experienced stress reached its lowest levels in the older age groups (Pattinson et al. 1979:17).

These findings, which are among the first to come from interviews of elderly residents in actual impact communities, help underline the importance of obtaining local residents' own reports on their experiences, in addition to aggregate-level economic data, in future research endeavors. They also point out the importance of considering social and cultural factors, as well as economic ones, in our explanations and predictions. The economic data that have become available to date do seem to imply a decline in well-being for the elderly boomtown residents, at least at the aggregate level--yet the people themselves do not report any such decline. Why not? I would suggest three sets of factors--one psychological, one social, and one cultural. Psychologically, the very fact that some of the older residents of boomtowns are relatively "set in their ways" provides an important source of internalized continuity in their lives at a time when many external changes are taking place. Socially, the elderly people of the growth communities I know best are quite well buffered, being supported and surrounded by a number of good friends; I have seen absolutely no evidence that the "senior citizens . . . are increasingly isolated, and have their meager network of relationships destroyed" by rapid growth (Brown 1977:5; for further data, see Freudenburg 1980). Culturally, the elderly residents of many pregrowth communities have strong beliefs in the importance of growth. To most of the older people of the boomtown, the presence of new retail outlets--a new K-Mart, Kentucky Fried Chicken, Taco Hut, Pizza Hut, McDonald's, shopping mall, and so on--can be a sign that the outside world has not "forgotten" their small community, a sign that their community will not become another ghost town. The new jobs in town--and the growth--are signs that "the young people can stay in the area," rather than needing to leave to find employment.

The Youth. The young people of growth communities, however, provide another illustration of the importance of including more than just economic considerations in our thinking. Our common wisdom is that the younger persons of a community--those who have just started their work careers, or who are planning to start them soon--are the one local group most likely to get the new jobs, most likely to increase their incomes, and best able to adapt to the changes in the community. As their elders often note, rapid growth in their hometowns can provide these youths with the opportunity to find work without moving away to some strange city. The logic is so direct and reasonable that researchers have apparently seen little need to double-check it against the young persons' own firsthand reports.

At least two studies, however, have actually interviewed the young people, and the results of these studies differ substantially from what had previously been expected. The first study compared high school students in a Colorado energy boomtown against the students in three relatively stable Colorado communities (Freudenburg 1979a, 1979b),[6] while the second study included high school students from all of the rural counties in Utah (Seyfrit 1978). Neither study found community growth to increase the likelihood that the students would plan to stay in their communities after completing high school. In the Colorado study, moreover, the students in the boomtown were somewhat more likely than the students in the comparison communities to say that they planned to move away after they graduated; in all four towns, but particularly in the boomtown, the students indicated that they would actually be less likely to stay in the area "if there were more energy-related jobs."

More important than their plans, however, at least in the context of the present paper, are the students' reports about their own well-being. Unlike the case among their parents and grandparents--some of whom appear to have benefited from the growth, and most of whom do not appear to have been greatly affected one way or the other--the students' responses revealed a clear trend, and the trend was overwhelmingly negative. They had a lower level of satisfaction with their community, more negative attitudes toward energy resource development, lower levels of satisfaction, and higher levels of alienation than did their counterparts in the three comparison communities--even though the longtime adult residents of the same boomtown did not differ significantly from the longtime adult residents of the same three comparison communities on the items that showed the differences among the adolescents (Freudenburg 1981, 1984). The students in the boomtown also showed a pattern of consistently negative evaluations on items that were not included in the adult questionnaire: They had more negative attitudes about their schools, their peers, their teachers, and even their own lives, as well as being more negatively disposed toward the energy developments taking place. They described a social situation that few people would find desirable, being significantly more likely to speak of fear, threats, and criminal victimization than were the students in the comparison communities. All of these findings, moreover, were based upon comparisons with other students of the same age who were living in the same general region, so in all likelihood the differences cannot simply be signs of general youthful cynicism or of "changes in the times," except as they represent changes taking place in the boomtown alone. Finally, these findings could not be explained by differences in sex, age, or class background, and an imposition of statistical controls for length of residence in the community showed that the boomtown/other differences among oldtimers were generally in the same order of magnitude as were the boomtown/other differences among newcomers (Freudenburg 1984).

It is not generally considered surprising that the children of the newcomers would have low evaluations of their own well-being: Although the literature has generally not discussed their situations, some of these young people have literally gone through a dozen years of schooling without ever spending a full year in one place. What is in many ways surprising is that even the students who have spent more or all of their lives in the boomtown show the same pattern of responses--not just in the case of a small number of "complainers," but taking the average of the longtime students as a whole.

As was the case in understanding the responses of the elderly residents, the best available explanations for the young people's responses apparently have relatively little to do with economics and a good deal more to do with sociocultural factors. The most important factors appear to be two in number: First, psychologically, the young people are disturbed in part because they are not yet as "set in their ways" as are their grandparents, or rather, because they do not yet know what these "ways" are, do not have a well-developed sense of self. "Unlike their grandparents, these young persons [do] not have 50 years' worth of momentum to keep themselves on course" (Freudenburg 1984:703). Second, socially, they are not as well-insulated as their elders: Unlike many of the adult locals of the community, who have learned to shop and drive at different times to avoid the crowds, but who have otherwise managed to continue living their pre-impact lives with relatively little interference from newcomers, the students come into contact with newcomers every day that they attend class. In short, the young people of the community may actually be more vulnerable to the changes than are their elders--yet because of their social situations, they may be forced to face the changes more directly.

A LOOK TO THE FUTURE

Perhaps the clearest need identified by the research summarized in this chapter is for future research that includes interviews with the actual residents of impact communities, and that monitors the residents' experiences and perceptions over time--emphasizing the sociocultural realm as well as economic and logistical matters. Economic factors and the adequacy of facilities and services are highly important considerations, particularly in rapid-growth communities; yet, as is becoming increasingly evident, it takes far more than just an adequate economic standard of living and an adequate level of services to support human well-being.

The need for broadening our inquiry exists both in the methods we use for measuring or inferring well-being and in the reasoning we use to make sense of our findings. The elderly persons in a boom community would be thought by the best available economic measures (and lines of reasoning) to be negatively affected by growth; in at least two communities they have not seen themselves as having been so greatly disadvantaged, and sociocultural explanations can give us some understanding of why they have not. Similarly, while the best available economic reasoning tells us that young people are fortunate to have an opportunity to live in a growing community, the youths in the two actual studies conducted to date did not appear to be so delighted, and sociocultural reasoning can provide an explanation. The clear preponderance of existing "well-being" research from growth communities, in short, consists of reasoned hunches, economically focused; testing existing propositions and findings against the actual personal experiences of locals is probably the greatest of our future research needs.

CONCLUSION

To return again to the theme that began this chapter and that is shared with the other chapters in this book, a given type of situation can differ dramatically in the implications it has for different groups of people. The energy boomtown provides a particularly clear case in point. Many of the persons involved in the policy debate over western U.S. energy developments have concluded that rapid community growth would be "a dream come true" for local residents. At the other extreme, some have argued that energy boom development is "a form of social and cultural genocide." These kinds of arguments, moreover, have not been limited to policy actors alone, since, as noted earlier, even social scientific researchers have often tended to see the advantages or disadvantages of development in relatively undifferentiated terms.

Both sides in the debate appear to be partially correct, but both also appear to be incorrect, and the errors appear to follow a systematic pattern: There are good empirical and conceptual reasons for concluding that rapid growth of the kind found in western U.S. energy boomtowns will have beneficial consequences for certain identifiable groups and that it will have negative consequences for others. As a result, both our policy decisions and our understanding of the social world in which we live can be improved by looking at the overall picture with this kind of increased attention to detail.

NOTES

1. This is Scientific Paper Number 7203, Research Project 0478, College of Agriculture and Home Economics, Washington State University. Portions of this chapter draw heavily from material originally published in Weber and Howell (1982); see specifically Freudenburg (1982a).

2. Both provide some discussion of length of residence--39 percent of the Gilmore and Duff sample had lived in the county for less than three years (Gilmore and Duff 1975:95), and Lantz and McKeown report (1979:46) that their population "was approximately evenly divided between oldtimers and newcomers." Neither study, however, provides a data breakdown for the construction workers' wives separated from the responses of other women.

3. In addition, the very image of "isolated" mobile-home dwellers, whether women or men, may contain more fiction than fact. Massey and Lewis (1979:85) report: "Only two of 114 respondents [from a sample of mobile-home-dwelling newcomers in Douglas, Wyoming] knew neither their next door neighbors nor anyone in the immediate neighborhood. More than 80 percent of all respondents knew other neighbors as well as one or both of their next door neighbors."

4. While the "permanent" newcomers are in some ways more visibly dissimilar from the longtime residents than are the short-term newcomers, even here the actual "value differences" between newcomers and longtimers may be relatively minor. Potentially relevant data on this point come from a statewide sample of three thousand North Carolina residents, which found "considerable value consensus" between urban residents who planned to move to rural areas and the rural residents who planned to stay where they were (Christenson 1979:338). The only significant difference was in the higher value that the "urban refugees" placed on recreation--a difference entirely explained by their younger average age. By contrast, rural residents who planned to move to urban areas did indeed have values that often differed from those of metropolitan residents.

5. In addition, some of the new and highly paid

jobs may be taken directly by persons who were previously unemployed.

6. This study utilized responses from all available high school sophomores and seniors in the one high school of each town. Questionnaires were filled out by the students during normal class hours within a peiod of approximately ten days in all four communities during the spring of 1977. Further details are available in Freudenburg (1979a, 1979b).

REFERENCES

Albrecht, S. L. 1978. Socio-cultural factors and energy resource development in rural areas in the West. Journal of Environmental Management 7:73-90.

———. 1982. Commentary. Pacific Sociological Review 25:297-306.

Blevins, A. L., J. G. Thompson, and C. Ellis. 1974. Social Impact Analysis of Campbell County, Wyoming. Laramie: Wyoming Environmental Institute.

Bradley, E. B., J. J. Jacobs, and A. Vanvig. 1979. Impact of Coal Development on Ranchers and Farmers in Wyoming's Powder River Basin. Laramie: Agricultural Experiment Station, University of Wyoming.

Brown, B. S. 1977. The Impact of the New Boomtowns: The Lessons of Gillette and the Powder River Basin. Washington, D.C: United States Government Printing Office.

Christenson, J. A. 1979. Value orientations of potential migrants and nonmigrants. Rural Sociology 44:331-44.

Clemente, F. 1973. Effects of industrial development on heads of households: Comment. Growth and Change 14:20-21.

Clemente, F., and G. F. Summers. 1973. Large Industries in Small Towns: Who Benefits? Working Paper RID 73.9. Madison, Wis.: Center for Applied Sociology.

Cortese, C. F., and B. Jones. 1977. The sociological analysis of boomtowns. Western Sociological Review 8:76-90.

Davidson, D. C. 1979. Overview of the boomtown phenomenon and its effect on women and minorities. In Energy Resource Development: Implications for Women and Minorities in the Intermountain West, ed. United States Commission on Civil Rights, 15-25. Washington, D.C.: United States Government Printing Office.

Denver Research Institute. 1975. Factors Influencing an Area's Ability to Absorb a Large-Scale Commercial Coal-Processing Complex: A Case Study of the Fort

Union Lignite Region. Washington, D.C.: Energy Research and Development Administration.
Dixon, M. 1978. What Happened to Fairbanks? The Effects of the Trans-Alaska Oil Pipeline on the Community of Fairbanks, Alaska. Boulder, Colo.: Westview Press.
Finsterbusch, K. 1980. Understanding Social Impacts: Assessing the Effects of Public Projects. Beverly Hills, Calif.: Sage Publications.
_____. 1982. Commentary: Boomtown disruption thesis: Assessment of current status. Pacific Sociological Review 25:307-22.
Freudenburg, W. R. 1976. The social impact of energy boom development on rural communities: A review of literatures and some predictions. Presented at the annual meeting of the American Sociological Association, New York.
_____. 1979a. People in the impact zone: The human and social consequences of energy boomtown growth in four western Colorado communities. Ph.D. diss. Department of Sociology, Yale University.
_____. 1979b. Boomtown's youth. Presented at annual meetings of the Rural Sociological Society, Burlington, Vt.
_____. 1980. The density of acquaintanceship: An overlooked variable in community research? Presented at the annual meeting of the American Sociological Association, New York.
_____. 1981. Women and men in an energy boomtown: Adjustment, alienation, and adaptation. Rural Sociology 46:220-44.
_____. 1982a. The impacts of rapid growth on the social and personal well-being of local community residents. In Coping with Rapid Growth in Rural Communities, ed. B. A. Weber and R. E. Howell, 137-70. Boulder, Colo.: Westview Press.
_____. 1982b. Commentary: Balance and bias in boomtown research. Pacific Sociological Review 25:323-38.
_____. 1984. Boomtown's youth: The differential impacts of rapid community growth on adolescents and adults. American Sociological Review 49:697-705.
Freudenburg, W. R., L. M. Bacigalupi, A. Clay, C. Landoll, and K. N. Deeds. 1977. Subjective responses to an energy boomtown situation: A preliminary report on research in progress in four western Colorado towns. Presented at the annual meeting of the American Sociological Association, Chicago.
Gale, R. 1982. Commentary. Pacific Sociological Review 25:339-48.
Gilmore, J. S., and M. K. Duff. 1975. Boom Town Growth Management: A Case Study of Rock Springs--Green River, Wyoming. Boulder, Colo.: Westview Press.

Gold, R. 1974. *A Comparative Study of the Impacts of Coal Development on the Way of Life of People in the Coal Areas of Eastern Montana and Northeastern Wyoming*. Denver: Northern Great Plains Resources Program.
———. 1976. Trespasses and other social impacts of Northern Plains coal development. Presented at the annual meeting of the American Association for the Advancement of Science, Boston.
———. 1978. Industrial trespass at Colstrip, Montana. Missoula: Institute for Social Research, University of Montana. Mimeograph.
———. 1982. Commentary. *Pacific Sociological Review* 25:349-56.
Guillaume, C. L., and S. R. Wenston. 1980. Child abuse in impact communities. In *The Boom Town: Problems and Promises in the Energy Vortex*, ed. J. Davenport III and J. A. Davenport, 85-98. Laramie: Department of Social Work, University of Wyoming.
Hogg, T. C., and C. Smith. 1970. *Socio-cultural Impacts of Water Resource Development in the Santiam River Basin*. Corvallis: Water Resources Research Institute, Oregon State University.
Ives, B., and W. Schulze. 1976. *Boomtown Impacts of Energy Development in the Lake Powell Region*. Albuquerque: Resource Economics Program, University of New Mexico.
Johnson, S., and E. Weil. 1977. *Social Aspects of Power Plant Siting: Ohio River Basin Energy Study*. Vol. 3-D, *Special Study Report*. Washington, D.C.: Environmental Protection Agency.
Lantz, A. E., and R. L. McKeown. 1979. Social/psychological problems of women and their families associated with rapid growth. In *Energy Resource Development: Implications for Women and Minorities in the Intermountain West*, ed. United States Commission on Civil Rights, 42-54. Washington, D.C.: United States Government Printing Office.
Lillydahl, J. H., and E. W. Moen. 1979. The economic position of women and their employment opportunities in energy boomtowns. In *Energy Resource Development: Implications for Women and Minorities in the Intermountain West*, ed. United States Commission on Civil Rights, 65-75. Washington, D.C.: United States Government Printing Office.
Little, R. L. 1975. Rural industrialization: The case of Four Corners. In *Societal Implications of Energy Scarcity: Social and Technological Priorities in Steady State and Constricting Systems*, ed. L. F. Carter and L. N. Gray, 108-31. Pullman: Department of Sociology and Social Research Center, Washington State University.
———. 1977. Some social consequences of boom towns. *North Dakota Law Review* 53:401-25.

Little, R. L., and S. B. Lovejoy. 1977. Employment Benefits from Rural Industrialization. Los Angeles: Lake Powell Research Project.

Massey, G. 1977. Newcomers in an Impacted Area of Wyoming. Rockville, Md: Center for Studies of Metropolitan Problems, National Institute of Mental Health.

Massey, G., and D. Lewis. 1979. Energy development and mobile home living: The myth of suburbia revisited. The Social Science Journal 16:81-91.

Moen, E. 1984. Voodoo forecasting: Technical, political and ethical issues regarding the projection of local population growth. Population Research and Policy Review 3:1-25.

Moen, E., E. Boulding, J. Lillydahl, and R. Palm. 1979. Women and Energy Development: Impact and Response. Boulder, Colo.: Institute of Behavioral Science.

Montana, State of. 1974. Draft Environmental Impact Statement on Colstrip Electric Generating Units 3 and 4, 500 Kilovolt Transmission Lines and Associated Facilities. Helena: Montana Department of Natural Resources and Conservation.

Murdock, S. H., and F. L. Leistritz. 1982. Commentary. Pacific Sociological Review 25:357-66.

Murdock, S. H., F. L. Leistritz, R. R. Hamm, and S.-S. Hwang. 1984. An assessment of the accuracy and utility of socioeconomic impact assessments. In Paradoxes of Western Energy Development, ed. C. M. McKell, D. G. Browne, E. C. Cruze, W. R. Freudenburg, R. L. Perrine, and F. Roach, 265-96. Boulder, Colo.: Westview Press/American Association for the Advancement of Science.

North Dakota, State of, and United States Department of the Interior. 1978. Draft West-Central North Dakota Regional Environmental Impact Study on Energy Development. Bismarck: North Dakota Governor's Office.

Pattinson, M., R. Weisz, and E. Hickman. 1979. Program Evaluation Report: A Study of the Impacted Population, Related Stresses, Coping Styles and Mental Health Needs in the Gillette, Wyoming Planning District. Sheridan: Northern Wyoming Mental Health Center.

Seyfrit, C. L. 1978. Energy development and migration intentions of rural high school youth. Presented at the annual meeting of the Southern Sociological Society, New Orleans.

Shields, M. A., J. T. Cowan, and D. J. Bjornstad. 1979. Socio-economic Impacts of Nuclear Power Plants: A Paired Comparison of Operating Facilities. Oak Ridge, Tenn.: Oak Ridge National Laboratory.

Summers, G. F. 1978. Rural industry: Myth and reality. Social Impact Assessment 34:4-6.

Summers, G. F., S. Evans, F. Clemente, E. M. Beck, and J. Minkoff. 1976. *Industrial Invasion of Nonmetropolitan America: A Quarter Century of Experience*. New York: Praeger.

Susskind, L., and M. O'Hare. 1977. *Managing the Social and Economic Impacts of Energy Development: Strategies for Facility Siting and Compensating Impacted Communities and Individuals*. Cambridge: Laboratory of Architecture and Planning, Massachusetts Institute of Technology.

Thompson, J. G., A. L. Blevins, Jr., and G. L. Watts. 1979. *Socio-economic Longitudinal Monitoring Project: Final Report*. Vol. 1, *Summary*. Washington, D.C.: Old West Regional Commission.

Trigg, M. 1976. Women face boomtown isolation. *High Country News* 8(1)4-5.

Uhlmann, J. M. 1978. *Providing Human Services in Energy Impacted Communities*. Denver: Rocky Mountain Regional Office, Economic Development Administration, United States Department of Commerce.

United States Bureau of Land Management. 1978a. *Draft Environmental Statement: Federal Coal Management Program*. Washington, D.C.: United States Department of the Interior.

_____. 1978b. *Final West-Central Colorado Coal Environmental Statement*. Denver: Bureau of Land Management, United States Department of the Interior.

United States Department of Housing and Urban Development. 1976. *Rapid Growth from Energy Projects: Ideas for State and Local Action: A Program Guide*. Washington, D.C.: United States Department of Housing and Urban Development, Office of Community Planning and Development.

United States Department of the Interior and United States Geological Survey. 1978. *Draft Environmental Statement: Development of Coal Resources in Central Utah*. Washington, D.C.: United States Department of the Interior and United States Geological Survey.

United States Energy Research and Development Administration. 1977. *Managing the Socioeconomic Impacts of Energy Development: A Guide for the Small Community*. ERDA 77-79. Washington, D.C.: United States Energy Research and Development Administration, Office of Planning, Analysis and Evaluation.

United States Environmental Protection Agency. 1978. *Action Handbook: Managing Growth in the Small Community*. EPA-908/4-78-005b. Denver: United States Environmental Protection Agency, Region 8.

United States Geological Survey and Montana Department of State Lands. 1979. *Draft Environmental Statement: Northern Powder River Basin Coal,*

Montana. Reston, Va.: United States Geological Survey.

Vander Muellen, A., Jr., and O. Paananen. 1977. Selected welfare implications of rapid energy-related development impact. Natural Resources Journal 17:301-23.

Warren, R. L. 1977. New Perspectives on the American Community: A Book of Readings. 3d ed. Chicago: Rand McNally.

Watts, G. L., J. G. Thompson, and A.L. Blevins, Jr. 1977. Socio-economic Longitudinal Monitoring Project: First-Year Progress Report. Vol. 1, Summary Report. Washington, D.C.: Old West Regional Commission.

Weber, B. A., and R. E. Howell, eds. 1982. Coping with Rapid Growth in Rural Communities. Boulder, Colo.: Westview Press.

Weisz, R. 1979. Stress and mental health in a boom town. In Boom Towns and Human Services, ed. J. A. Davenport and J. Davenport III, 31-47. Laramie: Department of Social Work, University of Wyoming.

──────. 1980. Coping with the stresses of a boom: Mental health alternatives for impacted communities. In The Boom Town: Problems and Promises in the Energy Vortex, ed. J. Davenport III and J. A. Davenport, 55-69. Laramie: Department of Social Work, University of Wyoming.

Wilkinson, K. P., J. G. Thompson, R. R. Reynolds, Jr., and L. M. Ostresh. 1982. Local social disruption and western energy development: A critical review. Pacific Sociological Review 25:275-96.

Part 2
The Case Studies

5
Work-Emergent Behaviors and Traits: The Segregation of Energy Workers in Boomtowns

Kristen R. Yount

INTRODUCTION

In rural boomtowns, energy workers do integrate into the communities in that they make friends, engage in social activities, and develop social support networks. However, they integrate into subcultures consisting of other energy workers and are largely segregated from the community as a whole. Most do not participate in church activities, clubs, classes, community projects and events, or in the political life of the towns. Instead, they play softball, fish, hunt, etc., with their coworkers. For the most part, their social life revolves around the bars in town and the social gatherings held by their work associates.

The purpose of this chapter is to provide a theoretical explanation for this sociocultural division, utilizing the concepts of occupational association and stereotyping and of work-emergent behaviors and traits. Occupational association identifies the tendency of people to associate in their leisure time with individuals involved in work which is the same or is similar to their own work with respect to skills and role relations. Occupational stereotyping refers to the ascription of certain traits to an individual on the basis of knowledge of his or her occupation. Work-emergent behaviors are defined here as a repertoire of behaviors which flow as a consequence of working within particular physical and social conditions of production. Work-emergent traits are self-concept traits that conceptualize or characterize these behaviors.

The theoretical perspective developed here stems largely from research conducted in Meeker, Colorado, a rural community experiencing growth due to energy development.[1] Six persons, including myself, collectively spent approximately one person-year during 1980 and 1981 collecting data through in-depth interviews with residents and participant observation work in homes, at community events, and at the bars and cafes in town. In addition, a questionnaire was administered in Meeker and in Walden, Colorado, a control town experiencing relatively stable growth. A summary of the survey results most relevant to the theory presented here is provided at the end of the chapter (for details of this research, see Lillydahl et al. 1982.)

OCCUPATIONAL ASSOCIATION

A Generalized Phenomenon

Within the social impact assessment literature, social divisions and conflicts are most commonly viewed in terms of a newcomer/longtimer dichotomy. This essay proposes an alternate paradigm that conceptualizes the primary basis of these divisions in terms of occupational association. In other words, the division between newcomers and longtimers can be attributed to the fact that most newcomers in boomtowns are energy workers.[2] Furthermore, the segregation of these workers is presented as a case of a more generalized phenomenon in which all individuals are segregated into subcultures that are largely occupationally based (for further discusion of occupational communities, see Salaman 1974). In Meeker, people in all occupations will tell you that they have a mixture of newcomer and longtimer friends. Indeed, of the longtime residents of Meeker, only 6.3 percent of the women and 7.2 percent of the men said they had not made friends with a newcomer during the last year. However, interview data indicate that their friends work in occupations that are similar to their own; i.e., professionals spend their leisure time with other professionals, ranchers with ranchers, etc. Public places such as bars and the golf course are frequented by both newcomers and longtimers. However, the golf course is attended primarily by business/professional people (including energy company managers), while one bar is dominated by ranchers and another by both newcomer and longtimer miners, construction workers, and oil rig workers. All newcomers to a small town face special problems integrating into the community, but it is occupational affiliation that primarily determines their subculture memberships and the community's evaluation of them.

Although people also congregate on such bases as age, sex, drug use, family ties, and religion, it is hypothesized here that the most pervasive basis of social integration is occupational.[3] This is so in any city or town. However, occupational networks are less noticeable in a city where many different kinds of production take place and many different locations for leisure activities can be found. In a small town, where two or three types of productive activity dominate and few places to congregate exist, the divisions stand out in relief, as a number of Meeker residents pointed out. For example:

> INTERVIEWER: Can you describe the men in town?
>
> MEEKER MAN (Professional): Well, I think there's quite a few different types that you've got. Your oil field, coal, oh, your energy people pretty much are one group and you have your businessmen and then you have your farmers and ranchers. . . . Those are pretty definite groups here in town. . . . Your groups associate pretty much with their own kind. They don't mix so much.
>
> INTERVIEWER: If you had to classify or categorize people . . . how would you do it?
>
> MEEKER MAN (Professional): Yeah. Well, I think you classify them a lot by their job anywhere you go. I can't think of anywhere in the country where you don't. It's kind of a pecking order, you know. There's executives and down to your laborers, and your executives don't hang out with your laborers. [laugh] Or they generally don't.
>
> MEEKER WOMAN (Professional): It's really funny because the professional people do tend to hang out together, the ranchers tend to hang out together. . . . [But] the ranchers and the professional people do not socially go together.

This phenomenon has been manifested for many years in Meeker between the ranchers and farmers on the one hand and the business people in town on the other:

> MEEKER WOMAN (Rancher): When I first moved here . . . you had the town people and you had the farm people. And never the twain would meet. There were a lot of things that the . . . town people and the farmers did not, you know, agree on. . . . There always was a

difference between city people and ranch people.

Furthermore, the energy workers in Meeker do not constitute a singular group. Rather, they affiliate on the basis of their particular kind of work, as this oil rig worker ("roughneck") noted:

MEEKER MAN
(Energy Worker): You know, there's roughnecks as opposed to coal miners or construction workers. . . . It's a little clique of people. . . . Coal miners are coal miners. They have their own family jokes about coal mining and stuff, you know. And they sit in the bar and they talk coal mining. And roughnecks sit over in the other corner, and they talk roughnecking. . . . The personalities are different I think.

Occupationally Based Social Activities

Several factors account for the tendency of people to associate with others in the same or similar occupations. First, a large proportion of social events are occupationally sponsored: The Woolgrowers and the Stockgrowers Associations hold their annual dances, while the energy companies hold annual Christmas parties and picnics. Many of the clubs in the community are occupationally centered (e.g., homemaker clubs and the Cowbelles, an organization consisting of wives of ranchers). Summer softball teams are sponsored by particular businesses and industries. Private parties are often given for the people at work or are organized on a neighborhood basis. Neighborhoods also tend to segregate people according to their type of job, since business/professional people live in certain parts of town, while many energy workers are concentrated in other locations, often in housing built by energy companies for their workers.

Shared Interests and Familiarity

Second, people congregate with those in similar occupations because they share common interests and feel comfortable with each other. They come to know the individuals during working hours, the modes of interaction are familiar, and no one must endure the tedious rituals of introduction. Furthermore, people like to talk about their work. Business is often conducted at social gatherings where people negotiate agreements, pursue the interpersonal politics of the workplace, and solve work-related problems. Because it is the topic people know the best and because it is so essential to their lives, work is on their minds much of the time. In the cafes and bars of Meeker, the most common topic of conversation is work. In fact, miners claim that "more coal is mined in the bars than in the mines." Thus, as several interviewees noted, there is a tendency for people to avoid events where another occupation dominates, because they feel uncomfortable, inadequate, and bored:

> **MEEKER WOMAN**
> **(Professional):** You get coal miners together, they talk coal mining. You get teachers together, they'll talk teaching. You get farmers together, they'll talk farming. And, unless you're willing to jump in there and talk about the pregnant cow that had to have a caesarean section, you just ain't gonna be . . . willing to listen. . . . If a guy was born and raised in a coal mine and that's all he knows, there is no way he is going to feel comfortable sitting around with a bunch of professional people talking. . . . Teachers can bore the tears out of people who are not teachers. . . . If you're sitting there with two people who are talking about something that you not only don't have any interest in, you have no knowledge of, and quite frankly you could care less, . . . it's very boring for you. . . . I think it happens no matter what profession.

Work Schedules

Work schedules are a third factor that hinders leisure-time interactions between different occupational groups. In Meeker, there are three basic conceptions of time. Business and professional people operate on a nine-to-five, Monday-through-Friday schedule, while energy workers usually work rotating shifts. Ranchers and farmers view time seasonally and are constricted by the regularities and the whims of nature:

MEEKER WOMAN
(Rancher): It's the hours that one works. A professional person is nine to five. Your miners have your shifts. They work different times in different weeks. Your farmers go by the season. In the summertime they might work from seven in the morning until ten at night. . . . When the hay is ready, the hay is ready. . . . A cow has a calf when the cow has her calf. . . . It makes a big difference in your party time.

For the energy worker, rotating shift work makes it difficult to schedule time for church, clubs, classes, political meetings, or any activity held on a regular basis. For example, one young oil rig worker attributed his lack of church attendance primarily to his Sunday work schedule. In addition, many transient workers are reluctant to invest the time in such organizations because they do not conceive of themselves as long-term members of the community. The fact that a number of workers leave their families behind in other towns also contributes to their absence from many family-oriented events, such as church and children's sports activities.

Occupational Stereotypes

A fourth and quite important reason why individuals do not affiliate with persons in disparate occupations is because of the particular stereotypes that persons in differing types of work ascribe to each other. In order to formulate a frame of reference for understanding what another person is like, one of the first questions an individual seeks to answer is what the person "does." Once that information is acquired, much of what the person's life and personality are like seems to come into focus. According to Becker and Carper (1956:342), occupational titles "imply a great deal about the characteristics of their bearers, and these meanings are often systematized into elaborate ideologies which itemize the qualities, interests, and capabilities of those so identified." Occupational information provides a broad guide as to the appropriate way to converse with the person, the topics of conversation that should be raised, etc. Knowledge of a person's job provides a rough idea of whether or not it would be advantageous or enjoyable to get to know her or him better.

In energy-impacted communities, energy workers are particularly susceptible to a negative occupational stereotype because they are highly visible as a group and because the people in the town receive largely negative information about them. For example, sizable numbers of the workers arrive in town at approximately the same time. They are nearly all men, and they are all strangers in a community where the predominant cultural theme is "everybody knows everybody." Their primary avenue of entry into the social life of the town is the bar, located in the middle of town. Furthermore, they are concentrated in high-density trailer parks and apartment buldings, a number of which have insufficient parking and no playground facilities. As several of these dwellings are constructed by energy companies for their workers, and members of the small town are quite knowledgeable of this fact, those who live in the residences are immediately pegged according to their occupational affiliation.

Most energy workers are invisible as individuals to many members of the larger community because the workers and other segments of the population have little reason to associate with each other and thus have few personal interactions. The workers who do receive public attention, primarily through Meeker's gossip network, are the "typifiers," who come to characterize all newcomer energy workers. These are the loudest, the rowdiest--the ones who get into trouble, write checks that bounce, are arrested for drunk driving, etc. For example, a male energy worker who keeps quietly to himself does not offer material for gossip, while a romantic affair between a worker and a young indigenous girl does provide an interesting topic of conversation. In sum, most of the social information concerning energy workers is selective information that involves some kind of trouble.

MEEKER WOMAN
(Rancher): The year before last there was quite an influx of the construction people and it seemed like every ambulance run, every fight in the bar, you know--they made a bad impression. And the residents are a little bit hesitant now. They're a little bit cautious about it all. . . . They were mostly single men with no place to go or nothing to get involved in, so they went to the bars and there were a lot of bar fights. . . . There wasn't any housing. So consequently, they were camping in the park a lot and there were no showers and they came in from work and they looked dirty. Meeker's not used to that kind of thing. Their

> initial impression was bad. . . .
> Families with high school-age
> daughters felt rather threatened by
> it. . . . I know there were several
> of the high school girls that got
> involved with the men and some of
> them ended up marrying them and
> other ones didn't, but there were
> some problems that way.

Because energy workers socialize in public drinking establishments and because of their concentrated housing arrangements, the workers are more likely than other members of the community to gain a reputation in terms of excessive drinking, fist fights, promiscuity, and the use of drugs such as marijuana. In fact, these behaviors can be found among many segments of the population, but they often take place in private homes rather than in public places. For example:

> MEEKER WOMAN
> (Professional): I was very surprised at some of the
> adults who smoke pot. . . . These
> are people who are in responsible
> positions. We're talking about store
> owners, [professional people]. These
> are your basic upstanding citizens
> that you hold up for models. . . .
> [But] they do it in their own home
> and don't get caught with it or
> don't get picked up by the police.
> . . . As long as . . . it is not
> brought to the public's attention
> . . . that's fine because nobody has
> seen the marijuana cigarette;
> therefore it does not exist, you
> see.

Finally, the negative regard for energy workers may be accounted for by blame displacement processes. While some residents of Meeker benefit because of energy development, many find they can't afford consumer goods or the inflated prices of housing; they can't afford to pay employees on the ranch or in a small business the same wages that large energy companies pay; they see their small town relationships and ways of life dissolving before them. It is difficult to find a concrete target to blame for the hardships imposed on them, for the larger social structure is obscured by its complexity, and the energy companies are viewed as remote, ominous, noncorporeal entities, necessary to our country's survival. However, the workers are corporeal and concrete. Because they are accessible and they maintain a negative visibility, they make likely targets for the venting of frustrations.

In sum, energy workers are socially defined as loud and rowdy hell-raisers who drink too much, chase women, and fight in bars. Occupational stereotyping, like any stereotyping, is self-perpetuating because it limits the amount and the nature of interactions among individuals. While not all of the workers fit the stereotype, those who don't are often avoided by business and professional people and by ranchers because of the existence of these beliefs. Most segments of the larger community avoid the places where energy workers go. For example, one bar, frequented primarily by construction workers, miners, and oil rig workers, was described in the following manner:

MEEKER WOMAN
(Rancher): Meeker's a nice little town. We do have one sore spot though, down at the [bar name]. That's Meeker's own little ghetto.

MEEKER WOMAN
(Professional): It got the reputation of being the place where drug pushers went . . . where people went in if they were looking for someone to go home with. . . . There were these different crews from different places . . . and there were high school girls coming in there picking up guys. . . . I would not walk in there myself.

MEEKER WOMAN
(Bartender): A lot of people think this is a sleazy bar and it's not. They don't know the people that come in here. They think they're a rowdy bunch of people. They're not a rowdy bunch of people--they just know how to have a damn good time. . . . They think you're going to get mugged or hurt, stabbed, beat up, brutalized--that your reputation will be tarnished.

Withdrawal from the Community

Energy workers are aware of the community's social definition of them. They overhear people talking about "trashy" people; they hear the complaints about the homes they live in. One theme of the workers is "They want our money, but they don't want us." Thus, the workers also avoid places where they feel uncomfortable and unwelcome, such as the golf course, because, "What do you think of when you think of a golf course? You think of your professional people that golf." Indeed, the workers choose segregation because their own subculture is quite sufficient to meet their social needs and because they feel used by and resentful toward the larger community:

MEEKER MAN (Energy Worker): Down through history and all this there's been so much--oh they show you these movies on TV where the miners are rowdy and they start barroom fights and all this. And people have been programmed to this type of thinking, you know, and when you say "miner," this is what they associate it with. . . . You're making probably better money than 99 percent of the people in the community. This starts it, you know, because they think, well okay, we can tolerate them maybe if they don't sit in the cafes or start any trouble. And every time they find out you're a miner, they're automatically on the defense looking for you to start trouble. . . . When we first moved into Meeker, the whole town resented it, terribly. . . . They didn't want the trash. This is what they looked at us as, as trash. . . . The bosses were accepted. But the actual working man, hell, we were just lowlife as far as they were concerned. . . . They wanted your money but they didn't want you. . . . Everybody's got their hand out, you know. And this makes coal miners stand back and say, well, I'm good enough to work underground . . . but I'm not good enough to eat in your cafe. . . . Most coal miners, they associate with other coal miners. They don't have the same type of social clique as most people do. Like I said, they're stand-offish.

When an occupational stereotype is a negative one, as in the case of the energy worker, one common response is to defend and romanticize it; to reciprocate by ascribing a negative definition to groups who view the workers negatively. For example, one oil rig worker characterized those in the established community who avoided him as "snobs," stuck in "boring ruts." On the other hand, he proudly introduced himself as "oil rig trash," commenting later that there is "nothing demeaning" about the term. In general, most energy workers who describe themselves with epithets such as "roughneck" and "tramp miner" imbue a colorful romantic characterization to this image, presenting themselves as the stuff from which songs are made: They are hard-working people, tougher and stronger than most. They are carefree vagabonds and rogues, wise in the ways of the world--free, independent, unencumbered, and accountable to no one. They are lovable, playful, mischievous rascals--rowdy, witty, and full of fun.

WORK-EMERGENT BEHAVIORS AND TRAITS

Theoretical Framework

In addition to stereotypical beliefs concerning people in certain occupations, another important factor contributing to occupational association concerns actual differences of norms among people in different occupations. Friendships are largely based on mutual acceptance of behavior, while individuals avoid groups who may condemn the way they act. And oil rig workers do act differently from ranchers. In general, ranchers are somewhat reserved and quiet. They don't talk a great deal, and when they do, they talk slowly:

MEEKER MAN
(Business Person): They're just real slow-paced. They just tend to their ranches more or less. They do things the Meeker way. If you want something done today, then you're impatient. They take their time. They don't get in a hurry.

MEEKER WOMAN
(Energy Worker): [Ranchers] talk so slow, they drive me nuts! I keep wanting to finish their sentences for them.

On the other hand, energy workers tend to be loud and boisterous. They move fast, talk fast, and talk a lot. They have a self-assured air about them and are assertive in their approach to strangers. They razz, tease, and heckle each other; tell jokes and make witty remarks. They wrestle with each other and slap each other's backs. They caravan down main street, yelling to one another while hanging from pickup trucks. As one miner said, they act like football players in a locker room after a game has been won.

To understand these behaviors and the sociocultural divisions that result from them, it is necessary to examine the varying conditions of production with which different occupational groups contend and to analyze the modes of behavior that flow from these conditions.

For example, the dominance of ranching and farming in Meeker's history has left its mark on the character of social life in the town. Much of the time, ranchers work alone or with one or two other people. They are essentially accountable to nature and to themselves. Ranch owners have no boss pushing them; they set their own pace within the constraint of their crops, their herds, and the weather. They rely primarily on themselves and their families and on their neighbors, who occasionally help with special tasks. As a consequence, when people are asked to describe the residents of Meeker, the most common replies are "friendly and helpful," "easy-going and slow," "independent and self-reliant."

While Meeker's production in the past was conducted by small, scattered groups of people (often by families), energy development implants a social work force or aggregate of large numbers of unrelated people into the community. And the workers bring their occupationally appropriate behaviors to town with them, engaging in modes of interaction which many residents find abrasive.

To summarize, it is hypothesized here that modes of behavior and corresponding self-concepts on the part of individuals stem primarily from their productive activity or the methods by which they obtain their subsistence.[4] Although the historical roots of this proposition can be traced to the dialectical materialist approach of Marx and Engels (1974), who originally stressed the influence of work life on the individual, the analysis presented here draws largely on the tenets of symbolic interactionism,[5] as expressed by George Herbert Mead (1972, 1974). According to Mead, selves emerge as individuals develop an ability to step outside of themselves and to view themselves as objects from the point of view of significant others in their lives. They take the role of the generalized other (or a representative conception of the community within their fields of experience) and react to themselves from the standpoint of these abstracted attitudes. Thus, the self-conceptions and behaviors of individuals depend upon their assessments of others' perspectives or definitions of them. In turn, their presentations of self contribute to the shaping of the definitions that others form.

In order to understand the emergence of the self and modes of behavior on the part of individuals, the present analysis focuses on the primary role played by the conditions, relations, and rewards associated with productive activity. In other words, individuals are profoundly shaped by factors such as the social relations in the workplace (e.g., authority relations, the numbers of people who work together, the interdependence required by job tasks), the stress involved with the job (e.g., danger, pace of work, work schedules, job security), the status accorded to the occupation (e.g., power, pay, prestige), the nature of the physical environment (e.g., indoors, outdoors, underground), the types of tools used (e.g., heavy machinery, paper and pen), and the types of skills required by the job (e.g., intellectual, physical, and social skills).

Work-emergent behaviors are those behaviors that help individuals to perform work tasks and to cope with their emotional responses to the problems and stressors of their productive roles. To the extent that behaviors either directly or indirectly facilitate the performance of work tasks, they come to be positively valued. On the other hand, behaviors that are irrelevant or dysfunctional to work are devalued or condemned.[6] Work-emergent traits are defined in a positive light and are encapsulated into ideal images or roles. The degree to which individuals are able to shape themselves to fit the idealized roles largely determines their feelings of self-esteem. In other words, to a great extent people assess themselves in terms of traits conducive to job performance.

The salience of these qualities to the individual stems from the great proportion of time that work absorbs in a person's life and from the subjective and objective importance of obtaining subsistence. That is, more time is spent mastering work-emergent behaviors than most other behaviors. During working hours, both the individual and others perceive the person engaging in work-related tasks and thus enacting work-emergent traits. These self-presentations carry over to leisure-time activities, shaping the perceptions others outside the work setting have of the individual. Because, as Mead would posit, people come to see themselves as they think others see them, work-emergent behaviors become established as central elements within the self-concept during both working and leisure time. Moreover, work-emergent traits obtain pivotal importance because of the importance of earning a living. This activity is not only the primary requisite of survival; it is also viewed as a means of achieving other salient goals such as social esteem, status, and self-actualization.

Occupational association contributes to the relationship between overall self-concept and work-emergent attributes because individuals are shaped by those around them, and their occupations largely determine who will constitute these reference groups (Salaman 1974). Because people congregate with others in similar occupations, their exposure to alternate groups that value different qualities of self is limited.

During the field research in Meeker, a number of underground coal miners were interviewed. A brief analysis of their work setting helps to concretize this theoretical framework at the empirical level (for a comprehensive analysis of work-emergent behaviors and traits in an underground mine, see Yount forthcoming).

Underground Coal Miners: Work-Emergent Behaviors and Traits

Traits and conditions. When miners are asked to describe all miners in general, three trait configurations are consistently indicated. First, they are described as competent (e.g., hard-working, knowledgeable, skilled, alert, and responsive). Second, they are depicted as hell-raisers, or rambunctious people who drink, party, and joke around a great deal. Third, they are portrayed as "tough," a term which has multiple meanings including assertive, self-confident, superior, impervious to physical pain and discomfort, and emotionally invulnerable to danger and to interpersonal degradation. In short, tough means social, physical, and emotional invincibility.

An examination of the stressors in an underground mine helps to explain why miners present themselves in these ways. First, the physical environment is extraordinarily dangerous and uncomfortable (dark, dirty, wet, and cold). Second, the job not only requires skill with heavy machinery, but also entails a great deal of physical strength and endurance. Third, the social relations entail an element of powerlessness; i.e., miners, relative to management, have little control over the work process. Fourth, with respect to coworker relations, miners are faced with a "competition/cooperation" dilemma: On the one hand, they compete with each other for prestigious work assignments and for recognition of skills under the constant observation and assessment of each other. On the other hand, the job necessarily involves a great deal of interdependence. Miners must work together in close coordination to accomplish difficult tasks and must be able to depend on each other's competence and willingness to work hard. More importantly, danger is omnipresent in a mine, and they must trust and depend on other workers to guard their safety.

These circumstances provide ripe breeding grounds for the generation of anger, frustration, fear, and depression among miners. However, because they work in confined quarters and in close cooperation, negative cognitive and emotional states on the part of individuals tend to be highly contagious and disruptive when expressed. In response, the group as a whole negotiates a definition of the situation to control emotional responses. In other words, in the face of danger, discomfort, and dismal physical surroundings, miners cope with fear, anxiety, and depression by maintaining self-presentations as brave, calm, and jocular, thereby indicating to each other that the environment is benign and tolerable. Thus, the self-presentations described above may largely be viewed as collectively derived coping techniques employed by miners to help them to deal with the strains of their work. Indeed, in any social situation where interdependence and danger are involved (e.g., a combat zone), a set of collective coping mechanisms will evolve and be enforced by the group as a whole (Bourne 1970; Grinker and Spiegel 1945).

Being Tough. Tough attributes emerge in a coal mine as valued qualities because they help to get the work done and because they serve to maintain morale. For example, toughness in the sense of superiority to others can be viewed as a compensatory idea that helps miners to rationalize and thus endure danger and physical discomfort:

MEEKER MAN
(Coal Miner): Miners . . . pretty well figure they are working probably one of the harshest environments there is, and I can cut it. So I'm not actually a step above anybody, but maybe I'm a little better, you know.

MEEKER MAN
(Coal Miner): It's something a lot of people don't want to do. And I like that too. They're scared of it. [laugh]

Tough in the sense of assertiveness may in part be assessed in relation to the frustrations in a mine. That is, it is easier to be assertive when you are angry, and work in a coal mine necessarily entails the thwarting of goals: Coworkers hold up production by laziness or incompetence. Equipment gets stuck in the mud or breaks down and parts are unavailable. Furthermore, bosses yell, cuss at, and deride workers on a daily basis. As one miner said, "They yell at their men like they were dogs or something."

Outside of the mine, assertive self-presentations can be viewed as an effect of the miner's productive activity. The physical conditioning that results from the job provides a sense of confidence in the miner's ability to defend him- or herself and to handle the physical pain of a fight if a disagreement should escalate--if push should literally come to shove. Moreover, the appearance of toughness is largely affected by a group presence. That is, miners usually attend social events together, and they extend the norm of mutual protection developed in the work setting to these events. Thus, an outsider's attack on one miner will be met by the group as a whole.

Because of the high degree of mutual reliance in a mine, it is important to each individual that all members of the team be tough. As a result, miners engage in a mutual psychological grooming in which they shape each other's self-concept by defining coworkers in terms of qualities functional to work. Lower-level supervisors in particular serve as important conductors in this social orchestration. Their job depends on high worker productivity, and attributes such as toughness facilitate production. According to the reports of miners, bosses (like army sergeants) often give "pep" talks to workers during which they define crew members as "mean" and "bad," etc., as opposed to "cry-babies" and "sissies."[7]

Hell-Raisers. One aspect of being a hell-raiser entails horseplay or kidding around--behavior for which miners are notorious. While at work, they play practical jokes, tell sexual and ethnic jokes, and continually "rag," "razz," "thrash," tease, and insult each other in a humorous manner. This behavior has evolved as a norm because of the multiple functions it serves in a coal mine.

For example, kidding around is used as a technique of mutual psychological conditioning, by which miners "toughen up" each other. Miners will cover other miners with grease and rock dust, screw lunch buckets to tables, nail each other's clothing to a timber, sneak up with their lights out to scare one another, etc. These jokes desensitize coworkers to their work environment by tapping their feelings of fear, vulnerability, helplessness, and frustration. In fact, a crew will "ride" other miners about those things that seem to bother them the most until the individuals stop expressing an emotional response to the topic. Social learning theory (Bandura 1970) suggests that those who play the practical jokes also benefit vicariously, learning how to manage their emotions by watching someone else cope with the situation.

As I noted above, kidding around also serves to manage the definition of the situation. When someone has made a mistake, the error is regarded as a humorous one to ease tensions. When miners are working in especially dangerous conditions, the joking helps to provide comic relief and to define the circumstances as benign. Moreover, when people are depressed or bored, joking provides replenishing uplifts that make the day go faster.

Razzing also allows tempered expressions of emotion. When miners become angry with other miners, they can get the issue out in the open and release hostilities without incurring conflict by using humorous insults and embarrassments. In addition, razzing provides an acceptable means of expressing affection: On the one hand, mutual protection in the face of danger promotes a sense of belonging and caring among miners that they describe as a camaraderie, a team, a family. On the other hand, compliments or expressions of compassion detract from a tough self-presentation because kindness and compassion are traits associated with emotional vulnerability. Sarcasm provides the solution to this dilemma. In other words, miners can tell the buggy driver that they admire his or her competence by telling the person that he or she is the "worst damn buggy driver they ever saw."

Kidding around is also a means of bringing workers into the group. The jokes are part of an initiation rite that tests new miners. If they pass the test, the razzing lets them know they are accepted. On the other hand, the jokes are also employed as a means of social control for the interdependent group. Depending on the context, the razzing can be used to ostracize those who hold up the work or who consistently threaten the collective coping tactics of the crew by complaining, moping, expressing fear, etc.

These behaviors, which originate in the work setting, also serve the nomadic lifestyle of many "tramp" miners, who move frequently and must establish social relationships quickly and often. In traveling from town to town, their personal histories and reputations are of relatively little importance. Rather, they are judged on the basis of their immediate behavior. Thus, many workers carry with them a repertoire of jokes, stories, descriptive and humorous slang, sarcastic remarks, and quick retorts. In short, they become adept at quickly selling themselves to others.

The consumption of large amounts of alcohol in bars is another aspect of being a hell-raiser and is also a major norm difference and point of abrasion between energy workers and the rest of the community.[8] Drinking, in fact, contributes to rambunctious behavior, because alcohol releases inhibitions. Public drinking can also be linked to the conditions imposed on energy employees by their work situation.

For the miner, the corollary of working hard is playing hard. According to the workers, they feel a need to celebrate getting out of the dismal atmosphere in the mine and making it through another day without being injured or killed. Further, dancing, drinking too much, driving too fast, etc., help to sustain the level of excitement they experience in the mine:

MEEKER WOMAN
(Coal Miner): You wonder, could I be next? And when you get out after eight hours, you're pretty happy that you're still alive. You want to go celebrate.

MEEKER MAN
(Coal Miner): It sounds crazy, but it's exciting down there. I mean, there's a lot of danger, but it's kind of like a high. You kind of get addicted to it. You look forward to it. It's a real rush.

Miners may get drunk even though they may have gone to the bar for other purposes, since bars are places where people are expected to drink. In the bar, miners carry on the business of working, discussing work plans and cementing relationships with those on the job, where the ability to get along is crucial. For example, buying a coworker a drink is a common method of resolving conflicts originating at work.

Many workers, especially nomadic or tramp miners, also go to the bar to relieve boredom and to escape unpleasant living environments. The men could read a book or watch television, but their homes are often cramped, poorly furnished, uncomfortable, and unattractive places to spend time. There are no recreation centers or movie theaters in Meeker and other such towns, and since energy development draws a large number of single male workers, there is an extreme shortage of women to date:

MEEKER MAN
(Coal Miner): There's nothing to do in this town. If you live on snob knob, fine--you can run with that crowd. But if you don't, if you live downtown, then you run with another crowd and there's nowhere to run. So you sit in the bar or you do nothing. Sit at home. Hang out in the laundromat or something. . . . There's no show; there's nothing really to look at. You can see this town in 20 minutes. . . . It's just kind of dull . . . either you hang out in the bar or you eat and sleep and that's it.

For tramp miners, the bar serves the function of a clearing house where they obtain essential information concerning living arrangements, eating facilities, and employment. The bartenders also provide an answering service for workers without telephones and a check-cashing service for those whose shifts conflict with banking hours. And the bar is a meeting hall where miners can learn about or reestablish contact with others they left behind in other towns. In addition, the bartender is almost always female, and she and the few other women in the bar are pleasant to the men. The women smile and talk to them, providing at least some reassurance that they are still attractive to the opposite sex--a reaffirmation they greatly need after spending so much time around other men:

MEEKER WOMAN
(Bartender): [This bar] is better than the Job Service Center. I've seen more people get jobs on oil rigs here. . . . I [give job information] all the time. I find people homes, countless numbers of people who want places to rent because I hear that stuff. . . . People new in town, I make a point of introducing them. . . . I sympathize with them . . . drink with them.

The workers may get exceptionally drunk for three reasons. First, they frequently drink on an empty stomach because shift work disrupts the appetite, because they often lack cooking facilities in their homes, because there is no food served in the bar, and because if no one cooks for them, they often won't cook for themselves. Second, the prevalence of shift work in the town has legitimized drinking at any time of the day. Thus, norms specifying appropriate drinking times, which tend to limit alcohol consumption, are disrupted by the work schedules. Night-shift workers, who have their after-work drink in the morning, may end up staying in the bar into the evening hours to talk with workers getting off the afternoon shifts.

Finally, alcohol consumption has symbolic meanings. It means that you belong to the group if you drink with the group--that you're one of the "boys." The ability to hold your liquor also symbolizes physical endurance and mental strength, and the workers often compete with each other, matching drink for drink, as a means of impressing others. Buying drinks is a norm frequently used as a method of winning acceptance and of indicating to others that you are not a leech--that you are willing to give. It is also symbolic of financial success. Miners make relatively high wages, compared to other blue-collar workers, and like many Americans, they engage in conspicuous consumption, which in their case, takes the form of buying everybody at the table a drink. The problem with this is that everybody else does the same, and the drinks keep coming all night (or all day) long.

QUESTIONNAIRE DATA

To summarize, the theoretical framework presented here accounts for the formation of distinctive subcultures in energy boomtowns largely in terms of differences in modes of behavior emerging from particular types of productive activity. Moreover, it is hypothesized that self-concept traits that correspond to or characterize these behaviors attain salience within the self-image of individuals. Questionnaire data, collected in Meeker and Walden, Colorado, suggest tentative substantiation for this last hypothesis. In a self-administered, confidential survey conducted in 1980, respondents were asked to check from a list of adjectives those words that applied to themselves and were also instructed to list three words to describe their personalities. The occupations of individuals were categorized, according to employment status and job skills required, into four main groups: (a) physical occupations (e.g., energy workers, truck drivers, mechanics, laborers, ranchers: n = 137); (b) business persons (e.g., store owners, office managers: n = 37); (c) tending occupations (e.g., teachers, nurses, health practitioners, waitresses, sales clerks, maids, orderlies: n = 104); (d) unemployed homemakers (n = 121).

Pearson correlation coefficients (statistically significant at the .05 level) indicate a general pattern of correspondence between self-concept and job category. Nurturant qualities ("nurturant," "gentle and soothing," "sympathetic," "kind and considerate," "devoted to others") are positively associated with homemakers and with individuals employed within the tending occupations who care for, wait on, or otherwise tend to the personal needs of others. These qualities are negatively associated with physical workers, who work primarily with materials, animals, tools, heavy equipment, etc., rather than with people. On the other hand, "independence," "competitiveness," and power-oriented qualities ("aggressive," "assertive," "dominant," "forceful") are most often self-ascribed by individuals engaged in physically strenuous occupations and are negatively associated with homemakers and with those in tending occupations. Business persons, whose work involves economic negotiations with others, distinguish themselves as "fair and reliable" and as "independent."

With respect to energy workers in particular, the questionnaire results are basically consistent with field research observations. Compared to other residents in the two towns, more of these workers characterize themselves as "aggressive," "dominant," "forceful," "competitive," and "independent." In addition, more of them are likely to ascribe an abrasive ("boastful," "coarse," "angry") social style to themselves and to also refer to themselves as "charming" and "attractive." It is interesting to note that, compared to other men in the town, more energy workers refer to themselves as "dependent," perhaps reflecting the interdependence required by their work setting. This was not true of other individuals in the physical occupations (truck drivers, mechanics, ranchers, etc.) who do not rely to the same extent on coworkers for task completion and personal safety.

Discussion

These data provide only initial and partial support for the theoretical perspective presented, which is still in the exploratory stages of development. A larger sample size is required so that oil rig workers, underground miners, etc., can be analyzed separately. And future research needs to control for variables such as age, sex, race, education, occupational history, and division of labor within the home. Furthermore, additional qualitative research is required to identify the conditions and relations of production within specific occupations, to assess the modes of interaction associated with the jobs, and to clarify and elaborate on the theoretical links between the two. Nevertheless, the results do provide sufficient grounds to warrant further research.

While the paradigm proposed here does not offer concrete indications for easing the sociocultural tensions in boomtowns, I believe that further development of the framework will lead to a deeper understanding of their origins. Moreover, studies concerning the impact of energy development on different age, sex, and racial groups would be greatly enhanced by special attention to occupational divisions and their social-psychological consequences. While the elderly, women, and minorities certainly face difficulties unique to their groups, the overall configuration of their problems may prove to be more a function of occupational affiliation and income than of age, sex, and race.

NOTES

1. This research was conducted with members of the Growth Impact Group, Research Program on Population Processes, in the Institute of Behavioral Science, University of Colorado at Boulder, under the direction of Elizabeth Moen and Jane Lillydahl. Funding was provided by the National Institute of Mental Health, grant number 33524. Special acknowledgment should be given to Elizabeth Moen for her insightful criticism and support.

2. By energy workers, I mean blue-collar workers employed by energy companies, e.g., miners, oil rig workers, construction workers. Energy company managers are considered to be business and professional persons.

3. Race is not listed here because of the lack of minorities in Meeker. Thus, few data were available concerning the relative impact of racial versus occupational segregation.

4. For the most comprehensive analysis of the impact of work on personality, see Kohn et al. (1983). Note that the relationship between occupation and self-concept in particular has not received systematic empirical assessment. For example, Wylie's (Wylie 1974; Wylie et al. 1979) voluminous review of the literature on self-concept does not discuss research linking work and the formation of particular attributes of self.

Also, note that the present analysis does not deny that the development of self-concept and behavioral patterns begins in childhood. This development can best be viewed as the result of directing a child's behavior into areas which adults believe will best prepare the child for productive roles later in life. Two factors, then, account for the congruence between self-concept components and traits generated by particular conditions of production. First, individuals with certain personality traits choose occupations suited to these traits, and the development of the attributes is perpetuated by the work. Second, certain traits emerge from involvement within certain jobs.

Moreover, racial and sex-role stereotypes also influence self-concept development. However, it is posited here that these stereotypes are rooted in occupational roles (e.g., the shuffling black can be traced to slavery; the miserly Jew to mercantilism; the helpless, dependent female to homemaking). Further, the social definitions are perpetuated because these groups are channeled into particular work roles. A discussion of the relationship between work-emergent behaviors and sex-role stereotypes is provided in Yount (1986).

5. The theories of Mead and Marx are basically compatible and complementary. Whereas Mead explains human action at the interpersonal level, Marx explains why particular modes of behavior systematically appear

among groups of people at particular stages in history by pointing to the central importance of their productive activity within the division of labor. For further comparison of the two perspectives, see Ropers (1973).

6. For example, a sociologist's ability to expound an analysis on social problems, politics, religion, philosophy, etc., is generally accorded respect among other social scientists. Among miners, however, there is a general disdain for intellectualism. Those miners with a college degree quickly learn to play it down because they are initially suspected of being uppity bookworms who haven't a lick of common sense because their lives have been spent in a book. Thus, they must make special efforts to prove their abilities at physical labor and practical know-how. According to one miner, "If you've got a college degree, you're better off to just keep quiet about it. They'll give you a hard time . . . [because] they think you won't be able to do the work."

7. Current theories of self-concept development lend credence to the proposition that work associates are exceptionally influential as reference persons. For example, according to Rosenberg (1979:Chap. 3), two important variables that help to account for the differential influence of others on the self-concept are valuation (the degree to which the individual desires the favorable opinion of particular others) and credibility (the degree to which the individual respects or has confidence in the judgment of others). With respect to work associates, particularly bosses, it may be hypothesized, first of all, that the individual desires their favorable regard because maintaining harmonious relations with them and winning their respect is not only important to the person's self-esteem, but can also be highly instrumental to success in the work place. Secondly, the individual accords credibility to their reflected appraisals because work associates see the products of the person's efforts and because they share with the individual similar goals and conditions and consequently value the same traits. Colleagues, more than others, are viewed as experts with respect to the individual's work-emergent or most salient traits.

8. Note that workers with families who live in town are less likely than single workers to frequent bars during their leisure time.

9. An in-depth analysis of how the productive activity of the homemaker generates socioemotional dependency as well as nurturance, submissiveness, and psychological distress is presented in Yount (1982).

10. Disaggregating populations solely according to class or income variables yields categories that are too broad. Many oil rig workers earn $48,000 per year-- more than some business persons. It is the conditions

and relations of productive activity, including economic rewards, that determine modes of behavior and sociocultural divisions.

REFERENCES

Bandura, A. 1970. Modelling therapy. In Psychopathology Today, ed. W. S. Sahakian. Itasca, Ill.: F. E. Peacock Publishers.

Becker, H. S., and J. W. Carper. 1956. Elements of identification with an occupation. American Sociological Review 21:341-48.

Bourne, P. G. 1970. Men, Stress, and Vietnam. Boston: Little, Brown.

Grinker, R. R., and J. P. Spiegel. 1945. Men under Stress. New York: McGraw-Hill Book Company.

Kohn, M. L., C. Schooler, J. Miller, K. A. Miller, C. Schoenback, and R. Schoenberg. 1983. Work and Personality: An Inquiry into the Impact of Social Stratification. Norwood, N.J.: Ablex Publishing Corporation.

Lillydahl, J., E. W. Moen, E. Boulding, K. Yount, S. Scott-Stevens, and I. Gallon. 1982. Quality of Life, Expectations of Change and Planning for the Future in an Energy Production Community: A Report to the People of Meeker and Walden, Colorado. Boulder: Institute of Behavioral Science, University of Colorado.

Marx, K., and F. Engels. 1974. The German Ideology, ed. R. Pascal. New York: International Publishers (originally published 1947).

Mead, G. H. 1972. On Social Psychology. Chicago: University of Chicago Press (originally published 1934).

_____. 1974. Mind, Self, and Society: From the Standpoint of a Social Behaviorist. Vol. 1. Chicago: University of Chicago Press (originally published 1934).

Ropers, R. 1973. Mead, Marx and social psychology. Catalyst 7:5-24.

Rosenberg, M. 1979. Conceiving the Self. New York: Basic Books.

Salaman, G. 1974. Community and Occupation: An Exploration of Work/Leisure Relationships. London: Cambridge University Press.

Wylie, R. C. 1974. The Self-concept. Vol. 1, A Review of Methodological Considerations and Measuring Instruments. Lincoln: University of Nebraska Press.

Wylie, R. C., P. J. Miller, S. S. Cowles, and A. W. Wilson. 1979. The Self-concept. Vol. 2, Theory and Research on Selected Topics. Lincoln: University of Nebraska Press.

Yount, K. R. 1982. Fascinating womanhood: Creating and re-creating the feminine stereotype. Unpublished manuscript, University of Colorado, Boulder.

———. 1986. A theory of productive activity: The relationships among self-concept, gender, sex-role stereotypes, and work-emergent traits. Psychology of Women Quarterly 10:63-87.

———. Forthcoming. Women and men coal miners: Coping with gender integration underground. Boulder: University of Colorado.

6
Ranchland: Impacts on Rural Communities

Patrick C. Jobes

INTRODUCTION

This chapter addresses the question of whether greater negative impacts occur in rural communities of ranchers as a consequence of energy development than would occur in urban communities with industrial employment. In order to answer this question, the structure of such communities must be examined. This differential impact is important for several reasons. Much of the current and future development of energy resources will occur in these highly vulnerable communities. Since they are especially likely to be especially disrupted, it is crucial that investigators and policymakers understand the unique impacts they encounter (Leistritz and Murdock 1981). Unless investigators measure the rural community as a unit of analysis, they will fail to describe the relevant fundamental impacts. Policymakers guided by such misinformation will be unable to protect such communities in the spirit of the National Environmental Policy Act (NEPA).

Ranchland is among the last vestiges of a traditional type of community-based social system which is referred to as a gemeinschaft. Like most vestigial structures, it exists largely because it was left behind in the evolutionary process. Some rural residents would claim to have retained the informal face-to-face style by choice. Certainly, they could have opted for the cities, as most former rural residents did. Nevertheless, the small number of persons involved and the wide landscape they occupy simply did not fit into the efficient model of urban industrial society (Kraenzel 1980). So, while those few who thought of their unique lifestyles and communities made choices to remain when others thought or chose differently, their choice was made possible because agricultural production continued to require a rural lifestyle rather than the larger, faster, and more specialized structures of urban society. When massive energy development occurs, rural residents discover they were only temporarily ignored by a system which had the potential for dominating them when it became profitable to do so (Jobes 1980). When previously unused resources are exploited through industrial technology, the structures of traditional communities, based as they are upon informal organization and primary interaction, are upset. Most frequently, they are affected by the rapid and sporadic in-migration of large numbers of unfamiliar workers engaged in development. However, I have observed one community that disintegrated due to significant out-migration, polarization, and bitterness which resulted from massive open pit mining.

Energy development may vary from a mine employing a handful of local-area residents to a generation/transmission complex with several mines and conversion plants. The former certainly implies relatively small impact in comparison with the latter. Social structure ranges from the ideal type gemeinschaft rural ranch community described throughout this chapter to gesellschaft urban society (Toennies 1940). The character of impacts warrants being considered in qualitatively different manners between gemeinschaft and gesellschaft. Some impacts, the kinds most frequently analyzed, may be thought of as quantitative and materialistic. Such matters as increases in the population, rates of deviance, and employment statistics imply a numeric dimension of impacts. Social impact research generally focuses attention at this level of analysis and prescribes material solutions such as more police and schools and better roads and sewers. However, the most important characteristic of change in gemeinschaft areas is likely to be a conversion to a qualitatively different type of social system. The greatest impacts are likely to destroy small agricultural communities based upon informal, face-to-face interaction among relatively unchanging residents over long time periods, frequently generations.

This chapter will take the position that ranchers in sparsely populated, relatively isolated, institutionally stable pastoral communities undergoing energy development suffer disproportionate social impacts. Although any community might be vulnerable to the kinds of disruption experienced by ranch communities, few other places exist which so closely approximate the ideal type of gemeinschaft. And other gemeinschaft-like communities are likely to be threatened by the presence of nearby energy development. Because of similar underlying conflicts initiated through the development process, the position taken in this chapter may apply to nearly all such communities. However, my comments will be restricted to ranchers in the Rocky Mountain West. The observations and conclusions in this chapter are derived from research over a decade in the northern Rocky Mountains. Some few small towns I have studied, particularly Douglas, Wyoming, have not undergone severe upheaval. However, even there, the outlying ranch communities were heavily impacted. In more remote communities, particularly Decker, Montana, from which the most negative generalizations in this chapter derive, the impacts have been socially devastating.

RANCHLAND AS GEMEINSCHAFT

The credibility of this chapter rests on convincing readers that gemeinschaft communities exist today in isolated places in the United States and that they require a qualitatively different perspective rarely used by social scientists or laypersons when analyzing social systems. Such communities are important. They are contemporary examples of concepts fundamental to sociology, yet increasingly ignored or mismeasured.

These communities are, admittedly, rare. They probably exist in only a few rural sections of the United States, and they are not perfect examples of the ideal type. However, they exist and fundamentally differ from the ubiquitous society of which most of us are a part.

I have personally worked with nearly a dozen small rural "boomtowns" and isolated rural communities. The residents in each have had widely divergent views about what the impacts might be before development and have been during and after development. The differences in the meaning of the changes are as great as in overt physical and social impacts. Both proponents and opponents of development generally agree that problems of interaction and organization have emerged. Both see the discomforting adjustment as service institutions try to meet expanded demands. Both acknowledge increased social disorganization. Both agree upon a quickened pace, unfamiliar and often undesirable residents, and a loss of the close, personal, face-to-face interaction they are accustomed to. What they disagree upon is the value attached to these changes. The proponents of change see them as an inevitable and defensible consequence of progress, where "progress" is taken as the evolution to a larger, more centralized, less personal form of service-oriented system. The opponents fatalistically see the destruction of an established community.

Social scientists take essentially the same perspectives as the residents they study. That is, they have opposing perspectives on whether isolated rural communities really are gemeinschaft. If they feel that modern isolated rural communities are essentially small varieties of urban society, then they are unlikely to see or be concerned about impacts of growth and change beyond those related to population characteristics and service needs. If they see them, as I do, as qualitatively different from larger urban places, they react to unique, particularly painful impacts. The situation is complicated by the fact that few social scientists have had a personal and professional lifetime in rural agricultural communities, particularly before energy impacts have even been considered. By the preboom phase when most researchers arrive, the gemeinschaft quality already has become obfuscated by the gesellschaft reinterpretation which is essential for handling the pressing problems of where the newcomers will live and how current roads, utilities, law enforcement, and schools can be made adequate.

There is, however, more at stake than an academic issue. If we "community romantics" are correct, then a crucial impact is frequently being ignored by impact analysts and suffered through by residents. If we are wrong, then mitigation should be devoted to coordinating and developing sufficient goods and services for a better community for both oldtimers and newcomers. If we are correct, though, mitigation must assume more protective strategies.

RANCHING GEMEINSCHAFT

The essential elements for the ideal type community are that it have small, isolated, and stable groups of interdependent residents. (None of these conditions exists perfectly in reality even among exotic tribes or cloistered monasteries.) Although these conditions might occur in almost any setting, they are most likely to be found in rural areas. These conditions create the primary interaction and informal social organization which further distinguish community from society. Over time, tacit norms governing what to do and how to do it evolve which are clear to community members, even if invisible to or mistaken by others.

No exact quantitative description of these conditions exists. They form an interaction which causes the particular population size to become relevant in terms of its independence from interaction with outsiders and the permanence of the institutions accomplishing essential tasks. An open country community with 150 residents which is 50 miles from the nearest town of 5,000 persons and which has had uninterrupted ranching performed by extended families for four generations probably is about as close to community as is likely to be found in the United States. It certainly is a contrast to 150 unfamiliar workers in a temporary construction camp adjacent to a city or 150 occupationally diverse suburban neighbors with nuclear families who move every four to six years.

Communities in ranchland are comprised of the residues of previous social systems. The residents are progeny of prior generations who lived there. These survivors remain, largely due to the support they have shared with community members in order to meet their individual and collective goals. The agricultural production is an updated evolution of pastoral herding. The family structure is more extended than can be found in less permanent families elsewhere. In general, then, ranch communities are comprised of people doing the same things in the same place that their forefathers did.

Such a summary is simplistic, of course. Many ranch children migrate away, while some few others, usually wives of ranchers' sons, move in. Newcomers have confided that they did not feel accepted as community members for many years. Other immigrants also move to ranchland. Wage and salary employment like fuel-truck driving, utilities, and ranch work provides jobs for a few outsiders, who may never be really regarded as community members, though their children will be, if they remain. To remain and be accepted requires that outsiders tacitly approve of the community, as it exists. This means that they provide community support and service, as expected of them, while acknowledging the desirability of local institutions and the style of life organized around them (Gold 1974).

Outsiders in a stable ranch community, then, are there largely through a selection process. They choose the area and at the same time are invited by the people who live there, since the established residents decide who will be wed, hired, and maintained. Newcomers are very polarized regarding energy development. Generally, they favor it more than ranchers, though some few, particularly city-bred ranch wives and educated ranchers and professionals, are likely to be the most adamantly opposed to development.

Most immigrants must be at least as emotionally attached to the lifestyle as community members, since the employment is demanding and usually offers low pay and little opportunity for advancement. Furthermore, employed outsiders can rarely expect to be regarded as the status equals of ranchers or merchants.

Ranch areas are stratified by race, property ownership, and income. The stratification is clearly evident in interaction systems. Ranchers associate with other ranchers and to a lesser extent with a smattering of higher-status professionals, managers, and business people, many of whom also own ranch land. Blue-collar workers tend to associate with each other and with lower-status and more transient professionals, such as teachers. Length of time in the community and property ownership are the most important determinants of groupings.

Stratification is unlikely to be perceived or discussed by the ranchers who are well entrenched in old and stable informal groups. But it is visible to newcomers, minorities, and landless professionals who are excluded from informal interaction while sharing formal systems with the ranchers.

CONTENT AND FORM

The most obvious characteristics of life in ranchland relate to content (Simmel 1971). Residents drive pickup trucks, ride horses, and wear jeans, cowboy boots, and hats even if they don't ranch. Country and western music and frequent drink help generate their good times. Direct, open, and frill-less conversation is typical, particularly among men. Traditional roles and values are regarded as virtuous, although some rugged shunning of convention is tolerated, if not necessarily appreciated. These and other substantively apparent characteristics distinguish ranchers from most urban dwellers, but they are not causally related to gemeinschaft interaction, though they may symbolize an important identity. They say, "I am different and a little old fashioned; I like things simple. I believe in personal independence (even if I behave in a nearly stereotyped way) from demands and fashions." In summary, styles of life, that is, substantively what people do, constitute the contents of community life and reflect an identity generally shared with others. They attract the attention of outsiders and are easily imitated. But the essence of ranch community lies deeper.

The visible characteristics of ranchers' lifestyles are largely independent of the forms of interaction created by the structures unique to gemeinschaft social systems. The most relevant differences distinguishing ranchers from others emerge from how these interactions are conducted. They are done with the same pool of persons, treated as whole persons, and they are performed with the expectation that all persons will contribute to the community when capable of doing so. The most important of these interactions involve the sharing of activities essential to the well-being of the community. Many of these shared activities are agricultural tasks, such as cattle roundup. Others center around service activities like running the school and the church.

Roundup

Grazing animals spread out over rough country which is immense from most other land-use perspectives. Forty or more acres frequently are required for grazing each cow and her calf. A good-sized operation will have two to four hundred cows, though big ranches have thousands. Usually cattle must be handled twice a year. In order to control reproduction and identification, they are rounded up, branded, inoculated, castrated, and separated, usually in the spring. Once separated and put out to range, the cattle must be rounded up in the fall in order to be shipped to market. The large size of the animals and their low density throughout great rugged expanses require a large temporary labor force if the jobs are to be efficiently performed. Ranchers draw upon the crew which is available, most frequently neighbors with whom they exchange labor. Sharing roundup also allows strays to be returned to their owners, fences to be checked, and, especially important for the community, residents to share tasks and reaffirm commitments to a style of life and to each other.

Roundup never is completely forgotten during the year, since it is a focal point of profit and activities. It provides great opportunities for being a collectively recognized hero, hard worker, and manager in a few days. Compared to the repetitious humdrum of feeding, repairing machinery, fixing fence, and myriad other essential, isolated activities of farm and ranch life, roundup is exciting to anticipate, experience, and savor.

Sheep Shearing

Shearing sheep, like other shared community work activities, is labor intensive. It requires skilled persons to shear as well as others to catch the sheep to be sheared, tie up fleece, and bag the wool.

Being especially labor intensive, sheep raising has been replaced by cattle ranching in most former sheep-raising areas of the United States. Many of the largest cattle ranchers have some sheep and had their origins as sheep ranchers, lending support to the ranchers' adage of "sheep for profit, cattle for respectability, and horses for pleasure." Farm flocks of one or two dozen may be sheared as a family activity, but commercial flocks, which occasionally number several thousands, require the coordination of dozens of persons. Large commercial operations with sheep have declined during the past half century, reducing the opportunities to share these tasks. Shearing usually is done by skilled migrant crews. Even so, it draws area sheep owners of all ages together to assist in the tasks supportive to shearing. It provides another opportunity for shared community participation and recognition around an essential function.

Shared Agricultural Activities

Contemporary shared activities are a legacy of the period of preindustrial agriculture when many more activities collectively engaged the community. Barn raising, threshing, sheep shearing, roundup, haying, and other shared activities typified shared community economic activities among independent agriculturalists to a much greater extent than they do today. The vestigial activities continue to be practical and meaningful for community operation and cohesion, however.

Agricultural activities which continue to be shared within the community can be described in both operational and symbolic terms. The few that persist as economically justifiable, such as roundup and haying, tend to have rich symbolic and ritualistic qualities. Those which are economically obsolete, if performed at all, continue with rare exceptions as lessons from the historic community. They provide an opportunity to get together almost solely to enjoy leisure time together while marveling over obsolete machines like threshers, horse-drawn mowers, and steam tractors. They recount the tasks, crews, and hardships now avoided by modern machines. The participants are intensely aware of and committed to a mystique romanticizing their lives as linked to a valuable and on-going historically important way of life.

The community knows approximately when each shared agricultural activity will occur. The activities are largely determined by the season, and each must be performed annually. An assumption that the activities will be performed repeatedly is shared by participants, lending a sense of an eternal cycle to life. More important, year after year the same persons share the same set of interlocking tasks with each other in the same informal and personal manner.

Rural agrarian communities dominated by shared agricultural activities reflect those patterns in all social institutions. One example of an institution where shared communal activities predominate is education.

The School in Ranchland: Informal
Organization of an Institution

Although consolidation of schools was common during

the 1950s and 1960s, many small communities continue to have high schools, and most have elementary (K-8) schools, which frequently have only one or two teachers. The elementary schools form an institutionalized base for common concerns and interaction. They require financing and administration by local residents. School trustees, whose major functions are hiring teachers and requesting and allocating funds, are elected, usually for three-year terms. Residents with children in school are expected to "take their turn." Frequently, one or two persons who are willing to serve and have become familiar with operations and procedures run unopposed, with local community approval, for several terms. I have interviewed several school board members who had attended the school they have since administered. One person was directly connected with his school for 55 years. Candidates who are new to the area and who are perceived to have an educational philosophy inappropriate for the local school often receive no votes except their own. I know of two elections in which such newcomers or outsiders ran unopposed and lost almost unanimously to write-in candidates. A few days before the election, telephone campaigns led to local unanimity for a familiar local resident willing to meet his (rural school board members traditionally are men) responsibility to community well-being.

Excitement rarely accompanies any aspect of rural school operation or administration. Elections are conventionally low-keyed and are supposed to reflect personal service to the community. There is essentially no reward, except for appreciation from community members, who realize the demands of the job. Hiring teachers has much of the same public emotional neutrality as elections, although personal emotions may be rather intense. Teachers are hired (and fired) as much for their anticipated approval by the community as for their academic credentials. Teachers, too, must fit into the close, informal, and personal network. If they cannot, they are inappropriate. I have known teachers to resign or be fired for introducing cross-country skiing into the curriculum, living too visibly out of wedlock, or assigning too much homework. In each case, the complaints from only one or two families led to the dismissal.

The other major official function of trustees is to request and allocate funding. They propose local mill levies and sign depositions for operations and maintenance. Generally, the levels of funding are so low that there is rarely much leeway for decision making. Community members rarely fail to support minimal funding for continuing school operation. The existence of the local school is proof of the community's competence to meet its obligations to current and future generations.

The local school also draws residents together for shared activities and symbolic events. In addition to the trustees, rural schools rely upon voluntary assistance by other community members. Annual maintenance days are performed by trustees and parents whose children attend. These usually involve installation of playground equipment, cleaning, and repairs. Parents usually are responsible for transporting their children to school and on field trips, and these activities also are shared and coordinated among parents.

In addition to the frequent and recurrent activities which draw participation by parents and trustees, a few especially important events command widespread community attendance. At least once each year, always at Christmas and usually at one or two other national holidays, the entire community attends a school performance and social function.

Preparation for the Christmas pageant usually begins about a month in advance. Teachers are expected to direct the entire program, which involves a play; organized singing; distribution of gifts by Santa Claus among children, parents, and teachers; and arrangement and distribution of favors for all persons who attend. Trustees allocate special funds for the performance and the favors. Teachers devote an hour or two each day for practice. Mothers sew costumes, while fathers rehearse lines.

Such performances are among the few mechanisms for publicly acknowledging the support from the larger community for the school and the teacher. They provide still other opportunities to share activities. They are symbolic affirmations of the community's ability to put together an event, linked to similar events of the past. They are noteworthy for their historical context and universal community attendance. They, perhaps more clearly than any other nonwork activity, personify the belief of the shared lifestyle of isolated rural areas.

MYTH AND REALITY

Ranch life is believed by ranchers and perceived by others to occur in a community which carries a direct, relatively uninterrupted tradition. People organize themselves and interact (Marans et al. 1980) "the way people used to." Although empirically correct for structural reasons already discussed, the perception also conveys a value judgment by residents that some elements of ranch life are more valuable than contemporary urban life. Ranchers are socially atavistic heroes, to themselves as well as to outsiders (Goldman and Dickens 1983). In effect, they maintain control of their world as individuals:

I've worked hard all my life and never had much to show for it but debt. But I wouldn't have done it any other way. And I could never have done it without her [his wife; women on successful ranches seem to glorify their lives at least as much as ranch men]. Despite the hardships of the weather, calving, the increased costs of everything, and unpredictable cattle prices, I never minded it. I've worked seven days a week most of my life, but it has been here, the most beautiful place a person could ever live.

Ranching seems to convey an aura of a whole lifestyle, from youth through old age, with interlocking gender roles: "There is always something new to look forward to. Each season means a different job has to be done. I've seen some suffering and death, but over the long run seeing the new ones [calves and foals] more than outweighs the hard times."

Ranchers see themselves as living a more desirable life than others. Economically, theirs is a livelihood possible to few persons since the land must be inherited or obtained at great price. Ranchers rarely mention that reality and instead focus upon the way of life which is a consequence of ranching. They carry a burden of living myth along with reality and feel remorse when they can no longer comfortably combine the two. Most hate to sell, even though their income may increase and their job demands decline by doing so. Their remorse involves more than retiring from a job; it is an admission that they must give up the style of life integrated around the work. Most retired ranchers speak apologetically about not being able to have done it any longer. I have never heard a rancher or former rancher regret his occupation and lifestyle. They interpret the immense number of hours, hard physical labor, relative economic hardship, and omnipresent threat from the physical environment and the economy as trials that only they, persons of special ability, could endure.

The point being made about myth concerning ranch life is that it is treated as reality by ranchers as well as by outsiders. Neither outsiders nor even most ranchers realize the structural bases for the uniqueness of isolated rural life. Outsiders are likely to think of it as a style, which can be adapted to increased and unfamiliar populations, new centralized forms of production, and larger, more diverse commercial sectors. They fail to understand that the community style of life is an adaptation to small, familiar, sparsely distributed agricultural activities capable of generating a minimal commercial sector. Ranchers, while aware of the numerous complexities of their social system, tend to be unaware of how important the structural antecedents are to what makes their community and their position in it vulnerable to destruction from external change.

Ranch communities are wholes at both intrapersonal and interpersonal levels. Urban society is fragmented because interactions in it are so specific and differentiated that face-to-face recognition of persons, rather than the roles they occupy, is lost even as interaction occurs. Efficiency and anonymity for the mass are gained at the loss of the person. Persons are protected, indeed prohibited, from acknowledging each other. Lacking a personally shared history, they must rely upon conventional symbols for their place in the interaction. Spectators can allude to the Yankees back in 1970 rather than to the fight in the local bar when one's nose was rearranged in the company of friends. Knowing the specific expectations of the reciprocal roles, urban persons may avoid having to care about the activities and concerns of the other person beyond the narrow limits of their interaction. Socialization among ranchers usually occurs with other community members. Interaction in the city is divided among coworkers, neighbors, family, and an enormous cast of supporting actors who are frequently unknown, like ballplayers on the local professional teams and shopping clerks.

Rural areas, on the other hand, engage persons in activities largely with personally familiar others. They offer little escape from being scrutinized. They force residents to acknowledge different values and, potentially, roles they share with other community members. Transactions generally involve multiple activities and concerns. Paying the checker at a market requires obligatory conversation in which the progress of the extended families of both cashier and purchaser, general politics and morals, local problems and administration of services, and, of course, the weather are mentioned. Such conversations are hardly idle. They simultaneously reaffirm social organization, help establish consensus, and recognize the individuals. They frequently imply things like, "I have to live with them, so I can't do what I would really like to do." They give primacy to maintaining personal commitments to each other in the community.

The small population lacks sufficient diversity to allow selective choice of friends and neighborhoods. Residents have to take what is there, which is likely to be local, conservative, and provincial. But whether residents like each other or not, they must share schools, churches, and other community activities or do without. Similarly, everyone in the ranch community is expected to do his or her share. (And his and her shares are likely to be traditionally gender related.) The small population precludes specialization that allows hiring someone to do hard, dirty, and painful jobs, like hiring and firing teachers and ministers, hauling children to school, and forming planning committees. It is difficult to remain either exclusive or anonymous.

CONCLUSION

The most common way large energy developments disrupt rural life is through rapid in-migration of many new, unfamiliar persons who are employed outside the existing agriculturally based economy. There are no acceptable roles for these newcomers in the relatively closed rural community. They are predominantly young men, frequently with divergent social backgrounds; their presence is accompanied by inconveniences, costs, and fundamental modifications in the community. Oldtimers are likely to become polarized around the multifaceted issue of development. Accustomed to accomplishing tasks with minimal conflict and arriving at consensus through informal discussion without outside interference, local residents become upset and disillusioned. At the same time, they are forced to adopt an impersonal orientation to accommodate newcomers and the change that brought them. Subtly and unwittingly, their traditional qualitative form of interaction and organization is exchanged for a modern quantitative one.

I have observed a less common type of disruption in ranch areas near the energy development site even when workers resided outside the community. In Decker, Montana, disillusionment followed blasting, ambient dust, and increased nuisances such as traffic, poaching, and trespassing. Embittered oldtimers began moving out, leaving behind a few hardened, impatient survivors who planned to stay, and a sad and apologetic majority who said they, too, were planning to move. Essentially no newcomers moved into the area, but oldtimers had ceased to share work or socialize. The community had disintegrated from within.

In both types of impacted communities, those deluged with newcomers and those which disintegrated from within, there is confusion and passive alienation. The realization strikes home that the community is no longer a relatively autonomous place comprised of familiar faces collectively performing tasks as a primary group. Residents are compelled to examine their community and their beliefs as a new way of life is juxtaposed on the old. They no longer see their neighbors as friendlier and more helpful than elsewhere or the place as more beautiful. The mystique is lost, as is the sense of community associated with it.

The ranch activities discussed in this chapter typify those in small, isolated agricultural communities in the northern Rocky Mountains. Their vulnerability to energy impacts occurs in large part because the ubiquitous effects of modern technology have left them as residual communities. Industrialization has gradually eroded the advantages of shared labor. By increasing the outputs of workers, mechanization has multiplied the number of acres and animals which each can handle. This has increased the scale of operations. It is not that individual effort has diminished so much as that it has been directed toward larger and more efficient operations.

The reduced labor needs in agricultural areas have been largely responsible for the reduction of rural populations and the demise of many small towns. Ironically, these trends may actually have strengthened many communities in the sense of gemeinschaft. The process has reduced the numbers of rural residents and communities. The propensity for intercommunity contact has been reduced as the size of the geographic areas for remaining communities has increased. The residual communities now frequently cover vast areas, formerly occupied by several communities. Even modern vehicles fail to compensate for the increased distances created between adjacent communities. Rural open-country and town-country communities in the northern Rockies frequently are spread throughout a thousand-square-mile area.

The point made is that the characteristics of small, isolated, stable communities such as the types described are qualitatively different from those of other communities. Thus, the lifestyles of their residents differ. Although communities may exhibit the same type of interaction and organization for decades, they are fragile when exposed to rapid development. They are small, face-to-face, personally familiar systems based upon sharing mutually valued activities over extended periods, preferably two or more generations. In less than a decade, they may lose their qualities through the introduction of sufficiently large, relatively mobile, and unfamiliar populations accustomed to institutions formally and impersonally providing goods and services.

Thus, ranchers who live in isolated agricultural areas suffer extensive negative impacts from resource development projects which residents of more gesellschaft places do not experience. The lives of the members of this occupational subculture are based upon the shared activities and interactions of these communities and are irrevocably altered when the character of the gemeinschaft community is changed by development.

REFERENCES

Gold, R. 1974. A Comparative Case Study of the Impacts of Coal Development on the Way of Life of People in the Coal Areas of Eastern Montana and Northeastern Wyoming. Denver: Northern Great Plains Resource Program.

Goldman, R., and D. R. Dickens. 1983. The selling of rural America. Rural Sociology 48:585-606.

Jobes, P. C. 1980. Changing Country, Changing Town. Research Report 165. Bozeman: Montana Agricultural Experiment Station.

Kraenzel, C. F. 1980. The Social Cost of Space in the Yonland. Bozeman: Big Sky Books.

Leistritz, F. L., and S. H. Murdock. 1981. Socioeconomic Impact of Resource Development: Methods for Assessment. Boulder, Colo.: Westview Press.

Marans, R. W., D. A. Dillman, and J. T. Keller. 1980. Perceptions of Rural Life in Rural America. Ann Arbor: Survey Research Center, University of Michigan.

Simmel, G. 1971. On Individuality and Social Forms, ed. D. N. Levine. Chicago: University of Chicago Press.

Toennies, F. 1940. Fundamental Concepts of Sociology, trans. C. P. Loomis. New York: American Book.

7
Women: Gemeinschaft in Boomtowns

Elizabeth W. Moen

INTRODUCTION

Is it possible or even appropriate to discuss women as if they were a minority, a subculture, or an ethnic group? Women are the majority of the population, and like men, they are to be found in every category of every social classification of people (except "male"). Thus, it is neither possible nor desirable to discuss the situation of women in resource communities as if all women have similar experiences. To do so would only perpetuate the stereotypes and assumptions regarding women in these communities that are commonly held by planners and policymakers in government and industry. On the other hand, theory and research suggest that members of a gender have a great deal in common: experiences, values, expectations, constraints, and worldviews that set the genders apart from one another.
Noting that writers from Georg Simmel to Kate Millett have mentioned the separate worlds of women and men, Bernard (1981) has shown, in her major study of the topic, how women and men live in single-sex worlds which are different both subjectively and objectively. There is clearly physical separation. Sometimes the separation is inviolate, and in the extreme case--purdah--it is almost complete. Laws and language also perpetuate separation, as do educational, organizational, occupational, and recreational settings. The male world, according to Bernard, is segregative, exclusionary, and even "in varying degrees hostile to the female world . . . it permits, encourages, and even prescribes behavior hostile to women" (1981:30; for a similar analysis from a more psychological perspective, see Schaef 1981).
Bernard, as well as others in many fields of inquiry (e.g., E. Boulding 1976, 1977; Joyce and Leadley 1977; Morgan 1984), has concluded that we are suffering from "ignor-ance" of the female world: "It is the male world that has been the major focus of

practically all research in the literature, history and the social sciences from Plato . . . right down to modern academic social scientists . . . virtually all of human knowledge is thus a male creation" (Bernard 1981:12-13). Further, the investigations of the female world that have been made are mainly concerned with oppression and victimization. We know much less about the power of women, the positive aspects of their lives, and the contributions they make outside their homes.[1]

In this chapter, I will examine the situation of women in energy resource communities, both as women in the world and as members of a female world. I will begin with a review of literature, develop a theoretical perspective, introduce the data, and then discuss the findings in terms of the consequences for women of rapid growth and change, gender segregation and differences, and women's contributions to the community. Although it is beyond the scope of this chapter to fully develop and test a theory regarding male and female worlds in energy resource towns, it is important to begin studying the relative influence of men and women in development planning and policy-making and how differences in the values and perspectives of males and females might affect the course and consequences of development.

WHAT DO WE KNOW?

Women and Development

We do suffer from ignor-ance of women in developing areas of the more and the less developed nations. Regarding economic development in general, women and their work have been ignored, stereotyped, and devalued. It is only within recent years that research has discovered or acknowledged that the status and condition of women, as compared to men, have not improved with economic development, either in contemporary developing nations or historically in the more developed nations when they were developing. Women lose status relative to men and are virtually absent from groups planning for change (see, for example, Black 1981; Dauber and Cain 1981; Morgan 1984).

In her critique of standard development theories, McCormack (1981) concludes that all perspectives accept continuing inequality between men and women, and even the newest notions of "development with equity" fail to consider equity for women. "The shock," says McCormack, is that

. . . patriarchy itself modernized. . . . Male preference, male privilege and male norms constituting standards of excellence are the outcome of a process which, in theory, should have given us a gender-free division of labor, a set of gender-free standards of achievement, and gender-free institutions (1981:28).

Now research is showing that the families of these women and the developing nations as a whole are being disadvantaged (particularly in the area of nutrition) because women have not been consulted or considered in planning, policy-making, or resource allocation. The failure of economic development programs in the developing nations is well characterized by the now-popular phrase, "The GNP is doing well, but the people are not." Black (1981), acknowledging that there is a female world, asks to what extent the worldwide failure of development is due to sexism, the resulting situation of women, and failure to take seriously women's distinctive experiences and values.

Rural Women in the United States

Although there has been a great increase in research on U.S. women, it has not extended to rural women or even to the rural family. Just as in the more general literature on women and development, rural women are stereotyped (as isolated "farmwives" and small town homemakers); their productive roles are ignored; the values which restrict women's activities to house and children are reinforced; and the expressive, supportive aspects of rural women's activities are overlooked and devalued (Bescher-Donnelly and Smith 1981; Haney 1982; Ploch 1981; Schumm and Bollman 1981; Joyce and Leadley 1977; Flora and Johnson 1978). There are, however, a growing number of exceptions such as the studies of U.S. farm women by E. Boulding (1980). According to Haney (1982), by understating the contributions of rural women to the home, farm, and community, the literature has contributed to policies that reinforce traditional gender stereotypes and the perpetuation of discrimination against rural women.

Most empirical studies compare rural women with urban women, rather than with rural men. This research suggests that although change is occurring, rural women maintain more traditional attitudes and behavior regarding marriage, family, and gender roles than do urban women. Rural residents are also following (though lagging behind) urban patterns of change in household formation and dissolution: The age of marriage is increasing, fertility and household size are decreasing, divorce is increasing, and female labor force participation is increasing (Flora and Johnson 1978).

Although rural women have a lower rate of participation in politics and face more opposition than their urban counterparts, it is also true that most women in the United States who have been elected to public office serve in local government in small towns and sparsely populated counties. Although they are less supportive of the Equal Rights Amendment than urban women, rural women are very concerned about receiving equal pay (Bescher-Donnelly and Smith 1981). Further, they are now forming new kinds of organizations which, unlike older organizations such as the Cowbelles (who promote the consumption of beef) and the Homemaker's Clubs, have the purpose of improving the image, status, and political clout of rural women (e.g., Rural American Women, American Agri-Women, and Women in the Farm Economy).

Perhaps the greatest and best-documented change for rural women, especially married agricultural women, has been their increased rate of employment outside the home. During the 1960s and 1970s, women accounted for most of the employment growth in nonmetropolitan counties in the United States. However, they remain concentrated in low-skill, low-wage positions (Haney 1982; Bescher-Donnelly and Smith 1981).

Women in Energy Boomtowns

Research and assessment of the social impact of rural industrialization have not been greatly concerned with the distribution of costs and benefits, and when distributional factors have been considered, the unit of analysis has frequently been towns or counties, rather than subgroups (race, class, gender, age) and individuals within towns or counties (see, e.g., Bloomquist and Summers 1982). With few exceptions, only men are studied. A more general, but most striking, example is Inequality in American Communities (Curtis and Jackson 1977), a very detailed, statistical study of patterns, processes, perceptions, and consequences of inequality in several U.S. towns. The authors generalize their findings to the communities as a whole even though the samples were composed entirely of male "heads-of-households" (including single males). All women (about 50 percent of the population) and all female-headed households (over 15 percent of all households) were excluded from the sample. The authors do not concern themselves with the validity of this procedure, nor do they tell how they defined head-of-household. Considering that the majority of poor households are female headed, it is likely that such a procedure excluded most of the poorest households from the sample of each community.

In Finsterbusch's Understanding Social Impacts (1980), there are no sections on distribution of impacts on women or minorities. The major reference to women is that "wives are bored." The author's references to "businessmen" suggest that he is unaware that a substantial proportion of small town (as well as urban) businesses are either co-owned or solely owned by women. In addition, a chapter on unemployment refers only to the unemployment of men and their subsequent loss of status and authority in the household and the community.

Similarly, in Social Impact Assessment in Small Communities, Bowles (1981) has little to say about the distribution of impacts and does not mention women. In The Socioeconomic Impact of Resource Development: Methods for Assessment, Leistritz and Murdock (1981) pay little attention to the costs and benefits of resource development within towns or among social subgroups. Leistritz and Murdock do, however, assume that women work outside the home.

Most of the research that focuses specifically on women in energy boomtowns has been done by the Women's Research Centre in Vancouver, British Columbia, and by the Growth Impact Group with which I am associated.[2] When the more general boomtown literature does mention women, it generally presents them as being the economic dependents of in-migrant workers or longtimer ranchers and farmers. In fact, social impact statements and other reports about the residents of energy boomtowns could lead to the following conclusion: Nearly all of the women in boomtowns are dependent homemakers married to construction workers. They all live in mobile homes, and although they suffer from chronic boredom, cabin fever, or more severe forms of depression, they would be quite content if only there were a decent shopping center and some recreation. The construction worker husband comes home after a hard day's work to find a bored, depressed, crabby wife. They fight; he gets mad and goes out to a bar. Later, he comes home drunk and beats her up. The solution to his problems (alcohol abuse and uncontrollable violence) is to solve her problems so she will be more fun to be around. If only it were so simple. There is, of course, research (e.g., Edwards 1980; Gill 1983; Gold 1984; Baker and Kotarski 1977) which attempts to present a realistic picture of the lives of boomtown women.

THEORETICAL PERSPECTIVE

As discussed in the introduction, this chapter is concerned with women in the world and the world of women. In considering how the female and male worlds might be conceptualized, Bernard (1981) observes that the female world is often discussed in terms of its place in the dominant social structure (class, caste, minority group, women as "nigger"), an occupation (the homemaker's world, the world of the Women's Page), a culture (a system of institutions such as the labor market or marriage), or an ethnic group (especially in regard to prejudice, segregation, and assimilation). Bernard, however, believes male and female worlds can be best understood via classic social science polarities such as Maine's status vs. contract, Toennies's kin-and-locale-based gemeinschaft vs. exchange-based, capitalist gesellschaft, Benedict's Apollonian (tradition-bound) vs. Dionysian (violent), Kropotkin's mutual aid vs. Spencer's survival of the fittest, Parsons's expressive vs. instrumental, and K. Boulding's integry (loyalty, love, trust, association, community, and grants of goods and services) vs. economy (competition, impersonality, rationality, self-interest, and exchange of goods and services).

According to Bernard, the first-named of each pair represents the female world and the second-named, the male world. Each world has a very different worldview or paradigm. Most of these theorists were not "wholly unaware of the gender related aspect of their conceptualizations." Some were quite explicit about the connection: "The nineteenth century world of industry and politics was seen in male terms as representative of male values and virtues, as one of harsh striving, or conflict and competition, and the female world was seen as a necessary counterpoint, a world of love and support" (1981:28).

Although K. Boulding did not specifically link integry and economy to gender, Bernard argues that "a good case can be made for the conception that historically the integry [the economy of love] has indeed been a women's world. . . . It has, that is, performed the integrating function of holding the whole system together" (Bernard 1981:27; see also E. Boulding 1976).

Acknowledging that the terms that represent the male and female worlds overlap to a considerable degree, Bernard chose for her study of the female world to focus upon gemeinschaft, which emphasizes the locale-based nature of its structure (community) and the love- and/or duty-based ethos of its culture. Since this chapter is specifically concerned with communities undergoing rapid economic development, I shall employ the broader concepts of gemeinschaft/integry and gesellschaft/economy to reflect the social and economic changes that occur. As such, the female world emphasizes the personal, integrative activity, community building, and grants of goods and services (e.g., volunteer activity). In contrast, the male world emphasizes the impersonal, profit, competition, and the exchange of goods and services.

Gemeinschaft and Gesellschaft in Boomtowns

One of the main concerns about energy boomtowns is increased rates of social problems in these communities. Most boomtown research that is guided by theory draws upon the concept of a rural-urban continuum, the loss of gemeinschaft and the rise of gesellschaft, to help understand increased rates of social problems. Rapid growth and change, weakening or loss of social bonds and social supports, and the increased bureaucratization and impersonalization of the formal structures that replace many of the informal support systems are thought to contribute to stress, mental and physical disability, and problem behavior (see Moen et al. 1981 for further discussion of the pertinent literature). The field of social epidemiology, which has shown that stress-related mental and physical illnesses may be mediated by social supports, also points to the importance of understanding and maintaining gemeinschaft/integry in communities undergoing rapid growth and change (see, for example, Cobb 1976; Kassover and McKeown 1981; Bougsty and Weisz 1985).

DATA

The data come from two studies of the social consequences of energy production in western Colorado. In the first study (conducted in 1978) of Craig, a genuine boomtown, and Paonia, a town then on the verge of rapid growth, data were obtained primarily through in-depth, semi-structured interviews with over one hundred women; a self-administered time-geography questionnaire; informal interviews and discussions with a cross section of community members and leaders; written documents; photography; participant observation; and self-administered questionnaires sent to energy industry employers (for details see Moen et al. 1981).

The second study (conducted in 1980 and 1981) was of Meeker, then an emerging energy boomtown which had grown at the average rate of 10 percent a year between 1977 and 1980, and Walden, a small, stable mining and ranching community. Data were obtained through a sample survey of households; surveys of businesses and organizations; structured interviews with community leaders, public officials, agency directors, and other influential residents; interviews with industry representatives; in-depth family studies; public documents; over one hundred in-depth, semi-structured interviews with a cross section of male and female residents; and participant observation (for details see Lillydahl et al. 1982).

Since there are gender-related differences in attitudes, values, behavior, etc., between rural and urban dwellers, in-migrants may be different from longtimers and be in the vanguard of social change in the community. To reflect the timing of growth in Meeker and capture potential differences, some data from the Meeker sample survey will be reported. The respondents were categorized as newcomers if they had lived in Meeker for five or fewer years and as longtimers if they had lived in Meeker over five years. The sample included 143 newcomer women, 135 longtimer women, 87 newcomer men, and 87 longtimer men.

RESULTS

Women in the World: The Social Consequences of Growth and Change

Contrary to the prevailing stereotype, energy boomtowns are populated by many kinds of families and households. Among the women, there are dependent homemakers, self-supporting women with and without children and with and without partners, women engaged in agriculture with and without men, older women on Social Security and pensions, married women who are employed outside the home because they prefer to be and/or because two incomes are needed, and women who like to work outside the home but cannot find a job or have husbands who disapprove. There are also unseen women, women left behind in another town with full responsibility for house and children because the only work their husbands can find requires continual travel from one construction site to another. Although their lives are greatly affected by energy production, virtually nothing is known about the women left behind.

Further, social problems in energy boomtowns are not confined to construction worker families. All the residents experience the stress that accompanies rapid growth and change, and social problems are found among all social categories both before and after growth occurs. Bored, crabby wives cannot begin to account for the existence of problems or their increase.

The majority of newcomer women have moved to an energy production community because their husbands have found a job or are looking for work as laborers, skilled craft workers, technicians, administrators, or professionals in energy- and non-energy-related fields. Many of these women had their own careers, were in the middle of their education, or were accustomed to working outside the home before they moved. Higher education is generally not available in or near the new community. Since there are few opportunities for the professional/managerial women, and energy and construction companies are still resistant to hiring women, the jobs that are available to these newcomers are mostly low-paying, dead-end "women's work" (see also Rollins 1980; U.S. Commission on Civil Rights 1978). Women who have come from larger towns are surprised and insulted by the wages (as low as $1.00 an hour in 1980) they are offered. Energy and construction companies do pay higher wages to their clerical workers than local employers are able to, but these wages are considerably smaller than those paid to predominantly male, unskilled laborers at these same companies. Thus, many newcomer women become involuntary full-time homemakers.

Middle-class women, who are generally more readily accepted by the local community, may throw themselves into volunteer work. Some women feel "used" by the community when they are continually asked to perform important volunteer tasks, but their work goes unrecognized. While some involuntary homemakers create very fulfilling lives for themselves, some become so obsessed with their home and family that they lose their own sense of self-worth and identity. Others become depressed and often find comfort in alcohol or drugs.

It is especially difficult for wives of migratory workers to find jobs because employers are reluctant to hire a temporary resident. Other forms of integration are difficult because many of these women are reluctant to establish friendships and other social bonds; they know these ties will soon have to be severed. Moreover, they and their families are often shunned by the rest of the community because of negative attitudes toward transient workers and mobile-home dwellers. The resulting stress felt by the family is compounded by the conditions of the husband's work. Because it is temporary, they may be forced to move as often as ten to twelve times a year. And although hourly wages are high, they may not stretch far enough to cover the times of unemployment and the costs of moving. Miners, who are also subject to layoffs, and energy-related construction workers have some of the most dangerous and uncomfortable working conditions in this country. Moreover, the shift work that is mandated by most energy and construction companies not only is hard on the worker, but also makes it extremely difficult for family members, who must adjust their lives to the continually shifting work and sleep schedules of the worker.

Longtime residents of energy production communities are similarly affected if they obtain work in construction or energy production, but they are also affected in other ways. Some gain a great deal through increased business, or by selling land and water rights. But others have a difficult time adjusting to the changes in their town. Many grieve the loss of community and way of life. Because of increased inflation accompanying rapid growth, those who do not benefit economically become relatively worse off. In some cases, more traditional couples find that the wife must go to work, and this necessity is stressful for the entire family. Elders on fixed incomes, most of whom are women, have few options except to tighten their belts tighter (or, as is being found throughout the United States, make the choice to "heat or eat").

Even when longtimer families do benefit economically, the women in these families may be hurt in the process. In this country, status is closely associated with earnings. When husbands go into higher-paying energy-related jobs or otherwise gain economically from the boom, although the entire household benefits in many ways, the status of the wife may be reduced unless she too gets a high-paying job (see also Ford 1978).

Self-supporting women, and especially those with children, are also hurt economically. Entry into the higher-paying energy-related jobs is quite limited, and these women do not have a spouse to bring in a second income. Thus, self-supporting women may have to leave town, take two or more jobs, go on welfare, turn to prostitution, or marry out of economic necessity. Moreover, with the recent cuts in federally funded social programs, self-supporting mothers who were able to work for very low wages because they could get daycare assistance now must drop out of work to care for their children. They reluctantly turn to welfare, but that too is being cut.

The majority of women who do get jobs in construction, mining, and other energy-related work are single mothers or young women who are trying to save enough money for higher education, to start a business, or to buy a home. Although these women make better wages than other women, they must endure, with the men, the dangers and hardships of that work, plus in many instances, a great deal of harassment from their male coworkers and supervisors. Such harassment ranges from attempts to embarrass and humiliate the women to pranks and noncooperation on the job that have resulted in serious injury (see Yount 1986 and Chapter 5 in this book).

To summarize, economic prosperity is one major benefit of a boom, but for most women the gain is derived from the advancement of their husbands, and in the process they may lose status relative to their husbands and in the community. On the other hand, some husbands and therefore their wives lose status because their income or occupational prestige is eclipsed or they are displaced in the community power structure by newcomers. Meanwhile, self-supporting women are likely to become severely economically disadvantaged because of their own low wages, inflation, and minimal job opportunities or assistance.

There are for women positive consequences of energy development, especially when supermarkets, laundries, fast food outlets, discount stores, day care, banks, insurance agents, health care specialists, etc., are established in the community. Our time-geography study (Moen et al. 1981) found that changes such as these may make it easier for women to hold jobs outside the home and give them more genuine leisure time if they no longer have to drive several hours for shopping and specialized services.

The foregoing was derived mainly from the four study communities. However, the strong degree of confirmation for these findings that has come from residents of other resource development communities, human service agencies, researchers, and attendees at numerous conferences gives some confidence that these conclusions do represent fairly well the general situation of women in western energy boomtowns.[4]

Consider, for instance, this report from Challis, Idaho:

> The plight of the women in the . . . Mobile Home Park is at least as desperate and demeaning as that of some women workers who are reported to be enduring sexual harassment on the job. . . . A double standard exists whereby their husbands . . . are given professional support and training for their new assignments, while the wives, who have often been uprooted from satisfactory roles in work, community, and family networks, are given no systematic assistance to help them fit into this new situation. Rather, they are put into the same position as locals in a typical Western boomtown: in exchange for the economic benefit of their husband's salary they are expected to bear the social costs of loss of community and sense of place. . . . Their importance as mothers and homemakers is given occasional lip service . . . but is clearly "second class" in the "real" world where status is measured in commitments of time and money (Gold and Sterling 1981:1).

Female and Male Worlds: Gender Segregation and Differences

Although change is occurring in rural areas, more traditional views about gender roles are still to be found, and in western rural communities activities continue to be highly gender segregated. A major complaint among women in the four study communities is that "it's a man's world." Not only do men dominate in industry, commerce, politics, religion, and public administration, but they also have many more options for their leisure time. The most available recreation is male oriented and considered "masculine," and bars, which comprise most of the "places to go" in town, are not considered appropriate places for women to spend much, if any, time. There are few recreational outlets or gathering places for women, particularly women with small children to attend. "Men have their hunting and fishing and bars; women have nothing" was also a frequent comment among women.

Energy production greatly increases gender segregation in the workplace, skews the gender ratio of the population towards males, and further masculinizes the community. The degree is especially related to numbers of newcomer construction workers, who are most frequently young, unattached males. But energy industry workers, who are more likely to be partnered males, also participate heavily in a virtually all-male society of coworkers.

The private sector responds to such population growth by providing more bars; the public sector responds, if money is available, by providing more recreational facilities such as a gym or basketball courts. Women benefit from some of these new recreational facilities, but their needs for gathering places to meet friends, for day care, for appropriate places for family dining and entertainment, for benches overlooking a playground, or even for a playground generally are not met.

Human services that are especially important to women in energy boomtowns are day care, recreation, and employment-related services and policies. Women in boomtowns and other rural communities have identified day care as a major need which would enable them to be employed outside the home, to tend to family errands and business in distant commercial centers, to have time to be with other adults or by themselves, and to alleviate the "cabin fever" that is common during the harsh winter months. The idea gets little support. The public sector says day care should be provided by the private sector; the private sector may be reluctant because local commercial interests are concerned that day care enables women to do their shopping out of town. Since there is still the feeling that mothers ought to be at home with their children, there is grudging acceptance of day care for children of women who must work outside the home.

Below, data from the sample survey of Meeker residents and a study of town and county administration are presented to further detail female and male participation and perspectives. The differences in male and female responses to the sample survey which are reported below are all substantively and statistically ($p \leq .05$) significant. In a more detailed analysis of the survey data via discriminant analysis, indicators of the main dimensions of gemeinschaft/integry and gesellschaft/economy enable the prediction of gender with over 80 percent accuracy, and gender accounts for up to 45 percent of the variance in the indicators. Among employed respondents, accuracy of prediction is over 90 percent, and gender accounts for up to 63 percent of the variance in the indicators.

Gender Segregation. In Meeker, nearly all of the clubs, organizations, and organized recreational activities established before and during the boom period were for men or women only. (The swimming pool was the major exception.) New energy-related employment was primarily for men, and in 1980 men held 80 percent of the elected and appointed positions on the 18 town and county boards open to Meeker residents. The 20 women who held such positions were concentrated on the hospital and library boards; one of the six members of the town board was a woman.

Planning and Policy-Making. Although few women have served on the city and county planning boards, or held political or administrative positions, they have influenced planning and policy-making for energy-related growth through two volunteer organizations, the Human Services Council and the Eastern Advisory Group of the Rio Blanco County Impact Mitigation Task Force. Women, along with ministers and other male human service providers, have played a major role in educating town and county leaders regarding the need to increase and expand human services (the formal counterpart of gemeinschaft/integry) and in lobbying for increased funding for these services. However, in 1980-1981 all energy impact funding requests ultimately had to be assigned priority by the county commissioners and mayors of the two towns in the county--four men and one woman. (Currently, the three commissioners decide, and all three are men.) These officials have placed a much higher priority on infrastructure and other capital improvements than on human services. (The situation is the same in most energy boomtowns.) By 1980, Meeker had sewer and water capacity for a population of 8,000, while human services for a then-current population of approximately 2,500 were stretched to capacity (see Lillydahl and Moen 1983 for more detailed discussions of growth planning and management in Meeker).

Beginning in late 1981 and culminating in the spring of 1982 with the closing of the Exxon-Tosco Colony Oil Shale Project, Rio Blanco and nearby counties suffered an unexpected bust because of the sudden cessation of nearly all of the shale oil development in the region (for details see Moen 1984a, 1984b). The stabilization or decline in population growth rates reduced the need for infrastructure and other capital expenditures, but the demand for human services remained the same or even increased in areas such as Aid to Families with Dependent Children, food stamps, job services, mental health, alcohol abuse, and domestic violence. Consequently, even with a decline in population, the town and county could not adequately provide human services to Meeker residents. Meanwhile, excessive infrastructure had still to be maintained.

<u>Employment</u>. Sixty percent of the women were employed, and 59 percent of these had full-time jobs. Over 40 percent of the employed women were in clerical or service positions, 10 percent were employed as nurses and teachers, and 10 percent held other technical and professional positions. Eighty-six percent of the men were employed (97 percent of these, full time); 30 percent were in technical and professional positions, and 25 percent in skilled crafts; 25 percent of the longtimer men were in agriculture, and 20 percent of the newcomer men worked as miners and operatives. Among the employed, 10 percent of the women, 19 percent of the longtimer men, and 59 percent of the newcomer men were employed by energy industries or related employers such as construction contractors for the project sites. (Since single, newcomer men were underrepresented in the sample, it is likely that 59 percent is low for the newcomer male population as a whole.)

Employment policies are especially critical for women. It has been found that, in addition to having economic resources, employed women have higher status in the home and the community and are more likely to feel fulfilled than homemakers (Ford 1978). In rural boomtowns, employment is especially important because it provides a meaningful way to spend time and helps newcomers establish social supports. In fact, in the Meeker survey one's workplace (not one's spouse's) was cited as the main place where most local friends were met. In Meeker, women, especially newcomers, were less likely than men to agree that there were good employment opportunities. There was considerable support for female employment: Nearly three-quarters of the newcomer women and one-half of the other respondents agreed that "I support employment policies which try to increase the job opportunities available to women in all occupations." However, this support was not unqualified. Reflecting traditional values, two-thirds of the newcomer women and three-quarters of the rest agreed that "there are some jobs in which men should be given preference over women." Nevertheless, 43 percent of the women aged 18 to 34 expressed interest in receiving training in traditionally male work: e.g., 30 percent were interested in truck driving, 23 percent in heavy equipment operation, 24 percent in carpentry, 10 percent in coal mining, and 15 percent in shale oil work. These are jobs which employers and the general public assume women do not want. There are few opportunities for job training in the area, and as occurs nationally, a variety of means are used to discourage or prevent women from seeking or staying in these jobs.

Day Care and Recreation. In Meeker, much of the day-care need has been provided by women involved in traditional marriages whose husbands' incomes are no longer sufficient to meet family expenses. These women have chosen to reduce the cognitive dissonance associated with employment by establishing small day-care centers within their homes. Among employed Meeker residents, women were more likely than men to believe that the availability of day care at their workplace was important. Fifty-six percent of the newcomer women and 36 percent of the longtimer women reported that having day care at the workplace was important, whereas only 12 percent of the newcomer men and 15 percent of the longtimer men thought day care was important.

There are fewer recreational opportunities and gathering places for women than for men in towns such as Meeker. Women, and especially newcomer women, in Meeker were less satisfied with their leisure-time activities than were men. When asked which aspect of the town they liked least, 42 percent of the newcomer women answered leisure-time activities, whereas only 14 percent of the longtimer men gave this response. Not having a place to go or to send young children poses an especially difficult problem for women whose husbands work night shifts, especially if living quarters are cramped, there are small children at home, and day care is not an option. These women must keep their children very quiet or take them out of the house while their husbands sleep during the day. This situation was described by one Meeker woman as the "kangaroo syndrome"--the mother walks up and down the streets or sits in the hotel lobby, the library, or a coffee shop all day, with her children constantly clinging to her.

Norms and Values. Although residents of rural areas are relaxing traditional gender-related norms, they still have more conservative views than residents of urban areas. In the Meeker survey, traditional views still obtained, although, as might be expected, women, and especially newcomer women, tended to be less conservative than men. For instance, men were more likely than women to agree that "in general, women who are full-time housewives and mothers are happier than women with careers." On the other hand, men were less likely to agree that "in general, full-time househusbands are just as capable of raising children as full-time housewives."

Reflecting both traditional values and gemeinschaft/integry (and probably the household economic situation), women were much more likely than men to stress the importance of their spouse's career. When asked to "list two things you do which make you feel the most useful and worthwhile," Meeker women were much more likely than Meeker men to list activities having to do with their family role (loving, tending, helping, caring for family members, being a good spouse or parent, contributing to success of family members)--i.e., activities representative of gemeinschaft/integry. Men, on the other hand, were much more likely to list activities having to do with work or general competency (working, doing a good job at work, success, doing my work well)--i.e., items representative of gesellschaft/economy. It is interesting that making money or providing for the family was rarely mentioned by either men or women. The second-most-mentioned kinds of activities for both men and women had to do with altruistic behavior (helping others, counseling others, having people rely on me, sacrificing for others). Men and women mentioned this kind of activity, which also represents gemeinschaft/integry, in equal proportions.

In discussing the male and female worlds of the rural United States, Flora and Johnson comment, "It is likely that farm women are socialized not to place a high premium on personal values . . ., stressing instead more holistic values" (1978:169). This seems to have been the case in Meeker. For example, men were much more likely than women to stress the importance of a successful career, whereas women were more likely to stress the importance of living a religious life and the importance of relationships with friends.

Summary. There was clearly gender segregation in the community and the workplace. There were also gender-based differences in attitudes, values, and norms. Men, and generally longtimer men, held the most traditional views, and women, especially newcomer women, held the least traditional views. Consequently, in-migration can be a catalyst for social change.

Contributions of Women

Just as throughout the rest of the world, most of the women in the four study communities hold more than one job and contribute to the community through paid employment and unpaid homemaking, reproduction, childcare, production (e.g., unpaid farm labor), and community service. The survey, family studies, and interviews all show that in the family, the community, and the workplace women are the main representatives of gemeinschaft/integry (Moen et al. 1981; Lillydahl et al. 1982). Although men are not absent from these activities, women are to a great degree the stabilizing, integrative, and community-building element of the town:

> Women, because of their central position in the household unit, are the key equilibrators of the family and the community as a social system. . . . They determine to a considerable extent the effectiveness of response of the members of their own families and of their neighborhoods and other social groups of which they are a part (Moen et al. 1981:8).

In the formal sector, they are joined by male clergy and other men who are concerned with human services and programs to facilitate social support and integration. For just as there are women who have "made it" in the male world by adopting appropriate values and behavior, there are men who have "made it" in the female world.

CONCLUSIONS

The literature on social impact assessment, rural industrialization, and energy boomtowns is similar to that regarding economic development in developing nations. Women are frequently ignored, or when they are mentioned they are generally treated as if they were all alike--married homemakers. Little attention is paid to impacts that might specifically affect women or to the important contributions that women can and do make to the development process.

Furthermore, as shown here, women are likely to be disadvantaged by economic development in the rural United States just as they are in developing countries. Boomtowns are controlled by men, who hold more traditional views regarding gender roles, and the towns are further masculinized by the energy-related growth and change. In addition, just as in the developing nations, public and industry planners and policymakers do not specifically consider the situations or the contributions of women. The result is that all women are at risk of losing economic resources and gesellschaft/economy-defined status in absolute terms, or, more frequently, relative to their husbands or other men with whom they are associated. At the same time, badly needed support in the form of adequately paid employment, day care, recreation, and social services may not be available to women. Consequently, they may develop physical and mental health problems that further impair their ability to adapt. The specifics depend upon the woman's place in the social structure of the community.

Women may be the "victims" of economic development, but they also make very positive contributions to the community. Consequently, it is important that women not be disadvantaged, not only because of the obvious injustice in such a situation, but also because of the roles women play in the community. As the primary representatives of gemeinschaft/integry, women are major stabilizing, integrative forces in the community. They bear the major responsibility for rearing children, maintaining the family, and performing many of the activities that make a town a community and that "hold the system together" (Bernard 1981:27). In the public arena, women are the ones who are most concerned with social consequences and services. If their ability to function in these roles is impaired, then their families and the entire town may suffer.

As the above data suggest, if women were to gain more political and administrative power without having to sacrifice values representative of gemeinschaft/integry, it is likely that these communities would have much more adequate (in terms of quality, quantity, and diversity) human services and programs, including those that are badly needed by women, such as day care, shelters, recreation, places to gather, job-training and placement services, and less discriminatory hiring policies. In addition, with increased female leadership (especially among newcomer women), traditional gender stereotypes and norms that constrain the social development of both males and females might be eroded at a faster pace. At the same time, the harsher, self-centered, profit-motivated aspects of gesellschaft/economy might be replaced with the more positive, integrative, and generous aspects of gemeinschaft/integry.

Many believe that without the gemeinschaft/integry of family, church, charity, and "women's work", which operate on opposite principles to those of capitalism's gesellschaft/economy, the latter will eventually destroy itself (see, e.g., Anderson 1976). Adam Smith expressed such concerns, and they are addressed in capitalist economies via the welfare state or grants economy. Without an economy of love (K. Boulding 1973) to counterbalance an economy of exchange, a society "operating according to its [male] logic would self-destruct" (Bernard 1981:36). Indeed, we are now witnessing a certain degree of self-destruction in the boom-bust cycle currently being experienced in western Colorado. Such rapid booms and rapid busts--both initiated solely by economic motives--can be destructive of individuals and entire communities (Gold 1984).

Sociologists have employed the concept of a rural-to-urban transition--from a society based on gemeinschaft to one based on gesellschaft--to help understand increased rates of social problems in energy boomtowns. By linking the concept of female and male worlds to the gemeinschaft and gesellschaft, Bernard has laid the groundwork for considerable advancement of theory. In stable communities and boomtowns of the rural West, this link holds, and as shown here, the transition associated with energy production not only disrupts gemeinschaft/integry-based social bonds and social support systems, but also legitimizes gesellschaft/economy-based values and behavior. Moreover, since energy development reinforces the gender-based division of labor, the male and female worlds and the wage gap between them are further separated and segregated.

Regarding social problems in energy boomtowns, theory is currently being developed and tested by the Growth Impact Group. To summarize:

> Energy development and subsequent urbanization may have both negative and positive consequences for the quality of life and economic resources of community residents. These impacts will not be distributed equally, and women are more likely than men to be negatively affected. Residents may adapt by accepting the consequences of development, taking action to improve their situation, or moving out. Residents with strong social support systems are best able to adapt, and residents who are less able to adapt are more likely to experience personal and family problems. Women, in addition to following the adaptation process of all residents, also are more likely to engage in integrative activities that reinforce, mend, recreate, and establish social supports and hence enhance the adaptive capacities of their families and the community as a whole. Women are able to do so, however, only when they have adequate resources, options, and autonomy. But because their needs are not met and their integrative activities are not valued by development planners, women are likely to lose status, and consequently social problems are likely to be more prevalent than they would have been otherwise.

Social problems in energy boomtowns are just part of the costs of energy production that are paid by the residents of the energy production community. And because these problems contribute to high levels of worker turnover, absenteeism, and inefficiency on the job, they also contribute to higher energy costs, which are borne by all citizens of this nation. Thus, the GNP may do well, but the people may not.

NOTES

1. The two worlds are not necessarily the exclusive provinces of females and males. Instead, they represent principles or clusters of characteristics that have been labeled (in modern Western cultures) feminines and masculines, reified as stereotypes about females and males, and realized through socialization, education, propaganda, and gender-segregated work. Yount's (1986) theory of work-emergent behavior is especially helpful in understanding the existence of the two worlds (see Chapter 5).
2. The Growth Impact Group is a multidisciplinary research group at the Institute of Behavioral Science, University of Colorado at Boulder. Our work is concerned with the social consequences of rapid growth and change in communities affected by economic development. The work reported here was funded by the Fleischmann Foundation and the National Institutes of Mental Health, under grant number MH33524. Much of the research reported here was done with Elise Boulding, Jane Lillydahl, Risa Palm, and Kristen Yount. I would like to acknowledge their work and also thank Barbara Gabella, Lillian Valenzuela, and Illana Gallon for their research and editorial assistance.
3. Bernard notes that gemeinschaft can be racist, sexist, bigoted, and provincial, as well as protective. In boomtowns, this shows up most clearly when longtimer men and women attempt to protect their own threatened sense of community and social support systems through the exclusion of newcomers (see also Bates 1978).
4. Freudenburg (1981) disagrees. However, he did not address the employment of women or assess the relative status of men and women. Instead, he used universal measures of happiness and satisfaction to determine if women were disadvantaged by energy development.

REFERENCES

Anderson, C. R. 1976. *Sociology of Survival*. Homewood, Ill: Dorsey.
Baker, G., and J. Kotarski. 1977. *Northern British Columbia Women's Task Force Report on Single Industry Resource Communities*. Vancouver, B.C.: Women's Research Centre.
Bates, V. E. 1978. The impact of energy boom-town growth on rural areas. *Social Casework* 59:73-78.
Bernard, J. 1981. *The Female World*. New York: Free Press.

Bescher-Donnelly, L., and L. W. Smith. 1981. The changing roles and status of rural women. In *The Family in Rural Society*, ed. R. T. Coward and W. M. Smith, Jr., 167-85. Boulder, Colo.: Westview Press.

Black, N. 1981. The future for women and development. In *Women and World Change*, ed. N. Black and A. B. Cottrell, 265-86. Beverly Hills, Calif.: Sage Publications.

Bloomquist, L. E., and G. F. Summers. 1982. Organization of production and community income distribution. *American Sociology Review* 47:325-28.

Bougsty, T., and R. Weisz. 1985. *Planning for Mental Health and Human Services in Boom-bust Communities*. Boulder, Colo.: Western Interstate Commission on Higher Education.

Boulding, E. 1976. *The Underside of History*. Boulder, Colo.: Westview Press.

_____. 1977. *Women in the Twentieth Century World*. New York: Sage Publications.

_____. 1980. The labor of U.S. farm women: A knowledge gap. *Sociology of Work and Occupations* 7:261-90.

Boulding, K. 1973. *The Economy of Love and Fear*. Belmont, Calif.: Wadsworth.

Bowles, R. T. 1981. *Social Impact Assessment in Small Communities*. Toronto: Butterworth and Co.

Cobb, S. 1976. Social support as a moderator of life stress. *Psychosomatic Medicine* 38:300-314.

Curtis, R. F., and E. F. Jackson. 1977. *Inequality in American Communities*. New York: Academic Press.

Dauber, R., and M. Cain. 1981. *Women and Technology: Impacts in Developing Countries*. Boulder, Colo.: Westview Press.

Edwards, F. 1980. Social impact assessment in Whitecourt, Alberta--a retrospective case study. Presented at the International Symposium on the Human Side of Energy. Laramie, Wyo.

Finsterbusch, K. 1980. *Understanding Social Impacts: Assessing the Effects of Public Projects*. Beverly Hills, Calif.: Sage Publications.

Flora, C. B., and S. Johnson. 1978. Discarding the distaff: New roles for rural women. In *Rural U.S.A.: Persistence and Change*, ed. T. R. Ford, 168-81. Ames: Iowa State University Press.

Ford, T. R. 1978. Contemporary rural America: persistence and change. In *Rural U.S.A.: Persistence and Change*, ed. T. R. Ford, 3-16. Ames: Iowa State University Press.

Freudenburg, W. R. 1981. Women and men in an energy boomtown: Adjustment, alienation and adaptation. *Rural Sociology* 46:220-44.

Gill, A. 1983. Women in northern Canadian resource towns. Presented at the annual meeting of the Association of American Geographers, Denver.

Gold, R. 1984. Ranching, Mining, and the Human Impact of Natural Resources Development. New Brunswick, N.J.: Transaction Books.

Gold, R., and A. Sterling. 1981. Challis Monitoring Report. Missoula, Mont.: Social Research and Applications.

Haney, W. G. 1982. Women. In Rural Society in the United States: Issues for the 1980s, ed. D. A. Dillman and D. J. Hobbs, 124-35. Boulder, Colo.: Westview Press.

Joyce, L. M., and S. M. Leadley. 1977. An Assessment of Research Needs of Women in the Rural United States: Literature Review and Annotated Bibliography. University Park: Department of Agricultural Economics and Rural Sociology, Agricultural Experiment Station, Pennsylvania State University.

Kassover, J., and R. L. McKeown. 1981. Resource development, rural communities and rapid growth. Minerals and the Environment 3:47-54.

Leistritz, F. L., and S. H. Murdock. 1981. The Socioeconomic Impact of Resource Development: Methods for Assessment. Boulder, Colo.: Westview Press.

Lillydahl, J., and E. Moen. 1983. Planning, managing, and financing growth and decline in energy resource communities: A case study of Western Colorado. Journal of Energy and Development 8:211-30.

Lillydahl, J., E. Moen, E. Boulding, K. Yount, S. Scott-Stevens, and I. Gallon. 1982. Quality of Life, Expectations of Change, and Planning for the Future in an Energy Production Community. Boulder: Institute of Behavioral Science, University of Colorado.

McCormack, T. 1981. Development with equity for women. In Women and World Change, ed. N. Black and A. B. Cottrell, 15-30. Beverly Hills, Calif.: Sage Publications.

Moen, E. W. 1984a. Voodoo forecasting: Technical, political, and ethical issues regarding the projection of local population growth. Population Research and Policy Review 3:1-25.

_____. 1984b. Population forecasting and planning: Some philosophical issues. Population Research and Policy Review 3:51-60.

Moen, E. W., E. Boulding, J. Lillydahl, and R. Palm. 1981. Women and the Social Costs of Economic Development: Two Colorado Case Studies. Boulder, Colo.: Westview Press.

Morgan, R. 1984. Sisterhood Is Global. New York: Anchor.

Ploch, L. 1981. Family aspects of the new wave of immigrants to rural communities. In The Family in Rural Society, ed. R. T. Coward and W. M. Smith, Jr., 39-53. Boulder, Colo.: Westview Press.

Rollins, C. E. 1980. A national resource: Women in energy resource development. Presented at the International Symposium on the Human Side of Energy. Laramie, Wyo.

Schaef, A. W. 1981. Women's Reality. Minneapolis: Winston Press.

Schumm, W. R., and S. R. Bollman. 1981. Interpersonal processes in rural families. In The Family in Rural Society, ed. R. T. Coward and W. M. Smith, Jr., 129-45. Boulder, Colo.: Westview Press.

United States Commission on Civil Rights. 1978. Resource Development in the Intermountain West: Its Impact on Women and Minorities. Denver: Rocky Mountain Regional Office, U.S. Commission on Civil Rights.

Yount, K. 1986. A theory of productive activity: The relationships among self-concept, gender, sex-role stereotypes, and work-emergent traits. Psychology of Women Quarterly 10:63-87.

8
The Yupik Eskimos of St. Lawrence Island, Alaska: A Social Impact Assessment of Proposed Energy Development

Ronald L. Little
Lynn A. Robbins

INTRODUCTION[1]

Indian tribes in the contiguous 48 states own a significant portion of the United States' energy reserves. Jorgensen (1984a) reports that tribes own approximately one-fourth of the strippable coal reserves, 4 percent of the oil, 10 to 15 percent of the uranium, and large quantities of the country's geothermal, tar sands, natural gas, and oil reserves. Tribes also lay claim to large volumes of water, water which is necessary for the processing and transportation of these energy resources. It is therefore not surprising that much has been and is being written about Native American involvement with energy development in the lower 48 states.[2]

Field research studies have reported that some aspects of native cultures, including economies, polities, and social structures, have been altered or disrupted by energy developments (Geisler et al. 1982; Jorgensen 1984a, 1984b; Jorgensen et al. 1978, 1983, 1984; Robbins 1980). Recent publications detail as well the attempts of Native Americans to protect their cultures, natural resources, and reservation ecosystems from negative consequences of energy development. For the most part, unfortunately, the conjunction of energy resource development and native peoples has resulted in harm to their cultures or yielded the people only limited beneficial impacts.

This chapter focuses on a relatively new dimension of the literature on Native Americans and energy resource development: Eskimos and off-shore oil development. More than 900 Yupik-speaking Eskimos reside in two villages, Gambell and Savoonga, on St. Lawrence Island, Alaska. This remote island, located south of the Bering Straits, is approximately 39 miles from Siberia and 120 miles from the Alaskan mainland. While sharing some cultural characteristics with native groups in the lower 48 states, Eskimo societies are unique in many aspects. An analysis of potential social impacts likely to result from off-shore oil development must consider the differences as well as the similarities.

A discussion of the St. Lawrence Island Eskimos is included in this volume for several reasons. First, because nearly 80 percent of their diet comes from naturally recurring resources, most of which originate in the waters of the Bering Sea, off-shore oil and gas exploration in Norton Sound and St. Georges and Navarin Basins portends potential alteration in the social structure of the Eskimo residents. Theirs is a subsistence economy, dependent upon the natural food resources of the sea and, to a lesser extent, the island. Their social structure is premised upon the continued existence of their current natural food base. Changes in the marine environment resulting from oil and gas exploration activities could readily reduce the availability of Eskimo food resources, especially marine mammals, thus forcing changes in the social structure of St. Lawrence Island.

Second, the island presents not only an important case study of environmental impact assessment issues, but also a rare opportunity to examine a New World culture which has retained many of its traditional elements, including an ancient, yet functioning, patriclan system. Third, by comparing the potential consequences of energy development for Eskimos in the Bering Sea with those experienced by Native Americans in the western continental United States, a more adequate assessment of these effects will be possible. The comparison will allow an initial estimation of the importance of traditional cultures as a factor in predicting the distributional effects of energy development.

Finally, St. Lawrence islanders have been and continue to be actively involved in the social impact assessment process. Intent on preserving the vital elements of their native culture, the two Indian Reorganization Act governments of Gambell and Savoonga have taken various steps to ensure that goal, including filing suit in federal district court to protect their interests.

THE ST. LAWRENCE ISLAND ESKIMOS:
AN ETHNOGRAPHIC SUMMARY

The ancestors of St. Lawrence Island's native population probably migrated from Siberia, near the Okhotsk Sea, sometime before the birth of Christ. At one time, perhaps as many as 5,000 Central Siberian Yupik-speakers lived on the island. In 1878, famine struck the island's people, then residing in several communities, plunging the population to a mere few hundred. Since the famine, the population has steadily increased; today islanders number just over 900. They live in two remaining villages, Gambell and Savoonga, both located on the north side of the island some 35 miles apart. Each village has an approximately equal number of Eskimo inhabitants and a few non-Eskimo personnel associated with community schools and churches.

The two most salient features of Eskimo life on St. Lawrence Island are the extreme dependence on the natural resource base, most especially marine mammals, and the strong ethic of sharing resources which is tied to this dependence. The nearly 80 percent of their diet which islanders estimate derives from naturally recurring resources is a proportion only somewhat less (20 percent) than the proportion which might have been observed 100 or 200 years ago. Anthropological observations by the authors in 1982 confirm this estimate. Using technology, skills, and social organization adapted to the requirements of the environment, island residents continue to hunt, capture, and consume what nature provides them. As would be expected, the people's underlying values and aspirations correspond to their subsistence activities, creating the fabric of their social structure (Little and Robbins 1983).

To fully appreciate the degree to which the two island communities rely on naturally recurring resources and the extent to which they are organized to pursue these resources requires first that the particulars of their subsistence activities and organization be understood.

Marine Mammal Hunting

The single most important subsistence activity in Gambell and Savoonga is the hunt for the several marine mammal species which seasonally inhabit the Bering Sea waters surrounding St. Lawrence Island. Most of the able-bodied adult male villagers are engaged in the subsistence hunting activities, with no evidence of declining interest or participation.

Walrus. In 1982, more than 300 islanders hunted walrus. They comprised 79 walrus crews, 41 in Gambell and 38 in Savoonga. An estimated 1,600 walruses were taken by St. Lawrence islanders in 1981, with Gambell hunters harvesting slightly over 1,000 and Savoonga hunters nearly 600. Although no estimate of Gambell's 1982 walrus kill is available from the authors' research data, consistent with previous years' totals, a conservative estimate would put the number at approximately 900. By contrast, in 1982 Savoonga had one of the worst hunts in its history, taking only 300 walruses.[3] Because Gambell shared its harvest with kin and friends in Savoonga, residents of the latter village had adequate walrus for the year.

Walrus is the islanders' most crucial resource, providing them with more food than any other single source. Almost the entire animal is eaten--muscle meat, liver, intestines, skin, some of the blubber, and the stomach and its contents, primarily clams. The parts are shared among crew members, their kin (particularly their patrilineal relations), and their friends. They are also shared with unrelated villagers, especially the elderly, widows, and women and children with no hunters in their households. The needy invariably receive walrus flesh and other edible parts of the animals. To those who give, whether those in need are kinsmen is immaterial. Hunters take great pride in being able to share the fruits of their labors without expectation of return. Each walrus hunter gives walrus products to an average of 10 households each year; his household receives similar subsistence goods annually, including walrus, from four other hunters.

Social relations coalesce around walrus hunting in such a way that major patrilineal clans are held together in an endless yearly round of hunting, butchering, distributing, and consuming walrus products. No one who calls at the home of a successful hunter is denied walrus parts. Additionally, because the people of Gambell and Savoonga are linked by kin ties, friendships, and the common value of sharing, intracommunity sharing is extended to all islanders. When one village lacks a major subsistence resource like walrus, the other village comes to its aid without hesitation, as Gambell did in 1982. The distribution network for walrus also extends beyond St. Lawrence Island to many Eskimos residing elsewhere, including residents of Nome, Anchorage, some other communities in Alaska, and a few households in the continental United States.

Bearded Seal. The most important of the seal species to the St. Lawrence islanders, bearded seal, is frequently hunted concurrently with walrus. Because of their large size, these seals are most typically hunted by crews. Throughout the spring, summer, and fall hunts, the seal-hunting crews are generally the same ones which pursue walrus. Only occasionally does a solitary hunter attempt to take a bearded seal without aid. A nonrandom sample of bearded seal hunters in 1982 indicated that 363 bearded seals were taken the previous year. By extrapolation, perhaps two and one-half times that number were actually taken by all St. Lawrence Island hunters in 1981.

Bowhead Whales. The spring bowhead whale hunt--brief, dramatic, exhilarating--brings joy and community solidarity unlike any other activity on St. Lawrence Island. Hunters state that the search for whales, with its quiet, intense expectation and the communal and masculine pride associated with it, is the most important task a man performs. In 1982, there were 22 whaling crews in Gambell and 10 in Savoonga, with Savoonga planning to add 2 new crews in 1983. More than 200 persons made up the 32 crews.

The progress of the whalers is transmitted by CB radio to keep people in both villages abreast of the hunt. When a strike is made, all island residents are made aware of it immediately. The news of a successful strike by crews from either village brings rejoicing to both over their mutual good fortune, for the sharing ethic is particularly evident in the distribution of whale.

Each community receives roughly one-half of each whale taken by the other community, with sharing behavior manifesting itself before the hunting season is over. Thus, Gambell residents may journey to Savoonga to receive their share of a whale taken by a Savoonga crew, only to have people from Savoonga arrive in Gambell one or more days later to claim their rightful share of a whale captured by a Gambell crew. The actual sharing of the bowhead takes place simultaneously with its butchering. A rationale common to western European thought would dictate that sharing be delayed until after the whale hunt is completed. By this logic, if both communities obtained an equal number or equal weight of bowheads, it would be unnecessary to trade whale products.

Such logic is inapplicable to the Eskimos of St. Lawrence Island. The costs of transporting whale parts back and forth between Gambell and Savoonga are apparently discounted as irrelevant by local residents. While the nutritional value of a bowhead whale, which generally weighs between 30 and 40 tons, must not be underestimated, neither must its symbolic and cultural value. The sharing of whale among the Eskimo islanders is of equal importance to its protein and caloric content.

As with walrus products, whale parts move not only within and between the villages, but into Nome and other communities as well. Muktuk (whale skin and subcutaneous fat) is a particularly important food, served on special occasions such as birthdays, holidays, and homecomings. Its use in these circumstances reinforces the importance of the traditional Eskimo diet and, more importantly, the special character of Eskimo culture. Because it is a major symbolic and ritual focus of island life, extraordinary efforts are made to distribute it to as many kinsmen and islanders as possible.

Resource Sharing. Hunting whale and walrus is associated with a specific form of social organization, the patriclan. With few exceptions, crews consist of closely related males (father/sons; uncles/nephews; brothers; and parallel paternal cousins, i.e., father's brother's sons). Occasionally, unrelated people join together, but they do so only when there are no close male kinsmen available to form a crew. The patriclans are thus directly and indirectly responsible for coordinating and conducting the most important subsistence functions. They not only hunt, but also butcher, store, and distribute the harvest. Because patriclan members sometimes reside in both Gambell and Savoonga, the two villages are united in a social system centered around mutual aid and common purpose.

Interwoven with the subsistence quest for food is the other dominant aspect of the island's culture: a fierce, insistent pride in sharing and giving. Many informants emphasized that islanders should and do give until it hurts, until there is no more to give. An example will serve to illustrate both the importance and extent of the sharing: One household in Gambell was recorded as giving subsistence products to 315 islanders in a single year. This ethic of sharing extends beyond marine mammals to all subsistence goods --fish, birds, birds' eggs, invertebrates, and land and sea plants--as well as to some products purchased from commercial establishments.

Summer Camping: Fishing, Hunting, and Gathering

Subsistence activities take the people to all corners of St. Lawrence Island, not only to coastal waters. There are few island areas which are not visited for the purpose of collecting some subsistence resource or in the quest for ancient ivory and artifacts. Modern technology--snow machines, all-terrain cycles, and motorized boats--has made the search for Arctic foxes, land and sea plants, marine invertebrates, fish, birds and their eggs, seals, and ivory much easier. These machines also bring nearly the entire island into regular use. The people of Gambell typically use the eastern half of the island, and the Savoonga residents the western half. With the exception of whales and walruses, most resources are rather uniformly distributed throughout the island and almost all major lagoons and rivers.

The Eskimos of St. Lawrence Island leave their villages in summer and early fall to fish, hunt a variety of seal species, and collect sea plants, invertebrates, and land plants. In 1982, approximately 325 Gambell and 420 Savoonga residents, over 80 percent of the island population, participated in the camps.

Gambell had 54 groups of campers, and Savoonga had 67. As with whaling and walrus hunting, the patriclans also provide the organizational base for summer camps. Most camping groups are composed of nuclear families, with two or more patrilineally related nuclear families occupying each site. Each family group averages many weeks of residence at its site. Islanders who do not camp regularly and for long periods each season usually do not because they cannot. The elderly, the handicapped, some men and women who hold full-time jobs, and some teenagers comprise the noncampers. Among the less than 20 percent of villagers who remain at home during the camping season, there are very few people who do not express the desire to camp.

These summer/early fall forays to resource collection and hunting camps away from the villages are economically essential aspects of the island's yearly round of subsistence activities. Additionally, they afford opportunities to visit friends, neighbors, and relatives outside the routines of village life. Quite apart from the fact that camping yields food resources indispensable to family larders, it strengthens the concern of these Yupik-speaking Eskimos for protection of the island and its vast natural resources. They take great pride in possession of a territory that is exclusively their domain. The time spent in summer camps appears to reinforce villagers' appreciation for nature unencumbered by man and his creations. Camping also enables them to leave the social and physical constraints of their village to achieve privacy and peace of mind in the solitude of nature.

Seals. Unlike the large bearded seal discussed in an earlier section, ringed, spotted, and ribbon seals are generally hunted by solitary hunters at summer camps. These smaller seals are a vital part of the island economy and are shared in much the same way as are walruses. In 1982, a sample of approximately 40 percent of Gambell's hunters reported taking 554 ringed, 459 spotted, and 19 ribbon seals in 1981. In total, Gambell hunters probably take about two and one-half times as many of these small seals as those reported by the sample. The considerable number of seals taken makes them an important food resource.

Fish. As might be expected of an island people, fish provide an important part of the diet of St. Lawrence Island Eskimos in both summer and winter. In winter, thousands of sculpins, halibut, and tom and blue cod are taken with hand lines. Summer camp fishing is different, focusing on five salmon species, Dolly Varden, arctic char, grayling, and whitefish. Both gill nets and fishing rods are used to land the catch. When islanders use rod and reel to fish the rivers and bays, subsistence harvesting and recreation have combined into a single, joyful activity.

Plants and Small Sea Animals. Each Gambell family annually harvests approximately 30 pounds of clams from the island's beaches and/or the stomachs of walruses. The Eskimos of Gambell and Savoonga also consume at least 12 varieties of marine plants and 24 varieties of land plants. These food sources yield nearly 170 pounds of sea plants and 120 pounds of land plants each year per household. The plant foods are nutritionally and culturally vital to the Eskimo diet, and their use frequently underscores a variety of celebrations, including homecomings and birthdays.

Birds. Every island family consumes hundreds of birds and bird eggs each year. The major species harvested include murres, auklets, seagulls, kittiwakes, and several species of ducks and geese. Murre, goose, and duck eggs are also collected and consumed in large numbers. A number of Gambell families shoot and consume or distribute over 400 murres a year, others as many as 600. Some families gather and consume or distribute over 60 gallons of murre eggs a year. When other species of birds and eggs are included in the harvest, the total is truly impressive.

Food Storage. In the past, storage of food was often a problem in summer, especially when large quantities were harvested over relatively short periods of time. Today, St. Lawrence Island Eskimo subsistence resources are stored in home freezers or in small lockers at the community freezer. Meat cellars are seldom used as they were in the past. The new technology has made the pooling and cooling of resources relatively simple, albeit relatively expensive. Foods can be stored for long periods, foods that in the past were difficult to preserve and were therefore consumed as quickly as possible or fed to sled dogs. By stabilizing the availability of seasonal resources, not only has frozen food storage made the husbanding of islander foodstuffs easier; it has also helped to ward off hunger among the villagers. Of equal importance, resource sharing can continue long after the hunts have ended, further reinforcing its cultural vitality.

COMMUNITY SOCIAL STRUCTURES

Patriclans

The most fundamental kinship structure of the people of St. Lawrence Island is the patriclan, a "non-local, corporate, compromised unilineal descent group in which post-nuptial residence is with the family of the groom and descent reckoning is through the father's male line" (Little and Robbins 1982:84). The continued strength and integrity of their patrilineal clan system, an essential part of their kinship structure for hundreds of years, is reflected in kinship terminology. The St. Lawrence Island Eskimos persist in referring to the father's brother's son as "brother" and the father's brother as "father."

As noted earlier, the several patriclans determine the social organization of most subsistence activities, from hunting to distributing a wide array of resources. Conversely, the social organization, technology, labor demands, seasonality, and monetary requirements of subsistence activities form the core of social life on St. Lawrence Island. Each household is tied to many others in the formation of hunting and collecting crews and in the reciprocal networks of sharing subsistence and other goods with kin, friends, and neighbors. The kinship structure determines and supports the social organization of the subsistence activities, and the subsistence activities reinforce kinship solidarity through the interdependences and continued interaction of the crews. For this reason, a decline in major subsistence resources would lead to serious adverse effects on the depth, breadth, and strength of the clans and other social structures. It would also erode that special communication of intense solidarity and mutual concern existing between the island's two villages.

Embedded within the patrilineal clans of Gambell and Savoonga is a well-defined hierarchy of authority defined primarily by age. Age overrides even sex in this patridominant kinship system. The eldest person in a clan, provided his or her health is reasonably good, is sought out for dispute resolution, approval of marriages, and advice about matters ranging from the beginning and ending dates of major hunts to major purchases and other personal matters. A clan head, directly or indirectly, also determines the distribution of subsistence goods by patriclan members. Treated with great respect, these clan elders are expected to be particularly restrained and judicious in their deliberations, to carefully weigh all sides of an issue, and to be available whenever needed. When clan elders do not reside in the same community as petitioning clan members and/or where issues arise, consultation may pose problems. Nevertheless, clan members must consult with the clan heads, who, in turn, must make themselves available.

Even though women may become clan heads, their status is achieved through their husbands. When they marry, women lose identification with the clan into which they were born, becoming instead members of their husband's clan. First, however, the husband must earn his bride by spending approximately a year performing bride service for his father-in-law or a surrogate father-in-law. The groom assists with a variety of tasks consistent with his sex role, including household work as well as participation in almost all subsistence activities conducted by the father-in-law and/or his crews. At the end of the bride service, the bride moves from her village to that of her husband. When husband and wife are from the same village, residence changes from the bride's parents' house or one near it to a residence nearer the groom's parents.

At the time a bride becomes a member of her husband's patrilineal clan, she becomes her in-laws' "daughter," "niece," and/or "aunt," depending on her place in the lineage. She is figuratively given away by the patrilineal clan of her origin. Her familial orientation changes, and her contacts with the clan of her birth greatly diminish. Her social orientation--visiting, subsistence activities and sharing, gift-giving, dining, and recreation--falls mainly within the orbit of her husband's clan. After marriage, women generally derive their prestige and pride from their functions in their husband's clan, assuming their new tasks and status unhesitatingly.

For the most part, St. Lawrence Island Eskimos tend to choose marriage partners from their own village. Only eight or nine Gambell women are married to Savoonga men, with an equal number of Savoonga women having Gambell husbands. Although some few women marry into mainland Eskimo communities, most marriages on St. Lawrence Island are intravillage.

Role Behavior

Women's Roles. Women on St. Lawrence Island prepare meals, care for children, keep house, maintain clothing, and collect land and sea plants and marine invertebrates. Their most important task, however, one expected of all of them during some time in their lives, is to prepare and dispense subsistence and other goods from their households. Some also sew skin garments for use by their families and for sale on the mainland. Many women search for old ivory and ancient artifacts at the old village sites and while at summer camp. Always in demand, artifacts bring significant income to the finder. Secondary sex roles involve keeping the family budget records, carving ivory, and in rare instances (one or two in each village), hunting alongside men for whales, walruses, and bearded seals. A few women aspire to or acquire positions of leadership on the island: A woman holds two elected offices in Gambell.

Men's Roles. The men of St. Lawrence Island do the hunting, fishing, trapping, and most of the ivory carving, teaching these skills to their younger male patrikin (sons, grandsons, nephews, younger cousins, brothers, adopted kin). They repair and maintain weapons, machines, and appliances as well as reload ammunition used in the hunts for marine mammals and birds. Men are generally expected to participate in village governments and institutions. They captain all hunting and collecting crews, risking their lives on rough, frigid seas and in harsh weather to provide food for their families and communities. Occasionally, men prepare meals and keep family budget records. Some make skin boats for whale hunting.

Children's Roles. Eskimo girls on the island help raise siblings, nephews, nieces, and children adopted by their parents or grandparents. They help with household chores, including meal preparation and laundry, and assist younger household members with formal education. Occasionally, they collect land and sea plants, marine invertebrates, and bird eggs. They are expected to stand in for the family's adult females in their absence. They also assist with skin sewing on some occasions and learn the valuable lessons of sharing with kin, friends, and others.

Boys assist the Eskimo men with hunting and fishing. They also frequently collect bird eggs, a dangerous undertaking for which they seem well suited because of their quickness and agility. They are trained to be strong, patient, enduring, and above all, generous. They run errands for their families, help elders with chores, watch after younger members of their households, and occasionally prepare meals and do general housework.

Elders' Roles. As discussed earlier, Eskimo elders are objects of respect and deference and generally head the patrilineal clans. Nearly all of them live with younger kinsmen, most frequently their married offspring. Elders watch over grandchildren and often raise their first-born grandchild. Married couples honor recently deceased elders by naming a newborn child after the departed. This practice originated from an old belief that the spirit of the deceased inhabits the body of the next child born into the lineage. Today, the practice mainly reflects respect for ancestors. The same respect manifests itself in the vital sharing which occurs among the islanders, with elders always receiving the entire range of subsistence goods.

Households

Most of the households in both Gambell and Savoonga are occupied by nuclear families consisting of parents or surrogate parents and offspring or surrogate offspring. There are also households comprised of extended families (parents and married offspring with children), grandparent/grandchild, siblings (brothers, sisters, or a combination of the two), and single persons. Many households have adopted children, often grandchildren fondly raised by their grandparents. In a few others, several people related to the household head, such as brothers, nephews, and cousins, live together. Households never stand alone economically; each is wedded to many others through the complex networks of patriclans, subsistence crews, sharing, and crafts production. These networks span not only households but villages.

The availability of new housing from the late 1970s through 1980 made it possible for many young married couples as well as single men and women to establish households separate from their parents and surrogate parents. Even so, in Gambell average household size in 1982 was 4.1 people; in Savoonga, with fewer single-person households, it was nearly 5. Families are large; the average number of children per adult over 35 years of age is nearly 4. In the past 12 years, the number of residents in each village has increased an average of approximately 2.3 percent annually, a doubling of the population every 28 years at the present rate of increase. The growth has occurred despite the fact 10 percent of the population migrates to the mainland.

Economics

Among a combined population of 913 people (455 in Gambell, 458 in Savoonga), Gambell and Savoonga had a total of 134 jobs available in the spring and summer of 1982. All but a few jobs are in the service sector of the economy, and most are dependent upon state and federal monies. More than half of Gambell's households and approximately one-third of Savoonga's have no wage earners (excluding carvers and garment makers), further underscoring the decisive importance of subsistence activities. Many of the jobs pay very low wages, and several of them are part time.

Relatively speaking, ivory carving is a significant source of income. There were 318 carvers in the two villages (111 Gambell, 207 Savoonga), with these artisans making important monetary contributions to their households. In total, ivory carvers earn approximately $250,000 per year. Additionally, some 90 seal skin sewers in each village contribute income to family coffers.

Families in Gambell pay an annual average of $3,800 for goods, mainly food, from local retail stores. Prices, by the way, are nearly double those in the lower 48 states. The major items purchased are cereals, tea, coffee, sugar, baby food, pilot bread, toiletries, soda pop, and cigarettes. Nearly one-half of the households in both communities receive food stamps valued at approximately $1,500 annually. In the absence of a significant wage economy and with only limited government assistance, expenditures for commercially manufactured or processed food average no more than $250 per month per household. A few families spend up to $800, but they are conspicuous exceptions to the norm. A small portion of family income goes for clothing purchases.

The islanders' major cash requirements directly relate to their subsistence activities and economy. In 1981, the annual cost of vehicles used for hunting and gathering, boats, boat motors, fuel, weapons, ammunition, and fishing equipment averaged approximately $6,700 per household. Some households spend much more than this, some considerably less. Nearly all households in both villages have a minimum of one snow machine and one all-terrain cycle, and most have an aluminum boat with at least a 40 horsepower motor. Families save scrupulously and diligently, to the extent of going without a second or third daily meal, to acquire the cash with which to purchase their transportation equipment. Gasoline costs alone for snow machines and other self-propelled vehicles average approximately $1,700 yearly for each Gambell household and $1,100 for each in Savoonga. While not all transportation expenses are directly related to subsistence activities, the majority of vehicle use is for hunting, fishing, and gathering.

Federal programs help cover the costs of some other essentials. For example, the U.S. Public Health Service provides medical care for islanders, but Eskimo families must nevertheless pay the one-way portion of a round-trip flight to Nome to receive anything more than the rudimentary service provided at local clinics. An energy assistance program helps defray the cost of home-heating fuel for some St. Lawrence Island households. With average annual home-heating costs per family at $2,700, the average annual energy assistance grant is $600 and rarely exceeds $700 for any family. Slightly less than a third of the households even receive monies from the program. Clearly, government aid covers only a portion of the expenses.

Local Government

Gambell and Savoonga each maintain three local governments: a city council, an Indian Reorganization Act (IRA) council, and a native corporation. Each government form has its own sphere of authority, even though some overlap occurs.

<u>City Councils</u>. Each city council consists of seven elected officials: mayor, vice-mayor, treasurer, and four councilmen. Administrative personnel are appointed

by the council. As with the other two government entities, the officers' terms are staggered. By the staggering of terms, organizational continuity and consistency are assured because experienced elected officials serve with those newly elected, thereby providing the latter with assistance in learning both the issues and their official roles. City councils have taxing powers over local businesses, provide police and fire protection, issue business permits, control road development within village boundaries, and maintain airstrips. They also are eligible for matching funds and for special grants for public buildings and other community improvements from the state and federal governments.

The city councils of both Gambell and Savoonga have agreements with the Alaska Village Electrical Co-op (AVEC), whereby the councils maintain electrical facilities and collect charges from customers. In return for these services, the city councils receive a monthly fee from AVEC. To date, Gambell has installed four wind machines to reduce its cost of power generation, which presently requires a charge to consumers of nearly 47 cents per kilowatt hour. Its city council intends to purchase as many as 45 such machines to further reduce costs. The Savoonga City Council is considering a similar plan.

State grants bring in far more money to the city councils than do local tax revenues. State benefits to the people of Savoonga amounted to nearly $100 per capita in 1981, rising to $190 in 1982. Gambell experienced a similar increase. Alaska's recent influx of revenues from North Slope oil fields has greatly benefited both villages. Those benefits reached their peak in 1983 when the communities each received state grants for new fire-fighting equipment and community buildings, including city offices, recreational facilities, learning centers, and libraries. Through special grants, the state of Alaska also recently funded the first phases of ivory co-ops being built in both Gambell and Savoonga. The total sum to be expended for each village's co-op is approximately $250,000, although details remain to be worked out.

IRA Councils. Each IRA council has a president, vice-president, and five council members. Gambell's council was chartered by the federal government in 1939 and Savoonga's in 1940. The councils receive funds from the Alaska Native Industries Co-operative Association (ANICA), native mercantile stores in each village, and federal grants. They have broad powers, many of which overlap those of the native corporations. Most powers pertain to the protection and management of resources on St. Lawrence Island and to native customs and crafts. Unfortunately, the IRA councils in both villages are chronically low on funds, making a difficult job even more difficult.

Native Corporations. By the federal government's legally mandated December 18, 1971, deadline, Gambell and Savoonga were faced with the options of: (1) taking fee simple title to St. Lawrence Island, including surface and subsurface rights, but relinquishing further participation in the Alaska Native Claims Settlement Act (ANCSA); or (2) participating as any native village may in the provisions of the act, but relinquishing all ownership claims to their island home. By the same federal mandate, both communities first were required to establish village corporations by which to implement the chosen option. After formation of native corporations in both villages and approval of their initial articles of incorporation by the Bering Straits Native Corporation established by ANCSA, the Eskimo people of Gambell and Savoonga voted for the first alternative and took fee simple title to their 1,205,000-acre island. In effect, the villages chose sovereignty over their land and way of life rather than a share of the $962 million disbursed to native corporations through the provision of ANCSA.

Shareholders of each native corporation elect a seven-member board of directors, who in turn elect three of their number as officers: a president, vice-president, and secretary-treasurer. The corporate shareholders in their respective villages are those enrolled Gambell and Savoonga native people born before December 18, 1971. Only they have the right to vote for members of the board of directors and to receive dividends. Shareholders in Gambell's corporation cannot own stock in Savoonga's, and vice versa.

Chartered by the Alaska Department of Commerce and Economic Development, the native corporations possess the same powers that any other Alaskan corporation has to manage resources and direct activities related to resource use and protection. Essentially, the two St. Lawrence Island native corporations own the island and its resources and thereby control both present and future resource development there. Because both native corporations are independent and cannot overrule decisions made by the other, they attempt to coordinate their separate efforts. When the native corporations were established, no firm guidelines distinguished their powers and functions from those of the IRA councils in the respective villages. The people of each community have, however, worked out amicable relations among their three local governmental entities. To date, all three have been able to avoid serious jurisdictional conflicts in both Gambell and Savoonga. In general, the native corporations have become responsible for resource use and protection, with the corporations of both villages exercising their power conscientiously.

In 1991, native corporation shareholders may sell their stock to any buyers they choose. As a result, there is mounting concern among the Eskimos of St. Lawrence Island about how to best serve and protect their cherished traditions and lifestyle. The people of Gambell believe that ANCSA places pressure on them to decide the questions involving disposition of corporate shares much too soon. They feel they need more time to collect and analyze information necessary to protect future generations. They especially fear the sale of shares to nonislanders.

The corporate boards and IRA councils in both Gambell and Savoonga recognize the difficult issues involved and have discussed the options open to native shareholders when 1991 arrives. Most of Gambell's leaders believe that the people of the island must proceed at their own pace to prepare for the future one step at a time. The leadership of Savoonga's native corporation and IRA council seems to concur. Several joint Gambell-Savoonga meetings of representatives from the two corporations and IRA councils have been held to discuss these matters in depth and to chart a course. The meetings have been held without rancor, jealousy, haste, or quest for exclusive power by any single organization.

Community leaders advocate that additional power be vested in their native corporations, allowing a prohibition of stock holdings by nonislanders. With respect to a related issue, there appears to be a consensus of opinion in the communities that they should not jump into any large energy development schemes at present, or even perhaps after 1991. As the surest means of attaining this result, islanders express a strong preference that property rights now vested in the native corporations be transferred to the IRA councils. The prevailing belief in Gambell and Savoonga is that such a shift will eliminate the risk that some native corporation shareholders might sell their corporation stock and create havoc for any unified, all-Eskimo energy development management strategy.

Public Service. The complexity of three separate political structures in each St. Lawrence Island village appears, for the time being, to serve the people well, permitting the management of the essentials of government with relative ease. Though strains exist within and among these institutions, often the most pressing concern is the demands placed upon the elected officials themselves. The same elected community leaders frequently hold positions on the Alaskan Eskimo Walrus Commission, the Eskimo Whaling Commission, and/or the Bering Straits School District.

They also maintain close ties with Kawerak, a regional nonprofit organization, and membership in many other specialized organizations. Few of the meetings of these groups are held on St. Lawrence Island.

In Gambell and Savoonga, there are 44 elected or appointed offices (23 in Savoonga, 21 in Gambell). Most of the officeholders are men, many of whom have previously held other official positions. Islanders believe their leaders should maintain close contact with constituents, kin groups, and subsistence crews, and that individuals considered best qualified have a duty to serve. And this is exactly what happens in both island communities. Public servants, although occasionally exasperated and often exhausted and overworked, generally continue to serve out of a deep sense of commitment and obligation. Some have vowed never to serve again, but they usually relent and run for office if a need arises. Most take pride in their service, realizing they form a core of leaders who rotate from one institution to another, gaining invaluable experience and a broad perspective on the interrelationships among their governing organizations.

St. Lawrence Island officials frequently hold positions of respect in their patriclans. These leaders are held in esteem for their hunting skill as well as their wisdom and knowledge of many matters of importance to the villages. Many are boat captains, a position which entails great responsibility and requires enormous amounts of time, not to mention money and organizational skills. The fact that leaders in one village often are closely related to leaders in the other accounts for some of the good will in governmental affairs between Gambell and Savoonga.

Elected and appointed village leaders oftentimes experience serious conflicts between the need to serve and the requirements of their hunting, fishing, trapping, and carving responsibilities, i.e., earning a living. They give top priority to their various subsistence pursuits. Other matters are clearly secondary, and the leaders make no pretense to the contrary. They also clearly prefer their traditional lifestyle to the segmented, bureaucratic demands of public life. Instead of attending meetings, these men would rather be at home with their families, kin, and friends. At home, too, the tasks of refurbishing equipment, reloading cartridges, and performing other work related to earning a living from the natural environment always await the officials.

Through government, professionalism has begun to come to Gambell and Savoonga. The city councils now have locally recruited, professional, full-time managers. Although the IRA councils and native corporations cannot afford managerial personnel, each does have clerical personnel, a beginning step toward bureaucratic specialization. These recent innovations presage specialization in local government affairs, specialization which eventually may replace some of the generalized duties of the present public officials. Embedded as they have been in the patriclans and other social structures tied to subsistence pursuits, leadership roles have, until recently, spanned government, kin, and other social responsibilities.

Religion and Education

Religion. Two Christian denominations are the focal points of religion in Gambell and Savoonga. Most dominant is the Presbyterian Church, which has been present and entrenched in Eskimo life since shortly after the turn of the century. Members number approximatey 365 in Gambell and 300 in Savoonga. The Seventh Day Adventist Church was established on the island during World War II and has 87 members in Gambell and approximately 10 in Savoonga. More than half of the members of both congregations attend services regularly.

Christian doctrines have proved appealing to the Eskimo people of St. Lawrence Island. Conversions have been numerous, with no evidence of heavy-handed proselytizing by missionaries. Old Testament themes of male-dominant lineages and respect for elders and tradition have found a comfortable niche among the island's patriclans with their attendant values. New Testament messages of communitarianism, brotherly love, humane and compassionate treatment of others, and forebearance in the face of life's unforeseen difficulties are consistent with the traditional subsistence lifestyle and sharing ethic of the people of Gambell and Savoonga.

It should come as no surprise that Christian churches play a significant social role in Gambell and Savoonga. The churches aid the needy and sponsor countless community gatherings unrelated to religious functions. Members of all ages, both male and female, engage in various church activities and assume church responsibilities with pride and general enthusiasm. In the Presbyterian congregations, women as well as men give the sermons. Some of the elderly Gambell women teach gospel lessons which expound Christian teachings but are illustrated by traditional Eskimo tales and legends. When St. Lawrence Island Eskimo people speak today of their treasured way of life, many of them include within it their Christian practices and Christian-sponsored social activities.

Christian doctrines have fundamentally altered certain aspects of traditional Eskimo beliefs and practices. Christian monotheism has replaced the island's traditional hierarchy of spirits. Man and Christian God alone are vested with eternal life. Animism, the belief that all things animate and inanimate possess spirits and that each is accorded respect and deference, has slipped away. Inanimate objects and nature's creations are no longer viewed as possessing eternal spirits; they therefore no longer require ritual acknowledgment as they did in the past (Hughes 1960:312-33). A remaining vestige of traditional Eskimo beliefs is a strong and persistent respect for nature and all living things and an abhorrence of cruelty and slaughter. In accepting Christianity, these Eskimo people have not lost their profound respect for the marine life they once worshipped. They continue to show great reverence for marine mammals, admiring their majesty, beauty, intelligence, and power. This respect will undoubtedly remain embedded in Eskimo life so long as the subsistence economy is the dominant means of obtaining food.

Education. Formal education for the children of Gambell and Savoonga is two-tiered. The Bureau of Indian Affairs (BIA) provides the staff and facilities for pupils in the first eight grades. State-funded high schools educate the older children in grades 9 through 12. Before the early 1970s when the latter schools were built, high school students were forced to leave St. Lawrence Island to continue their education. They were sent to boarding schools on the Alaska mainland, principally at Mt. Edgecombe, nearly 1,000 miles from the island. The boarding school experience had a special socializing effect, instilling values and skills dominant in mainstream American society. During the 1960s, Mt. Edgecombe, near Sitka, was particularly noted for a liberalizing ethic, stressing respect for the cultures and traditions of minority peoples, including Alaskan natives. Many St. Lawrence Island leaders, some of whom now live on the mainland where they hold important positions, were students at the school in the 1960s.

The public schools recently established in Gambell and Savoonga now absorb the high school-age students. The reasons they were built on the island, just as public schools were built in many other native communities in Alaska during the same period, were varied. They included protecting village cultural traditions, insuring that young people were no longer forced to leave families and friends, and providing the opportunity for young people to participate in the subsistence pursuits so vital to their families' wellbeing. Proponents of local high schools claim that the beneficial effects of local schools override the unique benefits of a mainland boarding school: Understanding of and adaptation to modern life can occur even while attending school on the island. Many graduates leave their villages for stints in military service, to acquire more education, or to seek work, but a large proportion of them eventually returns to the island.

CULTURAL CONSEQUENCES TO WESTERN AMERICAN INDIANS FROM ENERGY-RELATED DEVELOPMENTS[5]

Energy-related developments have had profound effects on many rural regions of the western United States, from the Grants Mineral Belt in New Mexico to the Skagit River in northwestern Washington. The consequences of these developments for American Indian societies have been summarized by Jorgensen (1984a) and analyzed at greater length in Jorgensen (1984b), Jorgensen et al. (1978) and Geisler et al. (1982). The experiences of the Indian tribes provide insights into, and perhaps warnings about, the likely consequences energy developments hold for the Eskimos of St. Lawrence Island.

Economics

The available evidence indicates that in practically all energy extraction or conversion projects on Indian reservations in the western United States, as well as in every energy-related project near reservations, decision making and financial control reside exclusively in the hands of national or international corporations. Reservation residents must simply abide by decisions made by others. New jobs created by energy-related developments on or near reservations go, for the most part, to non-Indians, even when preferential hiring clauses are included in the tribal/corporation agreements. The employment Indians obtain is often restricted to the construction phases of projects and is generally menial work, e.g., as laborers. When construction is over and operations begun, the few jobs Native Americans typically occupy are custodial or maintenance positions.

By way of illustration, Navajos obtained only 3,000 of the 47,000 energy-related jobs available on their reservation between 1957 and 1980, only slightly more than 6 percent of the total energy employment. As another example, during the peak of the construction phase at coal-fired power plants near the Northern Cheyenne Reservation, Cheyennes held 34 of the 895 jobs. After construction, their numbers dropped to six, slightly less than 4 percent of total plant employment. The six post-construction jobs were all custodial positions. It should be noted that this pattern is similar to the situation non-Indian rural residents encounter in seeking employment on energy projects near their communities. The preponderance of the jobs go to outsiders, not to local workers (see Little and Lovejoy 1979).

Tribal governments have fared no better than individual Indians in their financial transactions with energy companies. Accrued tribal revenues from mineral resources sold or leased, water allocations sold or leased, and rights-of-way granted have represented only a fraction of their actual worth. The revenues have also been small in comparison to the state revenues received from taxes on power production, transmission lines, and property holdings of those same energy operations. It is incomprehensible that tax revenues should exceed the value of the raw materials, but that is too often the case when Native American groups enter into contracts with powerful energy corporations. It should be kept in mind that by federal law the Bureau of Indian Affairs acts as trustee in representing tribal interests in contract negotiations with energy firms, a role it has frequently exercised to the detriment of Indians.

Both personal and tribal income of American Indians in the western United States are steadily losing ground each year in comparison with that of the non-Indian population of the United States. Public-sector income to Indians in the form of jobs, grants, contracts, and transfers in cash and in kind to welfare recipients far exceeded revenues from energy-related production through 1980, even though deep cuts in all public-sector transfers have been made in the past four years. Furthermore, personal and tribal income generated from jobs created by either the private or public sector as a result of energy-related developments is spent primarily either in off-reservation towns or in businesses owned by non-Indians. Thus, multiplier effects which could have improved the economic position of Indian tribes or communities have not materialized.

Conflict

As experience with energy developments on or near Indian reservations accumulates, one of the clearest trends emerging is an increased incidence of conflict. The conflicts have not been restricted to Indian/corporate strife. Tribal members have sued their own elected leaders in federal courts over contracts tribal authorities have signed with energy corporations. Indians whose traditional residences and resource areas for farming and stock raising have been threatened by energy-related developments have sued both energy corporations and federal agencies for failing to adequately assess the community's ways of life and the dependencies of the tribal people upon their traditional use areas. Residents in small hamlets on reservations have accused their tribal governments of failing to protect them from discrimination and of failing to protect their land from abuse by employees of energy corporations operating in their midsts. The turnover of elected and appointed officials in tribal governments has been high, and factional disputes within tribes often focus on issues related to energy development. Similar problems are also found in rural non-Indian communities (Little 1977, 1978; Little and Greider 1983).

Within Indian communities, households have been involuntarily relocated from their traditional residences and resources to accommodate mines, mills, electrical generation plants, railroads, and other industrial developments. Reciprocity-based kinship networks have been broken as relocatees have been forced to sever ties with kinspeople and friends. In some instances, sacred shrine areas and burial sites have been damaged by energy-related operations; in other instances, relocatees have been separated from them. Relocatees long to return to their home areas and grieve because their progeny may not reside there.

Other instances of conflict are illustrative of the nature and intensity of conflicts resulting from energy developments. In the Aneth-Montezuma Creek section of the Navajo Reservation, gas and oil operations conducted by Texaco, Phillips Petroleum, and other lessees for over two decades were almost completely staffed by non-Indians. It was alleged by the local Navajos that the non-Indian energy company employees ridiculed Navajo behavior, beat and mistreated Navajos on occasion, carelessly spilled oil around the rigs, and recklessly killed cattle and sheep grazing near roads or oil operations. Local Navajos had many other complaints, but when they took them to the tribal leadership for help, assistance was not forthcoming.

In response, Navajos in the Aneth region rebelled and took over the gas and oil operations, driving off the workers and completely shutting down operations. The rebels demanded that the oil leases be voided or renegotiated, that more Navajos be hired, that the oil companies make substantial financial contributions to Navajo education, and that discriminatory acts toward Navajos by oil company employees cease immediately. The oil companies made some concessions, but would not renegotiate the leases. The Aneth Navajos also castigated the Navajo Tribal Council for taking the money obtained from oil and lease royalties at Aneth--against the will of the local residents--while providing few resources and services for the Aneth people in return.

In another oil extraction project, the Wind River Shoshone and the Arapaho of Wyoming have alleged that over $3 billion worth of their oil was stolen by companies and persons engaged in extracting, storing, and transporting the oil. The allegations have been supported by a federal grand jury and an investigation conducted by the Department of the Interior. Indictments were filed, one person was convicted, one oil company recognized an "underpayment" and made restitution, and litigation continues.

The situation on the Wind River Shoshone and Arapaho reservation is not unique. An oil firm doing business on the Jicarilla Apache Reservation refused to open its books to the tribe. Under federal court order, it was forced to do so, and a $600,000 underpayment was found. The tribe assumed control of the oil operation.

The hostile and rebellious responses of American Indians to energy development projects in the western United States may be harbingers of native/native, nonnative/native, corporation/native relations when oil developments involving Native Americans elsewhere are at issue. They perhaps also presage village/regional corporation, village/village, or village/state relations regarding off-shore oil and gas development in Norton Sound and St. Georges and Navarin Basins.

COMPARISON AND CONTRAST OF ST. LAWRENCE ISLAND ESKIMOS AND WESTERN AMERICAN INDIANS

The consequences of energy development activities as they have affected reservation Indians in the western United States provide a framework from which to evaluate the potential effects of off-shore oil drilling activities on St. Lawrence Island Eskimos. In the absence of quantified and detailed time-series data on the subsistence pursuits of the islanders, it is very difficult to precisely estimate the nature and magnitude of potential future changes. Although general sociological and anthropological theories provide only rough estimates of likely social consequences, a comparison of St. Lawrence Islanders with Native American communities which have already experienced the impacts of energy-related development in part rectifies this problem. St. Lawrence Island Eskimo and American Indian communities share sufficient similarities to allow analogies to be drawn. To the extent unique characteristics differentiate the two groups, an evaluation of the Eskimo islanders' potential responses to energy development activities must necessarily focus on the differences between them. Examining both similarities and differences makes possible some hypotheses regarding the consequences to the people of St. Lawrence Island of altered patterns of availability of marine food resources as a result of off-shore oil and gas exploration and development.

A major difference between the island Eskimos and reservation Indians in the western United States is the uniqueness of the harsh and demanding arctic environment upon which St. Lawrence Island Eskimos are so dependent. Although many of the Indian tribes inhabit some of the least desirable land in their geographic region, none is situated in so hostile a climate as the islanders' Bering Sea home. On virtually all Indian lands, some subsistence hunting, gathering, farming, and/or herding occurs, but only on reservations where food production dominates (farming, stock raising) do the tribal Indians begin to approach the Eskimo islanders' level of dependency upon the natural environment. In a frozen land where cultivation of crops and domestication of livestock is impossible, the dependence on nature's wild harvests makes the people of St. Lawrence Island unique.

A second difference is the island's geographic isolation. The closest small city, Nome, is a regional hub located on the mainland 200 air miles distant, and air travel is expensive. With the social isolation imposed by geography, information access and dissemination are relatively limited and erratic. Information flows in and out via occasional travelers, letters, and telephone calls. Radio and satellite television also provide entertainment and news. Face-to-face interactions with the nonnative world are relatively rare, however, making movement into other social systems difficult. Because Savoonga and Gambell are not connected by a road, even intercommunity interactions are restricted. Boat, snow machine, and all-terrain cycle travel between the two communities is expensive, arduous, time-consuming, and frequently hazardous. Given the difficulties inherent in maintaining personal interactions and thus intercommunity ties, it is amazing that the two villages are so well integrated and demonstrate such solidarity and mutual support.

Western American Indian reservations are not nearly so isolated. All of them possess one or more paved highways, other all-weather roads, and numerous dirt and gravel byways connecting tribal communities with one another as well as with border towns and regional cities. Practically all reservation lands in the western United States abut or are checkerboarded with Anglo settlements and non-Indian towns as well, making native/nonnative interactions routine, albeit frequently strained. Regional cities much larger than Nome are readily accessible by auto and often by bus. Virtually all of these regional cities are within 100 miles of western Indian reservations, e.g., Billings (Crow and Northern Cheyenne), Gallup (Navajo), Flagstaff (Navajo and Hopi), Vernal (Uintah and Ouray Ute), and Farmington (Ute Mountain Ute and Southern Ute).

A third difference is that St. Lawrence Island Eskimos, while owning the surface and subsurface property rights to their island, do not own but a very small fraction of the natural resources upon which they rely for food. Even though subsistence foods make up nearly 80 percent of their diet, only a tiny portion comes directly from the island. The Bering Sea provides by far the greatest part. The fish and mammals of the ocean surrounding the island, as well as the sea birds and water fowl the native people harvest, are controlled by federal, state, or international government agencies. Western American Indians, on the other hand, own or control the wild fish and game which inhabit their tribal lands, as well as the waters which arise in or traverse their reservations. More importantly, they own and have immediate and easy access to domesticated foodstuffs, both plant and animal, which contribute so much to their overall diet.

The most obvious similarity shared by western American Indians and St. Lawrence Island Eskimos is their minority status. Besides ethnically and culturally, the two groups are minorities in two other senses of the term. First, they are numerically insignificant in face of the dominant nonnative population. Second, and partially because of their small numbers, they are both relatively powerless groups. Their lack of income and education combine to limit their access to the sources of power and their ability to use power to which they may obtain access. As a result, like other American minority groups, they experience discrimination and prejudice, and their rights and interests often go unprotected. Stereotyping abounds; many nonnatives believe that both groups are lazy, dishonest, always on the public dole, and therefore unworthy of continued federal or state protection or aid. In the case of Eskimos, epithets adapted from the lower 48 states demonstrate the widespread contempt for the local native people, e.g., "snow niggers." Their perceptions of rejection by the dominant society appear, however, to reinforce already-strong Eskimo and Indian group solidarity.

Another important similarity is the introduction and growth of universal achievement criteria and occupational specialization in Eskimo village and Indian tribal organizations (cf. Parsons and Shills 1951). Federal and state domination has brought with it alien government forms such as tribal councils and native corporations, as well as the formal rules and regulations of mainstream American society. The native peoples have had to adjust to formal job qualification requirements, restrictions on access to and use of natural resources, prohibitions against nepotism, and many other limitations unknown to them prior to this century. Legislation, such as the Indian Reorganization

Act (Wheeler-Howard Act of 1934) and the Composite Indian Reorganization Act (1939), and the establishment of federal and state bureaus, agencies, and offices which either administer native affairs or receive reports from and provide services to native peoples have all eliminated native autonomy to one degree or another.

Another similarity shared by tribal Indians and the island's Eskimos is their lack of economic and political independence. Dependency on public-sector funds characterizes both reservation and St. Lawrence Island economies. Control of commercially viable energy resources, from extraction through transformation to energy and its ultimate sale, is a prerogative held almost exclusively by energy corporations in partnership with federal and state governments. Both the decision making concerning energy-related projects and the income from their operation rest almost totally in the hands of nonnatives.

Yet another similarity is that both St. Lawrence Eskimos and western American Indians place noncommodity values on nature. Their views are unlike those of the dominant society which values the natural environment in economic terms. As do western American Indians, the people of Gambell and Savoonga view the elements of nature--land, water, air, animals, plants--symbolically, attributing to them native cultural values. Nature's creations symbolize persistence, continuity, and beauty and are regarded with respect and reverence. The native people expect that the current features of the natural environment will persist intact to support and gladden the hearts of future generations. As symbols, elements of the natural environment are integrated with labor, gifting, sharing, and helping customs.

The people of Gambell and Savoonga simply do not share the definitions of environment, ownership over nature's resources, and economic uses of those resources which prevail in the larger American society. As just stated, they do not treat the land, plants, animals, and air as commodities, although to a very limited extent they process seal and walrus skins and walrus tusks for the commercial market. They are, however, well aware of those definitions, ideas, symbols, and values in the dominant society (see McClelland 1961; Hofstadter 1967; Bennett 1979; Jorgensen 1972 for a discussion of American economic ideology in relation to competition, development, and the environment) which conflict with their own.

Eskimo island leaders further recognize that evaluating in economic terms the naturally recurring marine resources upon which their traditional culture depends is accepted as morally correct by the nonnative society. The acceptance of this economic interpretation by

America's decision makers tends to render the people of St. Lawrence Island powerless in opposing plans for oil and gas development in the Bering Sea. The noneconomic values island residents attach to their natural environment and its wildlife are viewed as irrelevant in the decision-making process and thus receive little or no consideration. The Eskimo islanders understand that public opinion and the dominance exercised over them by state and federal agencies, not to mention energy corporations, are rooted in the dominant society's economic and political power. That same union of economic control and intellectual leadership which has produced and maintained the powerlessness experienced by Native American societies elsewhere is what confronts the people of St. Lawrence Island now.

Leaders in Gambell and Savoonga are well aware of the social, political, and economic trends which are pressing for continued energy development. They realize the potential dangers inherent in off-shore oil and gas exploration and production in the Bering Sea, expressing dismay at its apparent inevitability and fully comprehending it could lead to the eventual demise of their traditional culture. While the Eskimo people of St. Lawrence Island recognize the threat, questions regarding the likelihood and magnitude of the threat remain.

CONSEQUENCES OF HARVEST DISRUPTIONS

For at least 1,900 years, the marine environment of St. Lawrence Island has provided sustenance to its Yupik-speaking residents. Today, their dependence upon naturally recurring food resources is not drastically different from what it was 19 centuries ago. Despite the introduction of processed foods in the last century, at present as in the past, they rely for their physical, not to mention cultural, survival on the wild harvests the Bering Sea provides. To disturb the natural state of the sea is to disturb the harvests and therefore the Eskimo people of Gambell and Savoonga.

Obviously, a healthy marine environment is necessary if the walrus, whales, seals, fish, and birds the islanders capture and consume are to continue inhabiting and passing through the waters near St. Lawrence Island. All of these creatures--birds, fish, and marine mammals--are dependent upon the biological production of the benthic life zones of the Bering Sea. Damage to the marine habitat, whether in the form of conditions limiting or ending marine life reproduction, interrupting normal seasonal marine life migration to the island, or causing marine life migration away from the island, would create a physical, psychological, and cultural calamity for the people of Gambell and Savoonga.

Available evidence indicates that a variety of activities associated with off-shore oil and gas exploration or production has the capacity to negatively affect marine environments. Boat, ship, and air traffic, as well as air and noise pollution, drive wildlife from traditional feeding, resting, or birthing areas. The most serious danger to marine life, however, is water pollution resulting from oil spills. Given the potential for human error--for example, a faulty weld on a pipe--and the capriciousness of nature--for example, a violent storm--it is not unreasonable to hypothesize that an oil spill will occur somewhere in the Bering Sea just as spills have occurred in many other ocean waters, an oil spill which will be carried in ice or water by ocean currents to the environs of St. Lawrence Island.

Such a spill would certainly have negative consequences for at least some members of the marine life chain. Whether the effects are first observed in marine mammals or microorganisms is irrelevant. Since the life chain is composed of interdependent partners, if one is affected, ultimately all are. The only questions are when, where, and to what extent the effects will manifest themselves. Even if the precise location, size, wind and current conditions, ice thickness, chemical characteristics of the oil, and all other important variables were known, an accurate and precise biological and physical assessment of the full extent of the consequences of an oil spill would remain impossible. Models specifying the important physical variables along with their interactions simply do not exist at present (LGL Associates 1984).

The social sciences suffer similar shortcomings. Well-articulated theories dealing with the social consequences of energy development for native peoples like the Eskimos of St. Lawrence Island, theories based upon reliable empirical evidence, have not yet been developed. Because sufficient information necessary for theoretical validation is not currently available, social forecasting and prediction must remain somewhat imprecise. Nevertheless, it is clear that reduction in the availability of naturally recurring marine species would have a negative social impact on the Eskimos' subsistence lifestyle. Any activity which limits the numbers of, or restricts the access to, the marine harvests on which they rely cannot possibly be viewed as beneficial to the islanders.

The reduced availability of marine species translates directly into reduced harvests. This necessarily follows because subsistence hunters must travel greater distances in search of their prey, thereby increasing the time spent traveling to new hunting and fishing grounds. The result is a decrease in the time available for actual hunting and fishing and thus a reduction in the subsistence harvest. Furthermore, economics and weather conditions may prohibit more distant hunting on many days when hunting closer to the villages may have been possible. If the incorrect assumptions were made that the St. Lawrence Island Eskimos spend little time hunting and fishing, that their efforts are easily rewarded, that current subsistence food harvests exceed their needs, and/or that the marine life would not be destroyed and only displaced a short distance from the island, it then would follow that the Eskimos' subsistence harvest levels could be maintained in the event of an oil spill. Such assumptions fly in the face of all evidence, however.

Even though a Bering Sea oil spill would undoubtedly reduce the availability of marine species and diminish subsistence harvests almost simultaneously, whether reduced harvests are linearly correlated with undesirable social impacts is uncertain. Field observations lead to the hypothesis that, in fact, the relationship between harvest reductions and negative social change takes the form of a negative inverse function. That is, the magnitude of negative social impacts appears to be proportionately greater than the level of harvest reductions which precipitate them.

Regardless of the precise form of the relationship, it is certain the St. Lawrence Island would not benefit from a reduction in the availability of the natural food resources upon which its people depend. In the absence of sound scientific evidence, predicting the precise magnitude of the social impacts which would result from an oil spill is impossible. While currently fashionable in some circles, it would be misleading to present a series of scenarios specifying the consequences for each of several levels of hypothetical harvest disruptions. It is more plausible and instructive to assume a moderate level of disruption in which a moderate number of marine mammals, fish, and birds perish or are driven from the traditional resource areas of St. Lawrence Island over time. Within this context, a discussion of effects of an oil spill on the traditional lives and lifestyle of the people of the island follows.

As the availability of previous numbers of subsistence species declines after a spill, hunting crews undoubtedly will increase their hunting efforts, making more and longer trips in order to maintain acceptable food levels for the island's people. In spite of their expanded effort, the subsistence harvest will begin to decline also, forcing the communities to draw down their stored food reserves. As a result of increased hunting efforts, scarce cash and/or credit reserves will also drop because additional fuel purchases will be required for longer, more frequent hunting forays. With both cash and food reserves beginning to shrink, an increased dependency on commercially processed foods will develop as the Eskimo people run out of native foods or elect to conserve remaining traditional foods for later use.

An increased reliance on commercial foods will further reduce cash and credit balances. As cash reserves for some of the island's population approach zero, the traditional sharing ethic will be extended to more fully include the remaining cash in the village as a subsistence commodity. Under these circumstances, its distribution across households will become more even. If instances of nonsharing occur and become public among the Eskimo villagers, negative sanctions will be brought to bear on the offenders. Besides sharing cash already on the island, its residents most probably will begin seeking new sources of credit from both local and mainland sources.

The longer harvest disruptions continue, and the greater their magnitude, the more serious the crisis for the Eskimos of the island becomes. Sometime before cash and food reserves reach a level where hunger is a serious threat to individual well-being, village officials will be forced to seek emergency relief from state and federal agencies. The people's initial reluctance to seek outside aid due to their sense of self-sufficiency will be overcome by their stark need. Concurrently, the credit lines of individual residents at the island's cooperative store and private retail stores will have been depleted, although the cooperative, as a member of ANICA, probably will have been able to extend credit for the longest period. Pressure on the private retail establishments, no longer able to shield themselves from criticism by appealing to bureaucratic rules and regulations ostensibly enforced by corporate managers located in Seattle, will mount. It is not unlikely that hostility toward the firms' owners, managers, and employees will develop, hostility which perhaps may even extend to their family members.

At the point the consequences of harvest disruption reach this level, some residents of St. Lawrence Island will opt to migrate to the mainland to find wage work. Their intention will be to send part of their earnings to kin and friends on the island during the crisis, but then to return there to their subsistence pursuits as soon as its natural resource food base rebounds to previous levels. The first to migrate will be younger single men and perhaps some few single women, for whom the move will be easier than for those with spouses or children. It is also the younger, more recent high school graduates who are likely to have more marketable job skills than do older Eskimos. Even so, many of the younger people possess only rudimentary mainland job skills, limiting them to menial employment.

Should harvest reductions continue, more and more islanders will move to the mainland. Younger married fathers will follow the unmarried men, leaving wives and children on the island where they can partially rely on the familiar traditional support structures there. Through leaving families behind, the costs of relocating are kept to a minimum, and the proportion of after-expense income available to support kin on the island is greater. A vicious circle thus begins: The longer and more serious the harvest disruptions, the more difficult it becomes for individuals and families to maintain physical and social cohesiveness and well-being. Migration to the mainland makes it increasingly more difficult to maintain family and community ties. With the loss of these ties follows a breakdown in community and island solidarity, which in turn undermines the patriclan structure.

At another social level, the island hunting crews, which initially responded to reduced subsistence harvests by increasing their hunting efforts, will show an increasing tendency to hunt less often and/or for shorter periods of time. Two factors reinforce the reduction in the frequency or duration of their hunting forays. First, as discussed earlier, because the need to husband scarce cash resources accompanies reduced harvests, the number of hunting trips will be restricted. Native subsistence hunters will confront the dilemma of electing to spend money for fuel, ammunition, and other hunt necessities, or to purchase foods to feed themselves and their families. Both individuals and crews will be forced finally to suspend hunting as cash and credit for gas, oil, shells, and other hunting supplies become totally expended. Second, to the extent that hunting success continues to be limited, many will opt to forgo hunting activities for pyschological reasons. According to exchange theory, hunters who are successively unsuccessful in their endeavors will hunt less often. Unless they meet with renewed success, they will cease hunting altogether.

Regardless of the cause, decreased hunting and hunting success will ultimately result in deterioration or even disintegration of the social structure of St. Lawrence Island. As discussed previously, both village and island social organization is centered around subsistence activities, especially marine mammal hunts. Without regular hunting activity and at least moderate harvest success, the extensive networks for hunting, collecting, processing, and distributing subsistence food resources will experience an immediate deleterious impact. Acquiring food and other resources through cooperative efforts will cease, a phenomenon similar to the experiences of native people in the lower 48 states and in other regions of Alaska. Production units such as whaling and walrus crews will no longer possess a reason to continue functioning in customary ways. Under the most extreme conditions, many traditional social units will simply cease to exist.

With the disintegration of harvest production networks on St. Lawrence Island, its traditional sharing networks also face potential collapse. With no resources to share, the various networks will begin to break down into small nuclear or extended family clusters, each struggling to maintain only its own well-being without the social, economic, and physical support the sharing networks once supplied. Redefined in this narrower, more restrictive manner, extending sharing beyond the family unit may come to be viewed as trivial, inappropriate, or unacceptable.

This more individualized interpretation of the social system, an interpretation stressing benefits to self and/or closely related kin only, to the detriment or exclusion of extended kin and other community residents, is commonplace in the larger American society but alien to St. Lawrence Island's traditional culture. In the event of state or federal aid to the Eskimo islanders to alleviate food shortages created by harvest disruptions, the abandonment of the traditional sharing ethic may be reinforced by government. The social welfare bureaucracy's orientation is to distribute relief aid to individuals or household heads, rather than to the patriclan heads and other community leaders traditionally responsible for the allocation and distribution of resources among the Eskimo islanders.

Should the consequences of harvest reduction lead to the deterioration or disintegration of the Eskimo people's sharing networks, the result will be, at least temporarily, a concomitant disintegration of the patriclan system, a kinship structure which has endured for thousands of years. Gambell and Savoonga will cease being integrated communities concerned for the well-being of all island residents. Lacking the social structure of the patriclans to determine resource allocation, the sharing ethic will be replaced by behavior and social structures more consistent with life in non-Eskimo urban environments (see Parsons and Shills 1951).

The Eskimo people of St. Lawrence Island are among the rapidly diminishing number of human cultures which derive their sustenance from the wild harvests nature provides them in their local environment. In the event persistent depletion of the natural food resources upon which they rely occurs, many aspects of the unique cultural characteristics of these central Siberian Yupik-speakers will be lost. The islanders are, after all, primarily hunters and fishers. To lose the opportunity to pursue their hunting and fishing activities threatens the essence of their way of life. Nothing occasions greater dread among the people of Gambell and Savoonga than the prospect of forgoing their present subsistence practices.

Island residents realize that their cherished way of life, with its social organizations, sharing ethic, mutual support, and social cohesion, depends on the continued availability of the various marine species they harvest. Their lifestyle and social systems can persist only so long as the marine environment remains unharmed. Their present social organization would suffer immeasurable damage if the naturally recurring food resources provided by the Bering Sea were rendered inaccessible for whatever reason.

Many, if not most, St. Lawrence Island Eskimos have serious misgivings about oil and gas exploration and potential production in the Bering Sea. In the past, the residents have declined corporate offers to utilize their island for industrial purposes. They understand they face obstacles in retaining their treasured culture and traditions, including their subsistence pursuits. To prepare themselves to meet the obstacles awaiting them, they have begun learning as much as possible about the development of oil and gas in their region. Through their increased knowledge, they intend to respond to the proposed energy developments in a manner which will further their own goals and wishes. To protect their interests, they recently filed a federal lawsuit challenging the thoroughness and scientific adequacy of an off-shore oil and gas lease environmental impact statement. Taking this action clearly reflects their awareness of what is at stake and their determination to protect their way of life. At the same time they practice their traditional ways, the people of Gambell and Savoonga are also practicing the "American way." It appears that St. Lawrence Island Eskimos will fight to protect their treasured heritage, using the techniques of mainstream society.

NOTES

1. The field research for this paper was conducted by the John Muir Institute, Inc., of Napa, California, under contract with the Outer Continental Shelf Office of the Minerals Management Service, Anchorage, Alaska. The authors and the institutions under whose auspices the data were collected express their gratitude both to the people of Gambell and Savoonga, Alaska, for their gracious hospitality and cooperation, and to the seven

native field workers whose participation was indispensable to the success of the study.

2. One of the most comprehensive books detailing Native American experiences with energy development is Native Americans and Energy Development II (Jorgensen 1984a).

3. Local hunters attributed the decreased Savoonga harvest to a persistent buildup of pressure ice which kept hunters from pursuing walrus on the open water.

4. International Whaling Commission rules limit St. Lawrence Island whaling crews to four struck whales, two each for Savoonga and Gambell. Whether the struck whales are ultimately landed is irrelevant; the hunting season ends when four bowheads are struck.

5. The material contained in this and the following section has been adapted and quoted from material first presented by Joseph G. Jorgensen (see Jorgensen et al. 1984:340-48), to whom the authors express their gratitude.

REFERENCES

Bennett, J. W. 1979. Land as space, place, and commodity. Draft manuscript for inclusion in Report on the Committee on Soil as a Resource in Relation to Surface Mining. Washington, D.C.: National Academy of Science.

Geisler, C. C., R. Green, D. Usner, and P. C. West, eds. 1982. Indian SIA: The Social Impact Assessment of Rapid Resource Development on Native Peoples. Monograph 3. Ann Arbor: Natural Resource Sociology Research Lab, University of Michigan.

Hofstadter, R. 1967. Social Darwinism in American Thought. rev. ed. New York: George Braziller.

Hughes, C. E. 1960. An Eskimo Village in the Modern Age. Ithaca, N.Y.: Cornell University Press.

Jorgensen, J. G. 1972. The Sun Dance Religion: Power for the Powerless. Chicago: University of Chicago Press.

———, ed. 1984a. Native Americans and Energy Development II. Cambridge, Mass.: Anthropology Resource Center.

———. 1984b. Energy developments in the arid west: Consequences for Native Americans. In Paradoxes of Western Energy Development, ed. C. M. McKell, D. G. Browne, E. C. Cruze, W. R. Freudenburg, R. L. Perrine, and F. Roach. Boulder, Colo.: Westview Press/American Association for the Advancement of Science.

Jorgensen, J. G., R. Klemmer, R. L. Little, N. Owens, and L. Robbins. 1978. Native Americans and Energy

Development. Cambridge, Mass.: Anthropology Resource Center.
Jorgensen, J. G., J. A. Maxwell, with V. Katchatag. 1983. Final Report of Ethnographic Baseline Village of Unalakleet, Norton Sound. Technical Memorandum NSI-4. Anchorage: United States Department of the Interior, Minerals Management Service.
_____. 1984. Effects of Renewable Resource Harvest Disruptions on Socioeconomic and Sociocultural Systems: Norton Sound. Technical Report No. 90. Anchorage: United States Department of the Interior, Minerals Management Service.
LGL Ecological Research Associates, Inc. 1984. Proceedings of a synthesis meeting--the Norton Basin environment and the possible consequences of oil and gas development. Draft report submitted to Outer Continental Shelf Assessment Program, National Ocean Service, Anchorage.
Little, R. L. 1977. Some social consequences of boom towns. North Dakota Law Review 53:401-25.
_____. 1978. Energy boom towns: Views from within. In J. G. Jorgensen, et al., Native Americans and Energy Development, 63-88. Cambridge, Mass.: Anthropology Resource Center.
Little, R. L., and T. Greider. 1983. Water Transfers from Agriculture to Industry: Two Utah Examples. Research Monograph No. 10. Logan: Institute for Social Science Research on Natural Resources, Utah State University.
Little, R. L., and S. Lovejoy. 1979. Energy development and local employment. Social Science Journal 16(April):27-49.
Little, R. L., and L. A. Robbins. 1982. Ethnographic Baseline: St. Lawrence Island. Final Technical Report SL1-4. Anchorage: United States Department of the Interior, Minerals Management Service.
_____. 1983. Summary: Ethnographic Baseline: St. Lawrence Island. Technical Memorandum SL1-2. Anchorage: United States Department of the Interior, Minerals Management Service.
McClelland, D. 1961. The Achieving Society. Princeton, N.J.: Van Nostrand.
Parsons, T., and E. Shills, eds. 1951. Toward a General Theory of Action. Cambridge, Mass.: Harvard University Press.
Robbins, L. A. 1980. Native American experiences with energy developments. In The Boom Town: Problems and Promises in the Energy Vortex, ed. J. Davenport III and J. A. Davenport, 21-32. Laramie: Department of Social Work, University of Wyoming.

9
It Doesn't Have to Happen Again: Reflections on the Nuclear Atmosphere

Simon J. Ortiz

When I was a boy, I remember my father saying, "I went outside that morning just before dawn. To be with the dawn, to say a few words in prayer for myself, for everyone, for the day, for the earth. And then looking to the southeast, I saw this shimmering light beyond the horizon. I said to myself, 'It is not the sun because it is too far to the south.' I didn't know what it was, but I knew it was not natural." Later, other people of Acoma Pueblo spoke about the strange dawn they had witnessed. They described that light being like something that danced on a wind which passed through them. They wondered what it was. One old man said, "I knew they were going to do something. They've done it before, and I knew they were going to do something again." Later, the people found out that it was an atomic bomb explosion that was the strange dawn which tremored with an unknown light through them. And that man's words were confirmed: They've done it before, and they were going to do it again.

Colonialism, which is exploitation of people and land by outside economic and political forces, has been a fact in the Southwest since the 1540s. First, it was the Spanish who came with their guns, horses, and a way of life previously unknown to the native peoples of the present-day U.S. Southwest. The conquistador demanded tribute and loyalty to Spain. Next, as actual colonization began, the demand was made for land, and land was taken, oftentimes the best farming lands of the native people. At the same time, souls were demanded by priests, "padres," of the Christian God. Though there was resistance, these were given also. What choice did the people have? They were faced with guns and a way of life that seemed to be all-encompassing. Many communities of Indian people, which came to be known as Pueblos, were destroyed. There were at least 92 Pueblos when the conquistador first came, and now there are 19, of which Acoma Pueblo is one.

At Acoma Pueblo, there is a story dating back to that time. A number of children, girls and boys, were taken south to Mexico, and a mission bell was given in exchange for them. Today, at Acoma, a wall surrounds the graveyard immediately in front of the mission, which is a massive edifice. The southern side of the wall has a hole in it. It is said that the hole is there for the souls of the children to return through. It is true those children were taken. They were taken after the conquest and razing of Acoma Pueblo in 1598 by the conquistador. Soon afterwards, the mission was built, and the people continue to tell that story in order to know the continuous history that they have been witness to since then.

Next, it was the Anglo-Americans who came upon the Pueblo Indian people. They also came with guns, horses, and a way of life that the people had gotten some idea about by then. U.S. colonization began in the 1820s and was a certain fact by the mid-1800s, when the U.S. claimed the Southwest. There was something more brutal in this period of colonialism. Though the Pueblo Indian people had lost land and lives to the Spaniard in the years before, something began to happen now that seemed to make life desperate. After the Pueblo Indian Revolt of 1680 resulted in the Spanish being driven away from the north (though they returned later), the Spanish colonizers became more accommodating. They recognized the native ownership of the land and the traditions of religious practice and self-government. In fact, they learned native practices and customs and began to live by them. Their people intermarried with the native people.

But there was something unholy and without any respect about the new colonizers. They were slick and fast-talking, and the skills performed by their lawyers, teachers, ministers, surveyors, engineers were totally overwhelming. The people could only be awed and fearful as they stood by helplessly. Their children were required to be good Americans by being forced to leave their homes to attend school. How else can you be truly a human being if you are not able to speak English, if you cannot turn away from your pagan ritualistic ways, if you are not an individual with the competitive drive to be number one? The people were amazed as they saw their lands be surveyed and diminish right before their eyes. They were dismayed as they saw their children turn away from the older ways, and they wondered what had come upon them. The Pueblo Indian people were dazed as they saw that locomotive steam engine coming from the east, and they watched numbly as its shiny road took their best remaining farm lands. Their leaders were confused as they signed documents that gave up their rights to land and water and a way of life. They tried to protest: "The land and the earth and our life are sacred." But the "wabuurlih," the American train, did not hear. It merely roared and shook the earth. The people and the earth trembled.

The process of colonialism is complex, and perhaps I've oversimplified it, but I am certain it has those basic elements that result in a people's sense of powerlessness, including loss of control over their land, their culture, their future. I feel though that the more we learn about this process, the more knowledgeable and assured we become that we can do something.

In the early 1950s, the uranium mining companies came to our local area. Anaconda opened up the pit called Jackpile Mine at Laguna Pueblo, which is a sister Pueblo to Acoma. It was simple enough. The federal government urged Pueblo Indian leaders to allow the mining to begin, and even if they didn't, it wouldn't matter. The U.S. Atomic Energy Commission needed to maintain and replenish its stockpiles. The Indian agents told the leaders: "This is your chance to get jobs. Look at how you're living, like uncivilized Indians. Enter the American mainstream instead of living like you are. Look at yourself; you should be ashamed of yourself: no job, no education, no haircut. Sign this paper." And so the people agreed, and they signed. Soon, most men of Laguna Pueblo were working at the Jackpile Mine, not in higher positions, of course; those were for the whites with education and sophistication and skills. But they were working, and they got wages for their labor. Economic life improved it seemed, but something else began to happen. Why is there so much alcoholism? they wondered. Why is there so much beating up and stealing going on? Why is there no one growing corn and melons and chili anymore? Why is there a lack of our traditional social and religious ceremonies? The people bought new cars and good clothes, and they fixed up their homes, but something else was happening.

Development of Indian lands has always resulted in incredible social, cultural, and economic changes. When the railroad came through Laguna and Acoma Pueblo lands, the people lost their farming lands. Because they had been mostly self-sufficient subsistence farmers, making their living that way, what were they to do? They had to take laboring jobs with the railroad company. They were moved to Winslow, Barstow, Richmond. This resulted in breakup of kinship systems, the clans. It created a weakening of the religious ceremonialism that had always sewn together the social fabric of the Pueblos. It led to a loss of that necessary respect for the community, for land, and perhaps even for life itself. As one may understand, this can be applied to what happens not only to Indian people but to other people as well. Because people lose control over their lives, lose respect for life and land, lose a certain sense of spirituality and moral responsibility, it is not long before they become a part of that force that has overcome them. This situation leads to acceptance of conditions that are detrimental to their social and individual well-being, and it even results in tolerance, if not outright advocacy, of public policies that do not guarantee a future for them and their children. This relates directly to the dilemma we face today and have been confronted with since the first plans were made for the detonation of the atomic bomb at Trinity Site in New Mexico.

New Mexico was chosen because it was the ideal site for such a horrendous event: It was chosen simply because national policy was based on the public belief that the land was occupied by a few jackrabbits, Mexicans, some cowboys, and a few remaining Indians who were vanishing anyway. The belief and attitude was that New Mexico was available, since it was wasteland anyway, for use in whatever way it was seen fit. And, of course, no one spoke up otherwise; besides, it was wartime, and everyone must do his share. Los Alamos laboratory had been established in the Jemez Mountains before that, the land for it taken from the Santa Clara Pueblo Indians. This same type of attitude and belief resulted in the opening up of the largest open-pit uranium mine in the world at Laguna Pueblo. It resulted in the exploitation of the Laguna miners at the lowest level of employment, and it resulted in the degradation of a native culture that had been held sacred for thousands of years.

When I was fresh out of high school, I went to work for a mining company at its mill operations at Ambrosio Lake. The area is north of Grants, which is a town about ten miles west of McCartys, the little Acoma Pueblo village where I was raised. The mines, which were underground, unlike the surface operation at Jackpile, had been operating since 1957 when uranium was found. Supposedly, a Navajo Indian from Bluewater had found a stone containing uranium ore and the rush was on; soon a half dozen and more mining companies were busy in the region. The myth about the Indian was a contrived truth, of course; explorations had been going on in the region since the late 1940s. In fact, the truth was that, as with the decision to explode the atomic bomb in mid-eastern New Mexico, the site that would be mined for uranium was accessible since it was on and near Indian lands, and there would be a source of nearby cheap labor. It was not only the labor of Indian people in that region but of the nearby Chicano communities of San Mateo and San Rafael and Grants, a small town that had known itself for a while in the early 1950s as the Carrot Capital of the World. The Bluewater Valley had been a farming region for a number of years, but there was hardly a living to be made from it. Acoma Pueblo, which is downstream on the Rio de San Jose, which flows through the Bluewater Valley past Grants, had known this for a long time. In all, there was need for employment in the area; for sure, this must have gone into the planning for mining operations in the Ambrosio Lake area.

I worked in the crushing and leaching operations of the plant until I moved into yellowcake, where the final product is processed. By this stage, the original uranium ore, which is plain-looking rock and sand, had been processed and turned into a yellow liquid. The liquid was passed into dryers, which took the water out. Yellow pellets were extruded and were then dried. After drying, the pellets were crushed into a fine yellow powder. The dust from the powder was constantly in the air. The main functions of the workers in that section were to make sure the machinery was maintained and kept in smooth-running operation and to pack the yellowcake into 50-gallon drums. We wore masks and company-furnished plastic overalls, but those seemed to be the only precautions we made. At that time, I never heard anybody talk about the hazards of radiation, if there were any. In retrospect, it seems to me that the company deliberately did not tell us anything. Why bother?--the workers were only Indians, Mexicans, Okies, Arkies, ex-coal miners from West Virginia, and ex-oilfield workers from the Gulf who had come to New Mexico looking for work since there was no work elsewhere. That seems to me to have been the reason why the mill superintendent did not tell us anything.

Exploitation is a simple enough matter. Get what you have to out of the workers; get what you have to out of the land. Don't worry about the consequences; economic development and growth demand it. Don't worry about the future; today's profits are the immediate concern.

In 1966, soon after a Texas natural gas company had laid its pipeline, which carried gas to California, through Acoma Pueblo land, there was an explosion one early morning. Flames shot hundreds of feet into the air. Old Man Tomato said, "I had gotten up because I always wake up so early, and I went outside to take a pee and look at the stars. And I saw this fire over the hill. I got frightened, and I thought it was hell coming from the east." The explosion destroyed several homes, and a couple of weeks later a gas company representative came to offer money to Acoma Pueblo. Some people recalled that elder saying in the 1940s: "They've done it before, and they are going to do it again."

To the west and north of Ambrosio Lake, which was a lake a million years ago, is a vast coal-bearing region. Since the early 1970s, major mining companies have been strip-mining the coal, which is used to fire power-generating plants such as the Four Corners Power Plant at Shiprock in northwestern New Mexico. This is all taking place on Navajo Indian land. Other regions of the U.S. have rich reserves of coal, but this is Indian land, which is accessible because in a sense the federal government still has immediate control. It has been stated national policy to develop domestic energy resources, and it just so happens, as has been much publicized, that Indian lands across the nation have much coal, oil, gas, uranium, and other resources ripe for development. Perhaps this is true, but I tend to suspect that it is somewhat like that Indian who was supposed to have found that chunk of uranium ore. And, of course, it's true in the sense that the vast resource of this country is Indian land, at least it once was.

The development, or exploitation, of Indian lands and resources has much to do with today's tense nuclear atmosphere. It is not only that so much of the basic element for producing nuclear weapons comes from the Ambrosio Lake region near Acoma Pueblo, but it is also the fact of U.S. history and the nation's attitudes, ideas, and approaches toward Indian land and people. Until lately, U.S. society has not had a high regard for the natives of this land. Indians have been cast in the image of the lurking savage, or the romantic noble one, or the helpless reservation ward, and therefore it has been easy enough to do whatever served U.S. society's self-interest. Perhaps we can regard the Indian as a symbol of what is happening to all of us in the present age. Indian lands had to be taken, whether by fraud or purchase--it didn't make any difference whether the Indians wanted to sell or not--in order for this nation to survive and push forward economically. At least this was the belief held; the only real asset was the vast land resource of this country. We have to develop this resource, it was said, and it doesn't really matter what the consequences are; we have to survive economically; we are the greatest nation in the world. The national economy is faltering; build up military defense in case we have to use it offensively; build more bombs. Why bother with informing the people of the horrors of limited or unlimited nuclear warfare; they're just people anyway. Besides, they need jobs. Tell them it's for their own good. It is a simple enough matter. They've done it before, and they will do it again.

Albuquerque, the city where my family and I live, is economically dependent largely upon military defense. Sandia National Laboratory, where the newest in military weapons design takes place, and Kirtland Air Force Base, combined, create the single largest employer in the city. When these are further combined with Los Alamos National Laboratory, White Sands Missile Range, and Cannon Air Force Base, the result is that New Mexico is to a degree economically dependent upon military defense, particularly nuclear weapons, and therefore the nuclear atmosphere. Laguna Pueblo, 50 miles to the west of Albuquerque, had been solely dependent upon Jackpile Mine until it closed in 1982, causing severe socioeconomic distress at the Pueblo. During the time of the mine's active operation, though there were certainly economic benefits from wage earnings and royalties, many social problems were encountered which practically overwhelmed the community. The incidence of alcoholism was extremely high, as was violence, and so forth. As I said earlier, the people wondered what had happened: why the values of caring for the land and the people no longer existed. At Acoma Pueblo, just several miles further west, the residents, though seeming to have prospered from the earnings of their men and women working in the mining industry at Ambrosio Lake, found themselves unsettled by the same social problems as at Laguna Pueblo. I recall my aunt saying, when she learned of the world's deepest uranium shaft being constructed by Gulf Oil on the western face of Kaweshtima, "What are they doing it for? Kaweshtima, it is our beloved sacred mother mountain. No wonder the young have no respect for the traditions anymore." Grants, not far to the west, has been a boomtown, and it has been as ill-planned as any boomtown ever was. It has had more than its share of problems and has been the cause of problems, such as the present one in which the town is the defendant in a suit filed by Acoma and Laguna Pueblos. Grants has allowed its sewage to run into the Rio de San Jose, which is a stream of water that in the prehistoric and historic past has served as the main water source for Acoma and Laguna Pueblos. Albuquerque and New Mexico are experiencing the social impact and most of the same problems that have been created by the kind of economic process undergone by Acoma and Laguna Pueblos.

It is wise for us, the American public, to concern ourselves with the kind of economy that we have, its history and its consequences. If we are to be morally responsible presently, then we have to assume responsibility for our history, especially economic history. Look at that American train, roaring and shaking the earth, as it took the best farming lands of Acoma Pueblo and left the people with very few choices. We have to study it, analyze it, and then make decisions. Look at our present economic life, study it, analyze it, and then make decisions.

One summer when my daughter was about four we were at my mother's home in McCartys. We had watched a TV program on the history of the atomic bomb from Los Alamos to Nagasaki to the present. The next day, she was outside playing, and suddenly I heard her scream terribly. I jumped up and ran outside and hugged her as she stood frozen to the ground. "What is it, baby? What is it, baby?" She was crying loudly into my shoulder. She turned her face then to the east and then shuddered and turned her crying face back to me. I looked, and there was only the mesa and further east a shoulder of the slopes of Kaweshtima, and above them was the thick grayish-black moil of thunderclouds that was the sky that day. And then she pointed her finger at a certain spot in the mass of clouds. "Look, look what happened?" a quivering in her four-year-old voice. She trembled. And then I saw what she was pointing at. It was a formation of cloud in the middle of the eastern sky. It was slowly turning and moiling and gave the illusion that it was something other than a raincloud. "It's okay, baby," I said, "It's the rain forming. It's only a rain cloud; the rain is good for the land." We watched the strange formation as it slowly dissipated into the massive thundercloud sky. "It's okay," I said once more, but she looked at me as if she did not quite believe me.

Too often, in the decades since that old man said, "They've done it before; I knew they were going to do something," his words have been prophetic. Those same words can be visionary though. It is up to us to work for that vision and for the true American dream, which will insure a secure, healthy, nonthreatening future for all people, the land, all items of life, even those things that do not breathe or move, everything. Life must continue. Even though it may have happened before, it does not have to happen again.

10
Reflections on Resistance to Rural Industrialization: Newcomers' Culture of Environmentalism

Allan Schnaiberg

THE INDUSTRIALIZATION OF THE COUNTRYSIDE

Among many other changes in the internal American economic structure (Blumberg 1980; Bluestone and Harrison 1982), the last few decades have witnessed the emergence of a number of forms of decentralization of industry. Although much of our attention has been on the shift from frostbelt or rustbelt to sunbelt, there are associated shifts that operate on a subregional level. This chapter focuses on one of these, the increased industrialization of rural areas, those smaller communities that have been largely rural villages or hamlets, or towns closer to rural than to major urban centers (in this chapter, these areas are coterminous with the census definition of "nonmetropolitan"). In contrast to the attentiveness of many sociologists to the sunbelt transformation, though, rural industrialization has been a topic of primary interest only to rural sociologists (e.g., Summers et al. 1976; Summers and Selvik 1979; Ford 1978; Dillman and Hobbs 1982) and economists (e.g., Lonsdale and Seylor 1979). Perhaps underlying this inattention by most nonrural practitioners is their assumption that such industrialization increases are small and largely irrelevant for most metropolitan populations and are, in any event, less substantial than major decreases in metropolitan blue-collar positions (Bluestone et al. 1981). Yet, about one-half of all new manufacturing jobs in recent decades have gone to rural areas (Lonsdale 1979:3).

One of the assumptions of this chapter is that rural industrialization is a significant feature of the overall changes in American industrial structure and that increases in these rural or semirural industries often exacerbate the plight of metropolitan labor forces, central cities, and urban minority groups (Bluestone and Harrison 1982). I start with the assumption that most modern rural industrialization investments could have been made in metropolitan areas (Bluestone et al. 1981; Quante 1976). Apart from energy or other extractive investments, little of the growth of rural industrial employment seems associated with geographic or local natural resource factors. Rather, rural relocation or expansion seems premised on the anticipation of higher profitability, or at least lower "transaction costs," in these locations (Haren and Holling 1979; Kale and Lonsdale 1979). Transaction costs are all those costs of linking buyers and sellers in the marketplace. Essentially, they include all the indirect costs of production and distribution, in my case especially the costs of "dealing with" regulations. The latter include both the costs of complying with environmental and other state regulations and the costs of evading them through flight or other responses.

The literature stresses a number of factors leading to these relocation decisions, "corporate flight" or "capital flight," as social critics (e.g., Bluestone et al. 1981) have labeled them. Included have been the desire to escape the financial and social costs associated with metro minorities and poverty problems and to reap the advantages of lower taxes and easier recruitment of labor also fleeing these metro problems (Bluestone et al. 1981; Quante 1976). To these benefits are added the local and state tax holidays often used by localities to attract new industry (Summers et al. 1976:12-13; Tweeten 1974, 1982). Availability of docile and cheaper nonunionized rural labor also motivates this capital flight, albeit to varying degrees. Industries using more labor-intensive technologies find such semi-skilled rural labor more profitable. In contrast, high technology industries requiring higher-skilled workers find this of less importance in relocation decisions (Summers et al. 1976; Erickson and Leinbach 1979).

Among the understudied transaction benefits of rural relocation or expansion has been the reduction of costs of environmental regulation. This factor is obviously of varying importance to corporate decision makers (Kale and Lonsdale 1979; Latham 1976; Hays 1981). The environmental movement's success in incorporating environmental legislation into the regulatory apparatus of the 1970s has led to substantial transaction costs for industries seeking regulatory approval or evading regulatory penalty (McKenzie 1979; Molotch and Logan 1984). A small part of rural appeal may be the rural availability of natural resource features--water or land areas with greater capacity to absorb pollution than already-degraded urban areas. But it is primarily the social and political structure of rural areas that permits lower environmental costs (Summers et al. 1976:13; Buttel 1982).

Specifically, the underlying assumption of this chapter is that the environmental benefit of rural location for many corporate actors is relatively higher social disattention to environmental disruption by rural populations and regulatory agencies. Basically, the argument here is that corporations expect that environmental enforcement will be less stringent in rural areas, lowering compliance costs (cf. Shulins 1984; Ogintz 1983a; Geiser 1983a, 1983b).

The following section elaborates the historical basis for this expectation. After that, I suggest ways in which these corporate expectations are likely to become increasingly invalid, because of the very social changes in rural and semirural areas brought by the phenomenon of rural industrialization. The essence of the argument is dialectical, viz., that locational changes in investment effected by industrial elites and their state supporters are likely to be self-limiting, due to the social changes that accompany such investments. Because of the changing composition of rural populations (Kasarda 1980; Long 1983; Wardwell and Gilchrist 1980), new "folk" resistance to rural environmental degradation is likely to develop, a process analogous to the socialization of labor in Marx's description of the early factory system.

SMALL COMMUNITIES AS SUITORS OF INDUSTRY

Corporate expectations about the regulatory climate in smaller rural communities have some firm basis in recent history. The decline of the family farm, the rise of capital-intensive agriculture, and the increased competition in food, fiber, and mineral-processing industries have all interacted to make for disinvestment and depopulation in many rural areas (Doeksen et al. 1974; Tweeten 1974, 1982; Summers 1982).

Agribusiness has combined costly machinery and migrant labor for cropping and processing in many areas. The resulting push factor of rural unemployment and the pull factor of metropolitan opportunity in education and employment have led to out-migration of the "brightest and best" of rural youth. At least, this was the dismal message delivered by many observers for the 1940-1965 period (e.g., Tweeten 1974). For many communities, then, a top priority in recent decades has been the attraction of new industry to replace jobs that have been technologically eliminated or competitively lost to metro firms. Moreover, with the loss of local wages and the capital stock of smaller industries, nonagricultural tax bases have shrunk (Tweeten

1974, 1982; Summers et al. 1976) and reduced the potential for communities to provide educational or other services. However, as with earlier studies of suburban development, social scientists analyzing rural development (e.g., Tweeten 1974, 1982; Summers et al. 1976; Summers 1982) have discovered anew the tradeoffs between increased rural investment and increased rural population growth. The latter requires substantial new community investment, especially for in-migrants with children (typical of rural in-migrants, as I note below), where large educational expenditures are required. This is the less-publicized problem of such growth, in contrast with the attention to "boomtown" problems (e.g., Wilkinson et al. 1982). To some extent, educational burdens have been offset by state sharing of revenues, but the new population growth still seems to require heavier local taxation, particularly on farmers owning large tracts of land. Thus, Tweeten (1974) argues that, while new investment may benefit the community as a whole, the benefits of such growth are not usually received proportionately by the people who pay the costs of it (see also Molotch and Logan 1984).

Despite these realities, underemployed local population groups and their local political representatives desperately seek inducements for new employers. For many such localities, their hopes have been and will continue to be in vain, since their locations offer few attractions to investors. However, they become an analogue of a pool of unemployed labor--a sort of reserve army of corporate suitors, bidding for new investments in many ways (e.g., McCarron 1983; Pear 1983; Edgerton 1983; Ogintz 1983b). And they, coupled with the large numbers of communities with somewhat better features (transportation, physical amenities, locations with high population potential), to a considerable extent have created an investors' market in relocation (Doeksen et al. 1974; Tweeten 1974; Summers 1982). With so many competing rural localities, investors can seek unusually favorable conditions for their investment.

Moreover, because of the negative impact of capital relocation on metro communities (e.g., Bluestone et al. 1981; Drew 1984; Rosenheim and Warren 1984), metro areas are also seeking new investors. While neighborhood and metropolitan social movement organizations (SMOs) often resist and critically evaluate new investments (e.g., Molotch and Logan 1984), the political administrations of metro areas (e.g., McCarron 1983; Arndt and Feigelman 1985) and of rustbelt states (e.g., Pear 1983; Ogintz 1983b) are growing ever more passionate in their courtship of new industries. At the extreme, the argument of this chapter may eventually lead to rural areas being by-passed because of courtship by metro areas. In part, this would be a result of growing immiseration in central cities, and in part, of a continuing out-migration of metro-area skilled workers who might have been more likely to mobilize in opposition to polluting investments (cf. Geiser 1983b). This heightening competition for investors only makes rural areas even more aggressive in their courtship.

For present purposes, it is the environmental regulatory conditions that I am concerned with. Among the relocation goals of corporate actors are a search for populations who will not press for too expensive a control over environmental additions and withdrawals (Schnaiberg 1980a)[1] and for local/state agencies who will likewise not press for too rigorous a set of controls. Obviously, this search for environmental disattention coexists with many other corporate goals, so that the present analysis is only a partial perspective on determinants of corporate relocation (e.g., Summers et al. 1976; Kale and Lonsdale 1979; Buttel 1982).

For many reasons, these community contexts for relaxation of environmental control standards are enhanced by historical shifts in environmental regulation. Much of the actual enforcement of environmental laws has devolved from the Environmental Protection Agency (EPA) to states. Furthermore, even the EPA itself is decentralized into ten regions, each responsible for supervising compliance in a region. Moreover, regional variation in EPA enforcement rigor has been noted earlier (e.g., Butz and Senew 1974). Thus, a corporate decision maker does not have a "featureless plain" of environmental regulation to operate in, but a highly variable distribution of enforcement forces (Hawkins 1984). Localities and state agencies help establish this variability, in terms of their perceived need for new investment, their sense of social, economic, and ecological competitiveness (e.g., Doekson et al. 1974), and their capacity for monitoring and enforcing environmental laws, ranging from basic air and water pollution to toxic and related substances (Buttel 1982). In effect, these conditions reflect values of natural resources versus economic achievement.

The recent dominance of rural development cultures has favored corporate elites in the investors' market. From the corporate perspective, reallocation of capital outside metro areas follows good business practice. Locational theories suggest the efficiency of a wider distribution of manufacturing facilities, with the flexibility of truck transport and decentralized marketing operations, including new electronic communications (Lonsdale and Seylor 1979; Bluestone et al. 1981).

In terms of environmental regulation, there are significant attractions of many rural locations. First, with lower population size and density, there are likely to be fewer conflicts between corporate waste disposal (air, water, and land) and population needs. Unutilized carrying capacity of these ecological systems will be higher than in densely populated metro areas. Moreover, there are more likely to be unused or little-used water and land areas where populations will not interact with waste sites, unlike the more crowded metro area (Summers et al. 1976). Second, some survey research indicates that metropolitan populations were in the forefront of environmental consciousness and that rural populations seem to have a more utilitarian cultural outlook on ecological systems.[2] Thus, corporate planners anticipate that environmental consciousness will be somewhat lower in rural locations, with local populations less likely than metro areas to label even low levels of waste disposal as a social problem. Third, even if there were individual complaints about waste disposal, a corporate planner might well expect that such individual complaints would have less cultural and institutional support for the creation of local social movements to oppose corporate waste disposal (or even new corporate investments). Limited local mobilization capacity should be further attenuated by the limited capacity of local individuals or groups to mobilize the political and technical regulatory forces in the state or the EPA regional office. Technically and politically unsophisticated local citizens typically have local representatives with similar social characteristics and cultural preferences, usually serving office on a part-time and largely unpaid basis. All of these traits differ from the cultural and social contexts of metro areas, where there are (1) more environmentally conscious individuals, who are (2) capable of social mobilization into new movement organizations and/or (3) mobilizable by a wide number of existing environmental social movement organizations (SMOs), including both local chapters of national organizations and local/regional SMOs; (4) such SMOs typically have or can obtain access to local monitoring or enforcement agencies, since (5) these agencies have full-time staff and litigative standing and (6) both the agencies and local political administrators have institutionalized concern and expertise in environmental protection (Shulins 1984; Geiser 1983a, 1983b). In essence, these differences are both cultural (differing values of environmental protection) and institutional (differing resource mobilization levels).

From this perspective, then, investors would be wise to seek a rural location to minimize their costs of compliance with environmental regulations. However,

I will argue that such investments themselves create social changes that are likely to produce local cultural and political changes that challenge this model. From a dialectical perspective, these new sociocultural antitheses I associate with the in-migration of newcomers who, I hypothesize, bring distinctive cultural values. Such cultural values conflict with the economic benefits brought by rural investment. The corporate synthesis of geographic relocation is, then, not likely to be as favorable in social outcomes as the previous analysis would suggest. I turn next to these antitheses.

SOME ROOTS OF RESISTANCE TO OR REJECTION OF INVESTORS

The first and perhaps most important antithesis to the rural marriage with industry is the compositional change in population of rural areas. Although depopulation has proceeded apace, partial repopulation has also occurred in many small towns and villages. Much of this repopulation is not a return migration, but a new in-migration of metropolitan residents and workers, seeking a variety of gains from their relocation. Thus, as has been increasingly noted by social scientists, the flight from the cities has led to a sizable formerly metropolitan population in rural communities (Beale 1978; Kasarda 1980; Long 1983; Wardwell 1982; Wardwell and Gilchrist 1980; Zuiches and Brown 1978). Hence, the socioeconomic composition, cultural value systems, and community locations of population subgroups now vary more independently.

Moreover, this new rural population with residential background in metro areas has socioeconomic traits associated with subgroup cultures that offer support for participation in social movements. And these same traits--particularly higher educational achievement-- have also been associated with higher levels of environmental awareness and cultural values supporting environmental protection (Schnaiberg 1980a:Chap. 8; cf. Mitchell 1980). There are, unfortunately, no systematic data on the social movement activity background or potential of rural in-migrants from metro areas. The best approximation we can do is to look for correlates of SMO activity. Of these, education and occupation seem to be the only ones available that have shown any systematic covariation with sociocultural support for political action in general and for strong values of environmental protection in particular.[3]

Zuiches and Brown (1978:65-67) show that for the 1970-1975 period, the college attendance level of metro-to-nonmetro movers is double that of the non-movers in the rural area (34 percent versus 17 percent); the proportion of upper-white-collar positions among men is about 50 percent higher in the former group (33 percent vs. 21 percent). This contrast is more meaningful than one including the total initial population of rural areas. Better-educated groups in the rural area are the most likely to migrate to metro areas (e.g., Tweeten 1974). Thus, they are unavailable for resistance to polluting investors.

The 1982 data (U.S. Bureau of the Census 1984:Table 22) show similar differences to the 1972 levels, although they are less pronounced. For both male and female metro-to-rural movers, there is about a 40 percent higher level of college attendance than for rural nonmovers (36 percent versus 25 percent). And upper-white-collar occupations characterize 29 percent of the male metro migrants, versus 21 percent of the rural nonmovers (U.S. Bureau of the Census 1984:Table 28). Recent differentials are smaller than those in the Zuiches and Brown (1978) report, partly due to the continuous socioeconomic upgrading of the rural population in the intervening decade (1972-1982). I believe this reflects continuing positive selection of metropolitan migrants, attracted by rural industrialization. Consistent with this, the reduced in-migrant/nonmover rural differentials are largely a result of increasing socioeconomic status of current rural nonmovers, rather than the lowering of status of the recent migrants.

Of course, past association of educational status with a culture of environmental awareness and social activism cannot automatically be projected into the 1980s. Geiser (1983a, 1983b) has argued that new toxic waste local movement organizations are constituted of working-class actors. This claim is supported only by unsystematic media reports and a few recent case studies (Hamilton 1985). One would suspect, along with Shulins (1984), that localized movements, dealing with immediate and concrete health threats, might indeed mobilize a wider range of groups with different values. But much of the new industrialization is both recent or in planning stages. Moreover, a larger share of it consists of relatively "clean" industries (cf. Bayles 1984; Barney 1985). Thus, resistance to these threats may still derive primarily from higher-educated citizens, who have stronger cultural values for dealing with less tangible environmental hazards (Hamilton 1985), rather than the working-class concern with tangible health hazards.

Such shifts in the socioeconomic and cultural composition (environmental awareness and social activism) of rural populations are partly independent of the economic trends in rural industrialization and job location. They reflect a variety of other metro push factors, including its polluted environment, and the cultural support for lifestyles that are less exclusively consumptive, but include high valuation of "unspoiled" and "peaceful" rural environments (e.g., Beale 1978). One part of this migration stream includes a large retired population (e.g., Marans and Wellman 1978); another includes those engaged in nonbureaucratic occupations--especially self-employment. Economic support bases for these groups rest on remittances from past metropolitan employment (including savings and pensions) or from providing goods and services to local consumers that are either "oldtimers" or "newcomers"[4] like themselves, and not on expanded local industrialization and its environmental degradation. Generally, the more recent the in-migration, the greater the likelihood that these newcomers will be employed in the new rural industries, though.

A second group of formerly metropolitan newcomers consists of workers who have moved to take up the new industrial employment in these communities. Their representation in rural in-migrant streams varies widely across rural communities. Since part of the corporate attraction to rural investment is the availability of cheaper, unorganized, local labor, the following argument about these newcomers seems most tenable: They are mostly managerial and technical workers, whose skills could not be available within rural labor pools (Zuiches and Brown 1978; Summers 1982; Doekson et al. 1974). Unskilled and semiskilled labor, such as that required for the mechanical or electronic assembly jobs, can readily be found in rural labor pools. Employers often recruit women who were previously not in the labor force (Summers et al. 1976; Erickson and Leinbach 1979; Summers 1982; McNulty 1985). Thus, in the absence of systematic data on this matter, it would seem probable that industrially employed newcomers are likely to be among the highest-skilled, best-paid, and most marketable workers in rural industries. Additionally, following the principles of marital homogamy, they would typically have more-educated and more-skilled spouses as well, something I will return to below.

One implication of this characterization is that this group has low dependency on local employers for future livelihood and thus has the freedom to resist local economic interests. They are workers with a more cosmopolitan culture, despite their current residence in the local rural area (Shulins 1984; Geiser 1983a, 1983b). From the descriptions above of other parts of the newcomer migration stream, such relative autonomy also characterizes many of these other newcomer groups as well. Thus, unlike many of the oldtimers in the population, many of the newcomers are less likely to be active suitors of new industry. They may be passive in the courtship of new industry, having found their niche in a rural environment, or even mildly-to-actively hostile at the courtship stage. Following the honeymoon period, when new industry produces higher environmental degradation than had been anticipated, they might then prefer a "clean" divorce to a "dirty" marriage.

Exceptions to this relative economic autonomy of newcomers are bound to be present. Newcomer entrepreneurs often seek to expand their businesses with new workers and wages, or to reduce their local taxes by encouraging new investments for local tax rolls. Others in this deviant category are newcomer industrial employees who dislike their jobs but want to stay in their newfound geographic area. And newcomers facing tightened labor markets may be less able to act on their cultural preferences.[5] But these exceptions are likely to be a small minority among metro newcomers. Generally, rural industrial workers from the community or the region remain more dependent on the new industries for their employment (Shulins 1984; Summers 1982; Tweeten 1982; cf. Geiser 1983a, 1983b; Hamilton 1985).

Conversely, in some communities, concern for environmental hazards among oldtimers may be even higher than for newcomers. Where these social groups experience vulnerability to hazardous products and wastes in both workplaces and residential areas (Geiser 1983b; Molotch and Logan 1984; Newby 1980), we may find more activism among employed oldtimers. Geiser (1983b) highlights recent toxic waste movements as focused on "local" rather than "cosmopolitan" concerns. For him, toxic waste hazards in local impoundments present clear and present danger to familial and worker health (since the impoundments are often adjacent to the workplaces) and thus lead directly to mobilization of impacted citizens. But such working-class mobilization often follows the consciousness-raising of many other national and regional social movement organizations in such conflicts (e.g., Derr et al. 1981; Gibson 1984; Graham and Shakow 1981; Graham 1983; Schnaiberg 1984), by redefining an abstract environmental problem as a concrete health crisis (Hamilton 1985).

Moreover, Geiser's work obscures the complexities of social movement mobilization even in the local arena around local issues. In the absence of systematic data on most of these local conflicts (cf. Hamilton 1985), my own analysis of media reports differs from Geiser's. Many of the key organizers of the local resistance movements seem to be middle-class, educated citizens. Part of my disagreement with Geiser's focus on working-class mobilization also lies in the apparent attribution of "working-class" to the category of "housewife," since women are key participants in many of these local struggles (Hamilton 1985) (see below). For me, then, middle-class metro newcomers usually are more diffident suitors of industry than are working-class oldtimers. The absence of socioeconomic attitudinal differences in Hamilton (1985) may, as he notes, result from the paucity of higher-status newcomers in these communities.

Although we have no systematic studies of the activism of these newcomer groups, information we do have suggests other self-selection factors that bear on their propensity to mobilize effectively to protect their new natural environments. To some extent, metro "refugees" are in flight from social problems of all sorts--their rural migration is a form of cultural retreatism (Merton 1957:Chaps. 4-5). Those in political withdrawal will not likely mobilize in their rural areas. However, since they have actively chosen to retreat to rural refuges, they may believe that they are culturally entitled to a protected environment in their refuge. This latter trajectory is more likely for people who have moved to a particular rural community because of its natural beauty or healthy natural environment, those for whom ecosystem integrity is a large part of their "quality of life" (Marans and Wellman 1978; Beale 1978; Summers 1982). For this group, who may also have made material sacrifices to achieve this, it is a matter of cultural equity that their refuge be environmentally secure. Such cultural equity commitment is less likely for migrants who have responded more to push factors, especially social problems in their past metro areas of residence. To these latter migrants, it is more significant that they are out of their metro environment than that they are in the rural environment. (They may feel cultural inequities more keenly if socially disadvantaged groups enter their new community, in contrast to invasions of the physical environment.)

What other political and sociocultural attributes are likely to influence newcomers' reactions to industrial suitors? With the fragmentary observations we have, some issues are very unclear. For example, the metropolitan and socioeconomic selectivity of this newcomer group (Zuiches and Brown 1978) suggests more activist political and social movement cultures than the oldtimer group is likely to possess. But subgroups that were in flight from problems of racism and poverty in the metro areas are likely to have a lower sense of political efficacy (Campbell et al. 1960; Balch 1974). They may have had less activism in their metro past and hence less propensity for future activism than non-migrant metro residents. Conversely, some of those fleeing the metropolitan area, in the past decade especially, may be precisely those social activists who found unacceptable the attenuation of progressive metro political movements due first to recession and later to Reaganomics. Since they were temporarily unable to fight metro problems, they chose flight from these environments instead. This may be especially true of social radicals of the 1960s and environmental activists of the late 1960s and early 1970s, who have chosen "voluntary simplicity" (Leonard-Barton 1981) with more personal control over the local ecological resources in the countryside. Such newcomers are, I suspect, an understudied force in much of the opposition to western energy development in "boomtowns" (Wilkinson et al. 1982). They are probably an obscure force in local resistance to waste dump siting, expansion, or even continued operation (cf. Geiser 1983b; Hamilton 1985). Indeed, because these ex-radicals eschew traditional middle-class-achievement values and behaviors, they may be a powerful force among the new working-class rural movements. For these formerly activist newcomers, past movement and political experience is likely coupled with a passionate desire to defend their retreatist environments. Many of them sought pastoral retreats away from the unwinnable battle to create a metro environment that had both social equity and environmental quality. For them, it is important to be in their improved rural natural environment, and not primarily out of the metro one.

In between these polar types likely lies a continuum of newcomers with varying degrees of political and movement experience or at least awareness. They are also distributed along a continuum of commitment to preserving the local ecosystems of their rural destinations. Generally, I would estimate that their median levels of political will (commitment to environmental protection) and political capacity (potential for mobilization of resources) are significantly higher than are those of oldtimers (Schnaiberg 1980b; cf. Buttel 1982; Wilkening and Klessig 1978; Newby 1980; Geiser 1983b).

Unlike the native-born rural population, they have generally chosen to live in these localities, and this raises their dissonance when local natural environments seem threatened by new industries. Conversely, these newcomers are freer to move than the oldtimers, and can thus reduce their dissonance by a subsequent flight. Yet, I suspect that this latter impulse is less powerful than the former one. However, this uncertainty forcefully reminds one that it is only the median levels of political will that are higher for newcomers than for oldtimers. If we observed distributions of environmental commitment, some oldtimer groups would be more committed than some newcomer ones (e.g., Geiser 1983a; Buttel 1982; Wilkening and Klessig 1978). That is, the distributions are likely to be partially overlapping. Likewise, some of the local oldtimer elites (especially larger landowners) are likely to have higher political capacity than do some high-status newcomers (Mansbridge 1980). Again, we should anticipate somewhat overlapping distributions.

On balance, then, newcomer groups should be more likely to mobilize opposition to polluting industries than should oldtimers, though oldtimers should be the mobilizers in at least a minority of communities. Especially powerful oppositional coalitions are likely to be formed when these two groups coalesce (e.g., Geiser 1983b).

SOME DIMENSIONS OF NEWCOMER POLITICAL WILL AND CAPACITY

In terms of their political will and capacity to fight against industrial pollution in rural areas, there are a number of reasons to anticipate cultural predispositions among newcomers from metro areas that differ from those of rural oldtimers (and even of some metro nonmovers). The following sociocultural selectivities of newcomers induce higher political will to fight for environmental protection.

1. Familial Commitment. Newcomers are more likely than rural oldtimers to be married and in the early stages of child rearing. This is in part because rural areas are perceived to be "good places to raise a family." Moreover, unmarried metro workers are unlikely to move to such areas, since they are unlikely to find spouses or significant others for enduring relationships. Moreover, far more social activity for mature workers is family-centered in rural as contrasted with metro areas.

In partial support of this, the most recent data indicate that among 25-to-34-year-old metro newcomers to rural areas, some 76 percent have children under 18. Among those aged 35 to 44, 86 percent have dependent children (U.S. Bureau of the Census 1984:Table 14). These two categories of adults comprise 57 percent of the total metro-origin in-migrant stream of working age (25 and older). For the total newcomer group aged 16 and above, 56 percent of the women are married with spouse present. Among those aged 25 to 34, some 62 percent are married with spouse present, and for those aged 35 to 44, some 83 percent are currently married with spouse present. The percentages for men in these latter two age groups are 60 percent and 66 percent, respectively (U.S. Bureau of the Census 1984:Table 28).[6]

2. Risk-consciousness. Because of their higher levels of education and media exposure, these metro-origin migrants are likely to be very concerned about environmental hazards for their children, as well as themselves. Their levels of ecological and health

knowledge and concern are higher than are those of oldtimers.
As indirect support for this, note that in Zuiches and Brown's (1978) analysis of the 1970-1975 metro migrants, twice as many newcomers had attended college as had rural oldtimers. For the most recent (1982-1983) migrants, about 36 percent of newcomers had some college, as opposed to some 25 percent of rural oldtimers (U.S. Bureau of the Census 1984:Table 22). These figures were quite similar for male and female newcomers, indicating the prevalence of shared socioeconomic traits in mates (homogamy) in these groups.

3. Spousal Support. Environmental and health awareness and concern are likely to be shared by both spouses, since the rules of homogamy in marriage produce couples that have similarity in socioeconomic background. This spousal or coparental reinforcement of environmental concern has a synergistic effect on the political will of the couple. In an unsystematic sample of newspaper clippings about female activists in recent toxic waste and other pollution conflicts, for example, I found some explicit reference to husbands' active support of wives' mobilization activities (e.g., Garland 1985; Hirsley 1984).

4. Perceived Efficacy. The higher education and media exposure of such newcomers relative to rural oldtimers make them more aware of the political efficacy of environmental movement organizations in metro areas, and thus offer a behavioral model for their reaction to perceptions of rural industrial pollution or other environmental degradation. Thus, social action becomes much more of an alternative to denial or flight, as contrasted with oldtimers. This is part of the individual newcomer's cultural predisposition and is reinforced by a shared culture among educated newcomers.

Geiser (1983a, 1983b) treats as unproblematic the mobilization of local working classes to toxic waste conditions. Yet, even if local groups are aware of problems, different cultural subgroups do not feel equally potent to do something about them. Varied sociopolitical backgrounds create rather different senses of the individual's and group's social or political efficacy (e.g., Balch 1974). Different activity patterns then emerge for various cultural groups at each stage of conflict resolution.

In the classical formulations of Merton (1957: Chaps. 4-5), individuals confronted with an awareness of a problem have at least five response options, only two of which (innovation or rebellion) can lead to social or political movement activity. Conformity, ritualism, and retreatism are the other options that have cultural supports as well as intrapersonal equilibria, permitting individuals other routes to reduce the strain of living with a hazardous condition. Nor are citizens restricted to only one option. For example, a member of the Environmental Congress of Mid-Michigan, fighting against dioxin pollution by Dow Chemical in Midland, Michigan, initially rebelled through active struggle as a member of the Congress and then retreated by selling her house and moving away: "I'm not comfortable . . . I refuse to allow . . . [city officials] to make decisions for me on what is safe or not. They're treating us as though we were test animals." (Bukro 1983a). Citizens do not necessarily react, then, even when they do perceive a problem, by organizing an oppositional movement. Such a view understates the complexity of individual motivation and cultural subgroup supports for alternative kinds of action (e.g., Locin 1984; Hamilton 1985; cf. Geiser 1983a, 1983b). Direct action to reduce hazardous risks for cultural or socioeconomic subgroups is probably their least likely response.

5. Social Deference to Newcomers. Newcomer couples are less likely to find two full-time jobs in rural areas than they were in metro areas. Therefore, the wife, who is more likely to be the one raising children (despite her educational achievement), may have time available for activities to mobilize social movements while she is at home. This capacity may be tapped because such social participation may permit her integration into the community, paralleling her husband's occupational integration. Because of the wage-earning spouse's high occupational status, moreover, local oldtimers will be more likely to respond to mobilization pleas originating from such high-status couples. Therefore, this potential is likely to be tapped because the nonworking spouse anticipates positive responses from oldtimers.

Mansbridge's (1980) study of a New England community's participatory democracy explicitly treats the tensions between newcomers and oldtimers (see Chaps. 7-9). She finds resistances to newcomers similar to that reported by Vidich and Bensman (1958) for a quite different community. She notes, however, that higher-status newcomers participate more than other newcomers. Moreover, their views carry more weight among oldtimers than do those of lower-status newcomers. Contrary to my emphasis above, though, she notes that women face serious resistance in formal political participation.

It may well be true that Mansbridge's account is true for many rural areas. But newcomer (and some oldtimer) women may turn to social movement activism precisely because they are less powerful in the formal political processes. Interestingly, in the convenience sample of community conflict clippings I drew on for this chapter, where women are participants in social movement organizations, they are far less frequently official leaders. This too may reflect the need to have male formal political leaders to reduce the resistance facing women in many local formal political forums, as well as in many environmental regulatory agencies (e.g., Garland 1985). There are exceptions, as in Utica, Michigan, where the director of the Michigan Toxic Substances Control Commission said: "Joan Peters showed us her survey, and we were impressed. . . . We got the Department of Public Health and some experts from the University of Michigan, and we had a meeting and we said, 'What can we do?'" (Sjostrom and Atlas 1983).

From the five factors enumerated above, the newcomers' average propensity to consider some mobilization activity, when they perceive a new environmental hazard from rural industry (actual or planned) seems substantially higher than for local oldtimers.

This difference in political will is, furthermore, matched by a political capacity of this newcomer group that is greater than that of oldtimers (and perhaps higher than that of metro nonmigrants) as well. Factors providing them with elevated capacities for social mobilization of resistance include the following:

1. Cultural Support for Activism. Because of the nonemployment (or underemployment) of one spouse, these well-educated newcomers (usually women) have greater time availability for voluntary social activity than their current metro counterparts and perhaps even than rural oldtimers (McNulty 1985). Given their metro past, they are more likely than local oldtimers to have some cultural legitimation for social movement organization and knowledge of more effective techniques of social mobilization for resistance to industrial polluters.

In numerous media reports, the role of women as community activists in local environmental conflicts is noted, at least in passing (e.g., Bukro 1983a, 1983b, 1984; Hirsley 1985; Atlas 1984; Fritsch 1983). Geiser (1983b) also refers to the role of women in organizing opposition to toxic waste generators or landfill contractors. Reporters such as Kersh (1984) have observed that:

> a growing network of crusaders prepare environmental battle plans. Their profiles are remarkably similar. Most of them are <u>women and homemakers who were uninvolved in civic affairs</u> until waste dumps came to their communities. Suddenly they plunged into the fray, devouring technical journals and arcane government regulations to become <u>self-taught experts</u>. "It's a long haul, especially when you

don't have an education in the area [of waste disposal]," says Sue Greer (emphasis added).

A similar view is expressed in Sjostrom and Atlas (1983):

Theirs is a guerrilla war waged from door to door in communities across America. Their only weapons against the cool discipline of scientists and the frequent callousness of public officials are passion, placards, and public opinion. . . . They appeal for answers, answers that don't often exist, in an emotional crusade that turns housewives into community organizers and their children into television stars. They plot strategy over coffee and besiege bureaucrats with pleas for help in the belief that if they make enough noise, someone will notice (emphasis added).

I have highlighted passages above because I believe they point to confusion among male journalists writing about "housewives" as if this categorization fully defined the socioeconomic and political statuses of these activists. In like manner, Hirsley (1984) reports about a campaign against Waste Management in Port Isabel, Texas, where "Ronald Boudreaux figures he's spent thousands of dollars on wife Deyaun's 'little campaign'" (emphasis added).

A more realistic account may be that written by Anne W. Garland (1985) about Mary Sinclair, an important figure in the early stages of the battle against nuclear power in Midland, Michigan. This female writer/editor, currently at work on a book about women activists, characterizes Mary Sinclair in terms of her educational background, previous occupations, and all the biographical details. For a substantial period, Sinclair was involved raising five children, during which time she would clearly have been identified as a "housewife." But both before and after that, she had worked as a technical librarian, had earned a baccalaureate degree in chemistry and English from a good liberal arts college, and had done technical writing for several organizations, including Dow Chemical. Her status as a sometime housewife seemed to dominate much journalistic coverage of her activism.

Her quasi-professional status was a limitation Sinclair herself was very conscious of: "Living in a community with a lot of Ph.D.s, most of whom were pro-nuclear power, I had to be very careful of credibility . . . I knew I wouldn't last a week if I wasn't absolutely sure of my data" (Garland 1985:65). To counter these barriers, she returned to school to gain additional M.S. credentials and knowledge, "because of all the animosity she had encountered from people in the community--especially from highly educated people who hinted that she didn't know much, since she was after all 'just a housewife'" (Garland 1985:108; emphasis added).

This community reaction by fellow citizens is probably shared by many male journalists and social scientists. The reality is that over one-third of the women newcomers from metro areas have had at least some college education. Since more than three-fourths have some dependent children at home, this helps explain why almost half (48 percent) of the married female newcomers are not currently in the labor force (U.S. Bureau of the Census 1984:Table 28). (These labor-force participation rates are similar to national levels as well for married women with spouse present [e.g., for 1978, see U.S. Bureau of the Census 1980].) A limited opportunity structure for well-educated women in rural areas (cf. McNulty 1985) probably offers trained women like Mary Sinclair only positions that underutilize their skills and experience. Because of these limitations and their own value preferences, many of these movement constituents probably combine familial responsibilities with volunteer work rather than paid employment, especially when their children are younger.

Garland's forthcoming study of such women will also likely reveal that many of these "housewives" had considerable organizational experience prior to or concurrent with their local activism. However, this is more likely to have been as volunteers (or in part-time or full-time work in prechildbearing years). While these activists may have had no formal political experience prior to the organizing around toxic waste or other issues, they likely had prior generalized "resource mobilization" experience (Turner 1981) in contexts ranging from church groups to PTAs. These experiences are highly valued by social movement organizations, along with members' commitments of time to apply these skills to SMO goals (Staggenborg 1985).

2. Spousal Support. The working spouse (usually the husband) in these couples is, because of their educational and middle-class background, more likely to support the social mobilization activity of the nonworking spouse than would the working spouse in an oldtimer couple. These newcomer spouses are more likely to offer social or emotional support or legitimation of social movement activity. This is because they share the wives' environmental consciousness, on the one hand, and do not feel as threatened by their wives' independent action, on the other. On both accounts, they stand higher on these dimensions than oldtimers. In two of my unsystematic sample of cases of female environmental activists, there is explicit acknowledgment of husbands' support. In the first, the husband was a lawyer; in the second, a successful entrepreneur.

Mary Sinclair talks about her family's joint commitment of up to $100,000 to combat a nuclear power plant in Midland, Michigan (Garland 1985:66; see also Hirsley 1984). While Geiser (1983b) describes coalitions of male workers and female activists in local health conflicts, the tensions in working-class families over female autonomy make this assertion dubious. Even in the middle class, where males have presumably accepted more egalitarian-feminist claims, ambivalence remains on the part of both genders (e.g., Bernard 1981).

3. Spousal Facilitation. Working spouses in newcomer couples are also likely to be of greater technical assistance than oldtimers in dealing with the details of potentially polluting industrial activities. They are more likely to be familiar with production processes, fiscal issues, and corporate reporting, because of their educational background and job histories. Because of their greater job mobility, they are also less fearful of using such skills to expose corporate policies, either on their own or through solicitation of coworkers.

Geiser (1983b) reports new local coalitions that combine men's workplace health concerns with women's community or neighborhood health concerns (e.g., Hamilton 1985). But even upper-blue-collar workers, particularly in the past decade of economic strain, are less likely than upper-white-collar workers to support their wives' organizing activities, for fear of corporate retaliation or other forms of "job blackmail" (Kazis and Grossman 1982). While the absolute levels of support of middle-class newcomer spouses may not be all that high, social science and journalistic accounts suggest that oldtimer wives find even less support from husbands (e.g., Wilkinson et al. 1982).

4. Network Supports. Because of past movement exposure, either directly or through metro media, the nonworking (and working) spouses are more likely to contact regional environmental or other social movement organizations for help in local mobilization. Help might include documentation of health hazards of some forms of pollution, sharing of organizing strategies used in similar communities, or having these SMOs directly mobilize the rural community.

Most media accounts of these local conflicts report little involvement of any extralocal social movement organizations. This may simply be a paucity of reports. One interesting exception is Geiser's (1983b:44) account of the conflict in Lowell, Massachusetts. Local groups were aided by a chapter of Massachusetts Fair Share, a statewide citizen action organization. Similarly, a local protest against the Navy ELF project in northern Wisconsin was buttressed by a group based in Madison, Wisconsin, where technical and student resources are concentrated (Locin 1984). It may well be that local group autonomy is generally preferred, because it reduces resistance of oldtimers to "outside agitators" (Locin 1984). Or the flow of influence from national and regional environmental organizations may be more indirect, stimulating consciousness-raising, providing a climate of supportive lobbying and legislation, or serving as a source for technical advice to individual activists. For example, when Mary Sinclair went back to school for a master's in environmental communication, she went to the University of Michigan and designed her own program. But a number of the activist-scholars at Michigan (such as James E. Crowfoot, who later formed a regular environmental action program) were already in residence at the time, thus offering her a supportive network.

5. Local Institution Use. Finally, because of their past educational exposure and higher respect for technical knowledge, newcomers are more likely to draw on technical faculty of local or regional postsecondary institutions. Newcomers in rural communities may be more likely to rely on local teachers who can apply the ecological and health impact models of these national researchers to local conditions. In this, they differ from both their metro regional and national SMO counterparts, which often seek technical inputs only from the research faculty of cosmopolitan research universities. They also differ from local oldtimers, who have less faith in technical expertise, perhaps apart from the agricultural extension areas (where there is a long and successful history of rural innovation, at least for larger landowners).

Hightower (1972, 1976) has documented the failure of land-grant institutions to funnel U.S. Department of Agriculture resources to smaller farmers, thereby increasing rural inequalities. On the other hand, there has been little focus on the role of nonagricultural disciplines in the two- and four-year colleges that are spread throughout rural areas as well as metro ones. If anything, their role has expanded considerably in the latest period of recession, for two reasons: (1) greater displacement of labor and drying up of opportunity, leading to higher demand for job retraining, and (2) reduced money available for education in more elite institutions (e.g., Griffin 1982).

All of the above five factors suggest that newcomers likely have more resources to mobilize in the initial organizing of resistance than do oldtimers (Hamilton 1985). Offsetting these propensities to some degree is the fact that they are newcomers, and thus mistrusted by many of the oldtimers whom they need to mobilize (Geiser 1983b; Hays 1981). The fact that they are of higher socioeconomic status than many oldtimers heightens their credibility to local institutions and perhaps even in face-to-face mobilization efforts (Mansbridge 1980). Their higher status enables them to form coalitions with oldtimers of higher status (independent professionals, newspaper editors, etc.), who themselves will confer greater legitimacy to the mobilization efforts. None of these political will/capacity differentials guarantees that newcomers will succeed in resisting investors. My hypotheses refer only to success in processes of mobilizing new adherents and constituents, not in effecting policy changes (e.g., Staggenborg 1985).

Hence, the newcomer groups often have stronger cultural values for environmental protection, and the socioeconomic and cultural supports for interposing their value preferences into the local community agenda. They are likelier to see the potential health and recreational impacts of many industrial processes well before their rural oldtimer neighbors do, and to demand that some local resistance be formed to affirm their cultural preferences for a pleasant as well as a healthy environment. Oldtimer groups may soon become adherents and even constituents of these new local movements. But it is the newcomers' cultural tenet of rebellion--supported by their belief in their efficacy --and their political mobilization capacity that together make them likely to produce the initial consciousness-raising and resource mobilization in these communities.

IMPLICATIONS OF THE ARGUMENT

The central argument of this chapter is that the physical and human resource development processes of rural industrialization create new forms of cultural resistance. Detailed arguments above suggest how these new cultural patterns are in fact imported into rural communities. It is clear that this resistance partly contradicts the commitment of most rural oldtimers to rural industrialization. A form of dialectical conflict can thus be seen emerging in the countryside, analogous to the early capital processes outlined by Marxists (e.g., Mandel 1978:267-68). Capitalists, they argue, sowed the seeds of their own demise. They concentrated labor power in factories for control and profits (the capitalist thesis). But they thereby also created socialization of labor, leading to a new culture of working-class consciousness and the mobilization of working-class resistance to exploitation, the very antithesis of what capitalists seek.

In our analysis, the socioeconomic setting is the community rather than the workplace. And the cultural equivalent of working-class consciousness is middle-class environmental consciousness. The resulting synthesis is a continuing tension between metro and rural domestic investment, on the one hand, and a tension between domestic investment and foreign investment, on the other (Blumberg 1980; Bluestone and Harrison 1982). Additionally, it suggests tensions between corporate attempts to reduce the environmental externalities of their industrial processes and their flight to communities that are less socially defended against depletion and pollution. Syntheses of these latter dialectical tensions will consist of varying mixes of corporate expenditures on research and development, on public relations to influence local suitor communities and enforcement agencies, and on relocational studies.

The central hypothesis presented in this chapter is that the possibilities for despoilation of the countryside are not limitless. Historical experiences of social resistance to corporate investment by metropolitan populations, and echoes of these even in less-educated rural populations (e.g., Hays 1981), provide some basis for future rural resistance to resource-intensive industries.[8]

There are numerous paradoxes associated with these historical consciousness-raising and migratory processes. Among these are the partial replacement of a rural folk by an ersatz "folk," a form of rural gentrification. These country cousins of urban "yuppies" have a culture that values a tranquil village-like environment more than singles bars and quicheries. But they also share a culture of activism in support of these values, based partly on skills and a sense of political efficacy that they share with their city cousins. When their turf is threatened by rural developers, they too rise in litigative and regulatory protest, mobilizing newcomer "folk," and perhaps oldtimer folk as well, and pushing for regulatory agencies to perform their statutory duties (cf. Hawkins 1984).

Skilled workers in both metropolitan and rural areas are motivated to resist because of the historical rise of a "new class" that incorporated environmental protection into its culture as an entitlement. This same class has inculcated values of political action to defend its cultural entitlements as well. Despite the recessionary and reindustrializing pressures on many workers in the last decade (Blumberg 1980), many of these values and social attitudes are likely to persist in "labor aristocracies" and technocratic white-collar groups that still have moderate-to-high levels of job security.

These "postmaterialist" (Inglehart 1977) behaviors, though, coexist with strong materialist determination to live in a sheltered private environment (Shulins 1984). Movements of the 1980s and 1990s are likely to be rather more localized and focus on immediate health and recreational effects (Hamilton 1985). This is in contrast with the more global survivalist environmental movements of metropolitan residents in the late 1960s and early 1970s (Shulins 1984; Geiser 1983b; cf. Schnaiberg 1980a:Chap. 9).

The last irony I will note is that along with this hypothesized rise of rural resistance to industrialization we are seeing the beginnings of metropolitan accommodation to capital movement. Rustbelt cities and suburbs of the Northeast and Midwest have great needs for new employment and expanded tax bases, after the disinvestment of recent decades. This condition makes protection of their environments seem like more of a postmaterialist luxury. Some of this accommodation is exacerbated due to the out-migration of former movement activists. Some is due to materialist pressures (employment, wages, taxes, property crimes) on such activists and their successors in the metro stratification system (such as the narcissistic "Yuppies").

Clearly, it is impossible to evaluate these factors at this point. But this rise of a metropolitan courtship of industry serves to forewarn us of the rapid political changes that capital flight can bring. And these twists within the domestic economy may find cultural echoes in the larger world system, even in peripheral countries. Resistances that we see today in rural areas from old and new "folk" groups may soon emerge in some groups in some Third World settings. Disillusionment with the fruits of capital investment in rural America (e.g., Summers 1982; Tweeten 1974, 1982) may arise in other settings as well, making the capitalist synthesis of investment abroad (Bluestone and Harrison 1982) a less attractive one for American corporate decision makers. Ironically, these outcomes are likelier to follow in the wake of resource development. Capital relocation is likely to create further environmental degradation abroad. But I hypothesize it will eventually also create the cultural and socioeconomic means for developing human capital to defend its threatened ecosystem.

NOTES

1. "Additions" refers to pollution types of ecosystem changes, which add new physical elements to the local system. "Withdrawals" refers to depletion types of changes, in which elements of the local system are removed.

2. See Schnaiberg (1980a:Chap. 8) and Dunlap and Van Liere (1978) for a review of some of the studies

arriving at these conclusions. Most studies found that higher-educated respondents expressed greater environmental concern and that metropolitan populations (even when education was controlled for) showed higher concern, although question wording seemed to alter responses quite sharply. Unfortunately, these attitudinal studies tell us little about patterns of social action, since they are primarily studies of attentive publics of social movement organizations, rather than of active participants in movement activities (cf. Mitchell 1980).

3. Social movement "adherents" are those in the broader public who show some attitudinal support of the goals/means of social movement organizations (McCarthy and Zald 1977). "Constituents," in contrast, are those with varying degrees of activity and commitment in SMOs. In general, constituents of most movements, including the environmental movement of the last 20 years, are disproportionately middle class (Schnaiberg 1980a:Chap. 8).

4. While I use the terms "oldtimer" and "newcomer" rather imprecisely in this paper, the distinction appears to be an important one in community studies (Vidich and Bensman 1958; Mansbridge 1980). "Oldtimers," in this chapter, refers to those born in the community or region, or migrating there at an early age. "Newcomers," as used here, refers to those migrating out of metropolitan areas as adults or near-adults. There is less basis to construct any hypotheses about resistance from other newcomers from rural areas (especially nearby ones).

5. As Blumberg (1980) and Bluestone et al. (1981) note, even those in a blue-collar and white-collar "labor aristocracy" have been vulnerable in recessionary periods, especially with capital flight to overseas production. Bluestone et al. (1981) note that in recent decades the capital development cycle has accelerated, so that plants in the sunbelt that were built with capital withdrawn or withheld from frostbelt regions have themselves been subject to abandonment. And of course, plant closings also impact on secondary employment--a "divisor" of employment, an inversion of the widely used employment "multiplier" (Bluestone et al. 1981; Meidinger and Schnaiberg 1980).

6. Although almost a quarter of the women in this metro newcomer group are formerly married, I suspect that a large share of these women have kinship ties in the local community and may not be migrating for new employment. This last group probably includes many widows retiring in these areas--e.g., among those aged 65-plus in the migration stream, some three-fourths of the women are formerly married.

7. There is a serious intellectual and political gulf between social scientists advocating collective

behavior versus resource mobilization perspectives on social movements (cf. Turner 1981; Mauss 1975). Because of its potential for integrating the concerns of both camps, the variable of "perceived political efficacy" (Campbell et al. 1960; cf. Balch 1974) that has been predictive in voting behavior studies has been largely absent from studies of participation in social movement activities.

8. There are many warnings in recent literature about the upper limits of total rural industrialization (e.g., Doeksen et al. 1974; Tweeten 1982; Summers 1982), as well as of the inequalities of the distributive impacts of such investment (Tweeten 1974; Summers 1982). To these limits we must add the increased competition of metro communities for investment dollars, often leading to even higher inducements to investors to locate in the metro area. The desperate plight of many metro communities (e.g., Arndt and Feigelman 1985), especially but not exclusively in the frostbelt or rustbelt states (Bluestone et al. 1981), is the subject of both journalism and social science. One indicator of the impotence of central cities is the spate of neighborhood and other grass roots movements that have begun a sustained critique of the costs of such inducements to industry (e.g., Harris and Black 1984; Leslie 1984). Essentially, such assesssments parallel the analysis of Tweeten (1974) over a decade ago, when he noted the rural impacts of new investment. Similar reassessments of rural investment by Summers et al. (1976) and Summers (1982) are as likely to apply to much of the new investment in central cities. In general, they are likely to be regressive in their net impacts on employment and wages.

REFERENCES

Arndt, M., and A. Feigelman. 1985. Gary grasping rays of hope where it can. Chicago Tribune, August 4.
Atlas, T. 1984. U.S. find no welcome mats in nuclear dump quest. Chicago Tribune, January 8.
Balch, G. I. 1974. Multiple indicators in survey research: The concept "sense of political efficacy." Political Methodology 1:1-43.
Barney, C. 1985. Toxic chemicals jar industry. Electronics Week, March 18, 32-43.
Bayles, F. 1984. Facing the health hazards of high tech. Chicago Tribune, September 2.
Beale, C. L. 1978. People on the land. In Rural U.S.A.: Persistence and Change, ed. T. R. Ford, 37-54. Ames: Iowa State University Press.

Bernard, J. 1981. The good-provider role: Its rise and fall. *American Psychologist* 36:1-12.
Bluestone, B., and B. Harrison. 1982. *The Deindustrialization of America: Plant Closings, Community Abandonment, and the Dismantling of Basic Industry*. New York: Basic Books.
Bluestone, B., B. Harrison, and L. Baker. 1981. *Corporate Flight: The Causes and Consequences of Economic Dislocation*. Washington, D.C.: Progressive Alliance.
Blumberg, P. 1980. *Inequality in an Age of Decline*. New York: Oxford University Press.
Bukro, C. 1983a. "Town that Dow built" is losing its chemical high. *Chicago Tribune*, March 20.
─────. 1983b. Ghost of toxic waste graveyard has state whistling in dark. *Chicago Tribune*, December 11.
─────. 1984. Fund for waste clean-up not so super, 2 towns say. *Chicago Tribune*, June 10.
Buttel, F. H. 1982. Rural resource use and the environment. In *Rural Society in the United States: Issues for the 1980s*, ed. D. A. Dillman and D. J. Hobbs, 359-72. Boulder, Colo.: Westview Press.
Butz, B. P., and M. J. Senew. 1974. *A Methodology to Measure the Performance of the EPA Regional EIS Review Process*. Report ANL/ES-41. Argonne, Ill.: Argonne National Laboratory.
Campbell, A., P. E. Converse, W. Miller, and D. E. Stokes. 1960. *The American Voter*. New York: John Wiley & Sons.
Derr, P., R. Goble, R. E. Kasperson, and R. W. Kates. 1981. Worker/public protection: The double standard. *Environment* 23(7):6-15, 31-36.
Dillman, D. A., and D. J. Hobbs. 1982. *Rural Society in the United States: Issues for the 1980s*. Boulder, Colo.: Westview Press.
Doeksen, G. A., J. Kuehn, and J. Schmidt. 1974. Consequences of decline and community economic adjustment. In *Communities Left Behind*, ed. L. R. Whiting, 28-42. Ames: Iowa State University Press.
Drew, C. 1984. Proud working class becomes "new poor." *Chicago Tribune*, December 10.
Dunlap, R., and K. Van Liere. 1978. *Environmental Concern: A Bibliography of Empirical Studies and Brief Appraisal of the Literature*. Bibliography P-44, Public Administration Series. Monticello, Ill.: Vance Bibliographies.
Edgerton, M. 1983. A new Silicon Valley? Du Page County thinks so. *Chicago Tribune*, April 10.
Erickson, R. A., and T. A. Leinbach. 1979. Characteristics of branch plants attracted to nonmetropolitan areas. In *Nonmetropolitan Industrialization*, ed. R. E. Lonsdale and H. L. Seylor, 57-78. New York: V.H. Winston.

Ford, T. R., ed. 1978. *Rural U.S.A.: Persistence and Change*. Ames: Iowa State University Press.

Fritsch, J. 1983. Waste dump site turning Antioch into raging bull. *Chicago Tribune*, April 3.

Garland, A. W. 1985. Mary Sinclair. *Ms.*, January, 64ff.

Geiser, K. 1983a. The emergence of a national antitoxic chemical movement. *Exposure*, February, 3ff.

———. 1983b. Toxic times and class politics. *Radical America* 17(no. 2/3).

Gibson, R. 1984. Chemical disclosure act surprises employers. *Chicago Tribune*, July 8.

Graham, J. 1983. Risk compensation—in theory and practice. *Environment* 25(1): 14-20, 39-40.

Graham, J., and D. Shakow. 1981. Risk and reward: Hazard pay for workers. *Environment* 23(8):14-20, 44-45.

Griffin, J. K. 1982. Community colleges take lead role in training for real life: Low costs lure job-hungry students. *Chicago Tribune*, December 12.

Hamilton, L. C. 1985. Concern about toxic wastes: Three demographic predictors. *Sociological Perspectives* 28:463-86.

Haren, C. C., and R. W. Holling. 1979. Industrial development in nonmetropolitan America: A locational perspective. In *Nonmetropolitan Industrialization*, ed. R. E. Lonsdale and H. L. Seylor, 13-45. New York: V. H. Winston.

Harris, J., and C. Black. 1984. Last chance for South Works. *Haymarket: Progressive Journal of Politics and Arts*, December.

Hawkins, K. 1984. *Environment and Enforcement: Regulation and the Social Definition of Pollution*. Oxford: Clarendon Press.

Hays, S. P. 1981. The structure of environmental politics since World War II. *Journal of Social History* 14:719-38.

Hightower, J. 1972. *Hard Tomatoes, Hard Times*. New York: Schocken.

———. 1976. Hard tomatoes, hard times: The failure of the land grant college complex. In *Radical Agriculture*, ed. R. Merrill, 87-110. New York: Harper.

Hirsley, M. 1984. Coalition rocks waste firm's boat. *Chicago Tribune*, May 20.

———. 1985. Gas stockpile detonates residents' nerves. *Chicago Tribune*, March 31.

Inglehart, R. 1977. *The Silent Revolution: Changing Values and Political Styles among Western Publics*. Princeton, N.J.: Princeton University Press.

Kale, S. R., and R. E. Lonsdale. 1979. Factors encouraging and discouraging plant location in nonmetropolitan areas. In *Nonmetropolitan Industrialization*, ed. R. E. Lonsdale and H. L. Seylor, 47-56. New York: V. H. Winston.

Kasarda, J. D. 1980. The implications of contemporary redistribution trends for national urban policy. *Social Science Quarterly* 61:373-400.

Kazis, R., and R. Grossman. 1982. *Fear at Work: Job Blackmail, Labor and the Environment*. New York: Pilgrim Press.

Kersh, S. 1984. Home-grown experts battle waste dumps. *Chicago Tribune*, April 15.

Latham, W. R. III. 1976. *Locational Behavior in Manufacturing Industries*. Leiden: Martinus Nijhoff.

Leonard-Barton, D. 1981. Voluntary simplicity lifestyles and energy conservation. *Journal of Consumer Research* 8:243-52.

Leslie, S. 1984. Take the money and run. *Haymarket: Progressive Journal of Politics and Arts*, December.

Locin, M. 1984. Navy plans tangled in Wisconsin woods. *Chicago Tribune*, February 12.

Long, L. H. 1983. *Population Redistribution in the U.S.: Issues for the 1980s*. Population Trends and Public Policy, No. 3. Washington, D.C.: Population Reference Bureau.

Lonsdale, R. E. 1979. Background issues. In *Nonmetropolitan Industrialization*, ed. R. E. Lonsdale and H. L. Seylor, 3-12. New York: V. H. Winston.

Lonsdale, R. E., and H. L. Seylor, eds. 1979. *Nonmetropolitan Industrialization*. New York: V. H. Winston.

McCarron, J. 1983. U.S. cities must market themselves. *Chicago Tribune*, December 4.

McCarthy, J. D., and M. N. Zald. 1977. Resource mobilization and social movements: A partial theory. *American Journal of Sociology* 82:1212-41.

McKenzie, R. B. 1979. *Restrictions on Business Mobility: A Study in Political Rhetoric and Economic Reality*. Washington, D.C.: American Enterprise Institute for Policy Research.

McNulty, T. J. 1985. Rural America orders fast-food style. *Chicago Tribune*, April 7.

Mandel, E. 1978. *Late Capitalism*, trans. J. De Bres. London: Verso.

Mansbridge, J. 1980. *Beyond Adversary Democracy*. New York: Basic Books.

Marans, R. W., and J.D. Wellman. 1978. *The Quality of Nonmetropolitan Living: Evaluations, Behaviors, and Expectations of Northern Michigan Residents*. Ann Arbor: University of Michigan Press.

Mauss, A. (with associates) 1975. *Social Problems as Social Movements*. Philadelphia and New York: Lippincott.

Meidinger, E., and A. Schnaiberg. 1980. Social impact assessment as evaluation research: Claimants and claims. *Evaluation Review* 4:507-35.

Merton, R. K. 1957. Social Theory and Social Structure. rev. ed. New York: Free Press.

Mitchell, R. C. 1980. How "soft," "deep," or "left"? Present constituencies in the environmental movement for certain world views. Natural Resources Journal 20:345-58.

Molotch, H., and J. Logan. 1984. Tensions in the growth machine: Overcoming resistance to value-free development. Social Problems 31:483-99.

Newby, H. 1980. Urbanization and the rural class structure: Reflections on a case study. The Rural Sociology of the Advanced Societies: Critical Perspectives. Montclair, N.J.: Allanheld, Osmun & Co.

Ogintz, E. 1983a. Toxic waste fear unites communities. Chicago Tribune, March 13.

_____. 1983b. Midwest states ride job-retraining wave. Chicago Tribune, August 14.

Pear, R. 1983. States investing in the future with technology aid programs. Chicago Tribune, September 4.

Quante, W. 1976. The Exodus of Corporate Headquarters from New York City. New York: Praeger.

Rosenheim, D., and J. Warren. 1984. Layoff study shows costly human toll. Chicago Tribune, October 21.

Schnaiberg, A. 1980a. The Environment: From Surplus to Scarcity. New York: Oxford University Press.

_____. 1980b. Political organization. In Mountain West Research, Abridged Literature Review, BLM Social Effects Project, 40-79. Billings, Mont.: Mountain West Research.

_____. 1984. The role of experts and mediators in the channeling of distributional conflicts. Presented at a conference on Distributional Conflicts in Environmental-Resource Policy, Berlin.

Shulins, N. 1984. Not in my backyard: Americans are saying NO to projects of all kinds. Chicago Tribune, February 12.

Sjostrom, J., and T. Atlas. 1983. Passion and publicity: Tools of toxin crusade. Chicago Tribune, July 3.

Staggenborg, S. 1985. Patterns of collective action in the abortion conflict: An organizational analysis of the pro-choice movement. Ph.D. diss. Department of Sociology, Northwestern University.

Summers, G. F. 1982. Industrialization. In Rural Society in the United States: Issues for the 1980s, ed. D. A. Dillman and D. J. Hobbs, 164-74. Boulder, Colo.: Westview Press.

Summers G. F., S. D. Evans, F. Clemente, E. M. Beck, and J. Minkoff. 1976. Industrial Invasion of Nonmetropolitan America: A Quarter Century of Experience. New York: Praeger.

Summers, G. F., and A. Selvik, eds. 1979. Nonmetropolitan Industrial Growth and Community Change. Lexington, Mass.: Lexington Books.

Turner, R. H. 1981. Collective behavior and resource mobilization as approaches to social movements: Issues and continuities. In Research in Social Movements, Conflict and Change, ed. L. Kriesberg, 4:1-24. Greenwich, Ct.: JAI Press.

Tweeten, L. 1974. Enhancing economic opportunity. In Communities Left Behind, ed. L. R. Whiting, 91-107. Ames: Iowa State University Press

_____. 1982. Employment. In Rural Society in the United States: Issues for the 1980s, ed. D. A. Dillman and D. J. Hobbs, 175-84. Boulder, Colo.: Westview Press.

United States Bureau of the Census. 1980. American families and living arrangements. Current Population Reports, P-23. No. 104, May.

_____. 1984. Geographic mobility: March 1982 to March 1983. Current Population Reports, P-20, No. 393, October.

Vidich, A. J., and J. Bensman. 1958. Small Town in Mass Society: Class, Power, and Religion in a Rural Community. Garden City, N.J.: Doubleday.

Wardwell, J. M. 1982. The reversal of nonmetropolitan migration loss. In Rural Society in the United States: Issues for the 1980s, ed. D. A. Dillman and D. J. Hobbs, 23-33. Boulder, Colo.: Westview Press.

Wardwell, J. M., and C. J. Gilchrist. 1980. The distribution of population and energy in nonmetropolitan areas: Confluence and divergence. Social Science Quarterly 61:567-80.

Wilkening, E. A., and L. W. Klessig. 1978. The rural environment: Quality and conflicts in land use. In Rural U.S.A.: Persistence and Change, ed. T. R. Ford, 19-34. Ames: Iowa State University Press.

Wilkinson, K. P., J. G. Thompson, R. R. Reynolds, and L. M. Ostresh. 1982. Local social disruption and western energy development: A critical review. Pacific Sociological Review 25:275-96.

Zuiches, J. J., and D. L. Brown. 1978. The changing character of the nonmetropolitan population, 1950-75. In Rural U.S.A.: Persistence and Change, ed. T. R. Ford, 55-72. Ames: Iowa State University Press.

Part 3

The Heuristic Device

11
Exploring Sociocultural Impacts: The Application of a Model

Raymond L. Hall

INTRODUCTION

Two basic but interconnected purposes constitute the rationale for this chapter. The first one involves a further explication of the foundation of and reasons why I generated the sociocultural model in Chapter 3 of this volume. The second purpose concerns the utility and applicability of the model as an "impactometer," as a potential gauge to explore positive and negative sociocultural consequences in energy resource development communities. Selected case study chapters contained in this anthology will be utilized to test the model. The model itself is a heuristic device geared to identify a select and limited number of crucial components of the social and cultural foundations of the groups treated in the volume-- women, Native Americans (Indians), ranchers, farmers, and miners. It is a simple but not simplistic model with a limited purpose: to isolate and discuss those elements or "variables" that exert the greatest sociocultural presence on particular groups usually ignored by scholars in the area of social impact assessment, and, to be sure, by developers of natural resources in rural areas. The chapter will proceed as follows: (1) a brief recapitulation of the state's role in resource development; (2) a short rationale for the model's simplicity; (3) the model's potential for practical application; and (4) a demonstration of its applicability vis-a-vis a number of chapters in this volume.

The State

The provision of an adequate if not abundant supply of natural resources for the American economy is ultimately a state (federal government) responsibility. The state, in turn, delegates a major part of acquisition and regulatory responsibilities to state and local governmental agencies. These three governmental tiers leave most of the actual exploration, development, production, and delivery of resources to private developers. However, despite the importance of the function of and involvement in resource development by other agents, the ultimate responsibility for the availability of natural resources rests with the state. This notwithstanding, social impact assessment (SIA) analysts in general have paid little attention to the state's involvement, mode of operation, and ultimate role in the resource acquisition scheme. This failure to consider the state as an important actor in the analysis of the natural resource development process is tantamount to a physician issuing a prescription for a sick patient while neither taking the patient's history nor providing him with a physical examination.

While ignoring the state's direct presence or very strong indirect influence, SIA specialists tend to limit their analysis to the following three general areas: (1) natural resource developers and the processes they use; (2) the economic and environmental climate in which the resource development takes place; and (3) the roles state and local agencies play in matters involving environmental and developers' interests. The analysis and assessment of these areas, of course, constitute monumental tasks, but they must not be allowed to cloud the analyst's vision at the expense of losing sight of the total development process. An exclusive focus on the natural resource product(s) and its immediate economic and environmental climate, while ignoring the role and involvement of the most important actor--the state--in the total process, is, at best, shortsighted.

In an attempt to correct this shortsightedness, a number of works have called to the attention of American social scientists the dynamic relationship between the state and its pervasive impact on the social structure over which it presides. In other words, by "bringing the state back in" one has a clearer vision of the sociohistorical evolution of the state and the role it plays in molding society-centered social, political, and economic phenomena to conform to the state's modus operandi. Among others, the works by Skocpol (1981), Nordlinger (1981), and Evans et al. (1985)--although addressing different facets of state involvement in the social structure--emphasize two common themes: (1) the primacy of state action on and control over domestic policies; and (2) (powerful) state influence among other states comprising the international system. (The discussion that follows will be limited to the first theme, although I am fully aware that resource development, or lack of it, in one state can quickly become a foreign policy issue.)[1]

The major contribution of these works emphasizing the relation between states and social structures is the focus on and explication of the administrative, legal, and

> coercive organization that forms the core of any modern state. . . . These have been identified as the likely generators of autonomous state initiatives . . . to explain why and when [they] pursue their own strategies and goals (Skocpol 1981:1-2).

In other words, these studies have found that strong states in particular (democratic or totalitarian) often go beyond the interests, demands, and wishes of social groups within their jurisdictions and make unilateral, momentous decisions to promote or resist "social change, manage economic crises, or develop innovative public policies" (Skocpol 1981:1).

This line of attack on the state as an autonomous decision-making entity contradicts quite a few influential works whose premise is that governmental outputs are the by-products of the dynamic interaction of the economic, political, and social forces located in the society's social system. Works using the society-centered orientation maintain that virtually all domestic (and foreign) sociopolitical and economic policy can be explained as the outcome of competition that produces winners and losers; the state itself is only involved, if at all, as a neutral arbiter. Skocpol cogently summarizes works that tend to take this "society-centered" approach:

> In place of the state, social scientists conceived of "government" as simply the arena in which social classes, or economic interest groups or normative social movements contended or allied with one another to influence the making of public policy decisions. Interest centered on the societal "inputs." Government itself was not considered to be an independent actor (1981:2, original emphasis).

Skocpol correctly observes that American pluralists and structural functionalists in sociology and political science (and other social sciences as well) were the major sources of

> society-centered ways of explaining politics and governmental activities. Even rebellious neo-Marxists began to theorize about the capitalist state [emphasizing] the social functions of the state as an arena for class struggles and as an instrument of class rule (1981:2).

While the society-centered approach in American social science is understandable,[2] it is nevertheless strange, given that the state's major role is to insure close continuity between its domestic and foreign affairs.[3] If a close reciprocal relationship must exist between society-centered functions and activities and state involvement, and I submit that it does, to focus exclusively on society-centered phenomena to explain state policy outputs is erroneous; only part of the picture is discernable. Such an emphasis assumes that the state has no agenda of its own. I would argue it does. The state not only has its own agenda, but it also sets the most important part of the agenda for society-centered change-promoting and change-resisting forces (see Hall forthcoming), given the dominant nature of the state. "Bringing the state back in" to reassess the state's interest and involvement in matters is a sound notion that merits much more attention.[4]

I am not suggesting that democratic states[5] tend always to take autonomous action in the face of unified opposition from "interest inputs" when the two have divergent definitions of a situation. (It is only when states are able to make decisions and pursue policies that may or may not mirror "the demands or interests of social groups, classes, or society" that one can refer to state autonomy (Skocpol 1981:4).) Rather, the more fruitful question is when and under what circumstances does the democratic state take autonomous action or make unilateral decisions--in this case whom to support in the resource development scheme--that may contradict society-centered interests.[6]

However, my purpose here is only to call attention to the curious absence of SIA research and analysis that considers that state imperatives transcend society-centered ones in the explanation of rural resource development. Therefore, acknowledging, if not analyzing (here at least), the state's role in the resource development process is necessary if for no other reason than to call attention to the fact that the development of rural natural resources, by whatever entity or unity, is more than a society-centered interest. It is a state responsibility.

The major point I want to make is that the state and natural resource development are closely linked, and the state's support, in whatever form, is with the developer(s). Therefore, as I develop the model of sociocultural impacts, remember that while the elements characterize society-centered sociocultural phenomena, the characterization is only part of a larger picture, one that may be shaped in varying degrees by the seemingly absent state.

For example, my discussion of ethnicity and the state in Chapter 3 suggested that power and ethnicity were closely related: Those with power in the United States tend to conform to ethnic/racial identities and dominate the state. I did not argue that the American state is merely a "tool" of the bourgeoisie superstructure used to subordinate the working-class proletariat, although that is true in many other states. In the case of the American state, however, it is more than that.

In summary, in developing the sociocultural model in Chapter 3, I did argue that development impacts are not evenly distributed across the sociocultural landscape where natural resource development takes place. Low socioeconomic status (SES) groups have a high probability of experiencing negative development impacts, while high SES groups have a low probability of experiencing such impacts. However, any group (or individual), socioeconomic status notwithstanding, may be negatively affected if the state (or its proxy) deems it necessary to do so in the "national interest" or the economic interest of a key client(s).

The Need for a More Responsive Sociocultural Model

The potential impact of resource development on a community is as pervasive as it is complex (see Finsterbusch and Wolf 1977; Cose 1979; Olsen and Merwin 1977). One of the more comprehensive and detailed impact models is found in a four-volume 1979 study conducted by Denver Research Institute (DRI) and Resource Planning Associates (RPA) for the President's Council on Environmental Quality, the Department of the Interior, the Environmental Protection Agency, the Department of Energy, and the National Science Foundation, among others. Entitled Socioeconomic Impacts of Western Energy Resource Development, the study had as its purpose, just as the name suggested, "to analyze the socioeconomic impact assessment process for western energy resource developments" (1979:iii).

The schematic diagram of the study identified real and potential impacts involving host communities and resource development. The study sought to include a comprehensive list of potential impacts on energy resource development communities, and especially to include sociocultural variables as an integral part of the assessment process. Under the general heading of "Sociocultural Characteristics," several variables--cultural values, occupational dominance, mobility, ethnicity, and human support systems--were included. The general heading and the variables subsumed under it pointed to "Societal Change." Another general heading, "Worker Social Characteristics," encompassing the variables of cultural values, ethnicity expectations, and desire to assimilate, also pointed to "Societal Change."

Concerned with theories of the social change that comes inevitably with resource development, the DRI study cited Wilbert Moore's definition of social change as being most applicable. Moore defined social change as:

> the significant alteration of social structures (that is, of patterns of social action and interaction), including consequences and manifestations of such structures embodied in norms (rules of conduct), values, and cultural products and symbols (Moore 1968:366).

Apparently, the authors were taken with Moore's definition of social change, but for their purpose, they did not take it very far. Likewise, they apparently liked Bell's definition of social change, especially the part that trichotomized society into social structure, polity, and culture where "each aspect [of society] is ruled by a different axial principle" (Bell 1973:12-13). Although the DRI study attempted to advance SIA theory by including social change and sociocultural variables, I would contend that it failed to explain and utilize Moore's definition and Bell's model in sufficient detail. The study merely called attention to the need for more theoretical analysis in the SIA literature. The most egregious shortcomings of the study vis-a-vis sociocultural impacts centered on the fact that its comprehensive design, its vast array of interconnected variables, subordinated the importance of sociocultural variables to political and economic considerations--particularly economic. Nevertheless, the DRI study took an important step towards calling attention to the paucity of studies that included sociocultural variables.

Unlike the multifaceted DRI model, the heuristic model below (see Figure 11.1), at first glance, is a simple one that includes a small number of sociocultural variables. It lists the basic variables that comprise sociocultural reality in any environment. They constitute the general social matrix of any group, whether it is defined by gender, race, ethnicity, or occupation. The model is designed to gather information to catalogue and assess each one of the variables in relation to specific groups. Specific examples include the following: <u>language</u> (Spanish in an English-speaking culture; <u>geography</u> (Native American reservations, ranches, mining camps); <u>history</u> (origins and duration of group occupancy of land subject to resource development); <u>religion</u> (beliefs and practices regarding sacredness of land); <u>gender</u> (do women possess a different "culture" from men?); and <u>race/ethnicity</u> (are some

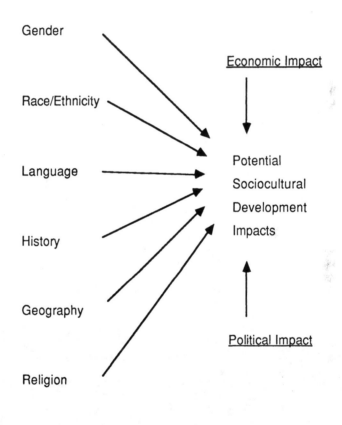

Figure 11.1 Schematic Diagram of Potential Sociocultural Impacts

ethnic or racial groups more subject to the disruption of their lifestyle through natural resource development than others?). This small number of sociocultural variables can be used to construct a group's total "picture," or profile, which can then be examined in relation to the potential impacts that group may experience as a result of natural resource development.

In Chapter 3, I discussed the rationale for the development of the model and the reasons for selecting the specific limited number of macro variables or elements (components). Each of the lower four elements in the diagram is a generally accepted component of culture--<u>language</u>, <u>history</u>, <u>geography</u> (territory, space, place), and <u>religion</u>. <u>Gender</u>, although included in the diagram as a sociocultural element, could also include some, if not all, the aforementioned elements, for women may characterize, for example, their history and place, in ways that differ from those of men. However, here, for the sake of simplicity, <u>gender</u> itself constitutes part of the model, Along these same lines, <u>race/ethnicity</u> also contains all the aforementioned elements. However, the model contains <u>race/ethnicity</u> as a sociocultural component.

The model also contains what I have labeled "latent economic influence." The location of this factor suggests that it is an ever-present influence in the area of the sociocultural components. The reason for its location is quite simple: It represents the latent influence of the state and, as stated earlier, its transcendent power in society. That is, if groups block a developer's access to natural resources, the state usually sides with the latter. If the natural resource is crucial from the state's point of view, it has and may invoke--or allow state or local officials to do so --the power of eminent domain.

The model can be utilized in areas where rural resource development is taking place--or, in any natural resource development community--to gather specific sociocultural information. While the model tends to favor gathering qualitative information that a quantitative thrust might miss or consider unimportant, it is not incompatible with quantification. In fact, it might be difficult in a field setting to omit quantifiable information, depending upon the particular analyst or intent of the study.

The model can be used as a guide for a small sociocultural study to be included with studies concerned with economic and political considerations. The model may be used as a mechanism to generate information on potential and real impacts that can be shared with a wide variety of planning groups, agencies, and organizations specifically concerned with such impacts. Moreover, since most impact studies involving poor and minority group communities tend to be designed in the absence of input from them, the sociocultural model is amenable for use by those groups directly affected by the development project(s). The model should be applied in advance of and not after the implementation of the resource development process. Further, the model may be used by two or more groups simultaneously in order to generate and compare results; conflicting and/or complementary information could then be sorted out with a view towards finding an acceptable compromise.

The basic purpose for using the model would be to identify both potential and real, positive and negative sociocultural distributional impacts. Depending on the socioeconomic status of the particular community under consideration for natural resource development, positive and negative distributional impacts might occur simultaneously. For example, natural resource development tends to generate a higher level of economic activity in the community for wholesalers and retailers. They, in turn, make available more goods (and services) to the community in general. However, what of individuals and groups unable to take advantage of the increased goods and services if the development projects do not elevate their earning and thus consumption potential? What of groups that may be evicted from their land in the community to make way for the development project(s) because the natural resource sought is located under their (tribal, ethnic, racial) land?

When should the model be applied? Briefly, it should be applied when a rural site occupied by one or more groups has been selected for natural resource development. This is especially important when the group, for whatever reason, has been only tangentially involved in the planning process for the resource development. Discovering potentially positive or negative impacts and explaining and discussing them with the particular group(s) may expedite the development process by speeding it up or, if the negatives are too out of balance with the positive impacts, lead to abandonment of the project altogether. In either case, the sociocultural facts would be known in advance.

How should the model be applied? After identification of the group(s) residing in the area(s) where natural resource development is being considered, the model should be applied to accomplish a number of purposes, as for example:

1. To determine the social identity of the group (ethnic/racial, gender, occupational).
2. To specify whether the group's native language is other than English; if so, a mode of common communication both written and oral must be

>   established through interpreters and bilingual individuals.
> 3. To consider the group's perception of its historical link with the American mainstream. Does the group consider its history a part of or apart from American historical traditions?
> 4. To explore how the group perceives its relation to the land on which the group members reside. Is the land rented? From whom? Do they regard the land itself to be sacred? What part of it constitutes ancestral burial grounds? Do they own the land as individuals or is it considered to be group property? What is their perception of excavating land for potential natural resource development? Would the group accept relocation with proper remuneration, or is the land itself part of the group's history?
> 5. To examine to what extent the group's religious belief or orientation has an influence on its worldview. Specifically, are ethnicity/race, language, history, and geography all aspects of the group's religion? Is the land, for example, a spiritual link in the group's sociocultural existence, in its lifestyle?

These specific questions and others stemming from the sociocultural components should provide enough information for both the developer and the group(s) involved to determine how, or even whether, the two principals should proceed. If so, after the developer's wishes are known, the process, as stated above, can proceed more expeditiously or not at all.

Other uses may be made of the model. To illustrate, I shall apply the sociocultural model to four cases involved in this volume--women, racial/ethnic groups (Native Americans), miners, and ranchers.

THE APPLICATION OF THE MODEL

Women

> Because of our social circumstances, male and female are really two different cultures and their life experiences are utterly different.
> --Kate Millett

> Most human beings live in single-sex worlds, women in a female world and men in a male world, and . . . the two are different from one another in a myriad of ways, both subjectively and objectively.
> --Jessie Bernard

There is no tradition of research on women in energy resource development communities, only a scattering of references to them here and there in some recent works, with most of the commentary devoted to the impact of these kinds of communities on the traditional women's roles, as mothers, housewives, and homemakers. If recognized at all, women tend to be seen only as dependent appendages to their husbands, for it is the women who are charged with ministering to their families' needs. "Domestic tranquility," if it is to characterize the home, is solely the woman's responsibility. Even the recent literature on the topic of women in energy resource development arenas, except some of that written by women themselves, is desperately in need of corrective measures. Moen (Chapter 7) has it right when she succinctly sums up the literature on social impact statements and statements about women in boomtowns: They live in mobile homes, bored, depressed, and dreaming of shopping centers and recreational outlets. Their construction worker husbands come home only to find them in one or a combination of these sad psychological states. They argue; he goes to the (male) bar and gets drunk, after which he comes home to beat her up. The whole vicious cycle could be broken only if she could get her act together. As Moen observes, "If only it were so simple."

Beyond these stereotypes, keeping in mind that stereotypes are gross (and sometimes grotesque) exaggerations of a reality with a grain of truth, women play quite functional roles, for themselves and their families, in resource development communities. In fact, women in boomtowns appear across the full socioeconomic and family spectrums just as they do in any other town: Some are single, others are married, some are dependent homemakers, others are working women; many have children, others do not; and so forth. They work, and they are housewives, mothers, and homemakers. But these roles are merely everyday realities that characterize work and family life in any community. The issue of importance for our purpose is: To what extent does an energy resource development community impact on the sociocultural aspects of women's existence?

To begin with, the question itself implies that women may have an existence, in some fashion, that is different from that of men. In Chapter 3, I alluded to that possibility, relying heavily on Gilligan's (1983) work on the differences between male and female children's moral development and Erikson's (1976) discussion of culture. What these two works suggest is that although men and women both share the larger American culture, there is, using Erikson's notion, an "axis of variation" within the larger culture that may be dichotomized according to gender. Such a dichotomy is based on the "different voice" Gilligan, Bernard

(1981), and others observe and hear in the articulation of women vis-a-vis their perception and interpretation of social reality. To suggest that women possess a different "culture" from that of men is difficult to verify empirically. However, numerous references suggest that within the deep structure of the psychic dimensions undergirding perceptions of reality between men and women there is indeed a divergent set of gender views on some different issues. Thus, in this sense, women may possess a subculture that is in important ways different from that of men. Logical consistency would dictate that men, too, possess a subculture if their worldviews are different from those of women. Therefore, the combination of the two subcultures constitutes the large culture, although they may be analyzed separately.

Moen's research has revealed a myriad of problems, disappointments, stereotypes, and disabilities experienced by women in boomtowns, and it also has uncovered a few underlying differences between men's and women's views, supporting our hypothesis that perhaps the differences are undergirded by different cultural perceptions. More women than men in Meeker believed "that househusbands are as capable as housewives of raising children." Women also were more likely than men to be of the opinion that "if both spouses work, the husband should do half the housework." Women felt much more strongly than men about social bonds.

Regarding the model, Moen's chapter clearly demonstrates that gender is used as an instrument of domination. Where women's views differ from the normal stereotype of "woman's place," these views are regarded as deviant, and several kinds of sanctions are employed to engender conformity. In essence, distribution impacts in energy resource development for women are generally negative. The few gains, in terms of low-wage employment and enhanced voluntary associational participation by the spouses of middle-class male workers, do not offset the large-scale social and "cultural" disadvantages suffered by the vast majority of women in boomtowns.

Of course, the present conclusion that the relationship is negative does not mean that it will remain so in the future. More research is needed, with a specific focus on women in the energy resource development arena.

Native Americans

Little and Robbins (Chapter 8) begin their discussion of the cultural consequences of energy-related developments on western American Indians with the observation that Indians have no control over the development process, pointing out that

> the available evidence indicates that in practically all energy extraction or conversion projects on Indian reservations in the western United States, as well as in every energy-related project near reservations, decision making and financial control reside exclusively in the hands of national or international corporations.

Indians have no voice in the development and implementation of policy. Little and Robbins note that the few jobs obtained by Indians are restricted to the most menial employment categories of the construction phase of projects. Once the construction phase is completed, Indian employment is usually restricted to maintenance and custodial jobs, still menial and low-paying occupations.

Beyond individual occupations, Little and Robbins indicate that Native American tribal governments and collective bargaining groups have fared no better in terms of obtaining substantial financial rewards from energy-related developments on or around lands they own. They refer to the Reagan Administration policies, i.e., the state, as being injurious to Native American economic benefits. What is astounding about the economic picture is that Native Americans in the western part of the nation are "losing ground each year in comparison with . . . the non-Indian population of the United States."

What of the sociocultural impacts? "One of the clearest trends" resulting from energy developments on or near Indian reservations has been an increase in conflicts. The conflicts have included Indian/corporate strife as well as Indian versus Indian as a result of corporate game playing. By providing one group or individual(s) with more favorable benefits, the corporate developers have used the divide and conquer tactic. Moreover, "Indians whose traditional residences and resource areas for farming and stock raising have been threatened by energy-related developments have sued both energy corporations and federal agencies for failing to adequately assess the community's ways of life and the dependencies of the tribal people upon their traditional use areas" (geography in the model).

In short, Little and Robbins go on to detail the many ways in which Native Americans have been victimized by both developers and the state. Some examples include the involuntary relocation of Indians from their traditional residences because of the opening of mines, mills, electricity generating plants, railroads, and related developments. Family ties have been broken and friendships severed as a result of the intrusion of development schemes, schemes with no benefits to Native Americans. Little and Robbins continue by indicating that the examples of personal mistreatment, economic and political powerlessness, and hostile and rebellious responses to development may be but harbingers of the conflict to come when oil developments are at issue. They conclude, after exploring a number of similar examples throughout North America, that, in essence, Native Americans could expect no diminution of the incursion of natural resource developers to disrupt and destroy their way of life.

Native Americans in the Southwest

Simon J. Ortiz, a Native American from New Mexico, though not a social scientist, has written nothing if not a clear and powerful essay (Chapter 9) on the sociocultural impacts experienced by Native Americans (and by extrapolation Mexican Americans or Chicanos) in the Southwest. Ortiz's orientation as a writer, poet, essayist provides him with a unique vantage point from which to view the impacts stemming from rural resource development. In that part of the United States, these two groups (blacks may be included) fall at the lower end of the socioeconomic scale.

Ortiz's essay begins with his father recalling what turned out to be the explosion of an atomic test bomb in his home state of New Mexico in the 1950s. Not that testing atomic bombs there was unusual in those (or these) days. His father's point was that those who would suffer directly and indirectly from the nuclear fallout were not informed of the tests--not to speak of the potential hazards. Large and significant events regularly took place without anyone informing Native Americans. And in reference to the aforementioned experimental nuclear explosion, an elderly native man casually observed: "I knew they were going to do something. They've done it before, and I knew they were going to do something again."

"They've done it before, and they were going to do it again," observes Ortiz as he points up the many, many times Native Americans in the Southwest, from the 1500s forward, have had _it_ done to them: The Spanish did it with their guns and disrupted the native way of life. ("The demand was made for land, and land was taken, oftentimes the best farming lands of the native people.") But the Spanish colonizers became more accommodating. They recognized the native ownership of the land and the traditions of religious practice and self-government. In fact, they learned native practice and customs and began to live by them. Their people intermarried with the native people. Following the Spanish, in the 1820s, came the Anglo-Americans "with guns, horses, and a [different] way of life. . . . by the mid-1800s, . . . the U.S. claimed the Southwest." According to Ortiz, "There was something unholy and without any respect about the [Anglos]." The native children were forced to leave their homes to learn English; natives were forced to abandon their religious practices and rituals; their lands were surveyed and diminished "right before their eyes"; the remaining best lands were taken by the railroads; and native leaders, mesmerized and confused by the power of the new invaders, "signed documents that gave up their rights to land and water and a way of life. They tried to protest: 'The land and the earth and our life are sacred.'"

Ortiz's discussion of the history, geography, land, language, religion, culture, and so forth, provides evidence to be used in the application of the sociocultural model as it relates to Native Americans. He states, "Perhaps I've oversimplified it [the process of colonialism], but I am certain it has those basic elements that result in a people's sense of powerlessness, including loss of control over their land, their culture, their future."

But none of this happened all of a sudden. In the 1950s, uranium mining was introduced, aided and abetted by the federal government. "The federal government urged Pueblo Indian leaders to allow the mining to begin, and even if they [the leaders] didn't, it wouldn't matter. The U.S. Atomic Energy Commission needed to maintain and replenish its stockpiles" (the transcendent state). Willingly or not, the natives took jobs in the mines, "not in higher positions of course; those were for the whites with education and sophistication and skills."

Despite the low-level and low-paying jobs the natives had, their "economic life improved it seemed, but something else began to happen"--alcoholism, stealing, and fighting among themselves broke out; corn, melons, and chili were being grown no more; traditional social and religious ceremonies almost ceased. The people were victims of modernization, a euphemism for the ever-present latent and sometimes manifest economic functions that control us all. Some benefit; others suffer.

In sum, Ortiz's essay highlights all the components of the sociocultural model as they relate to negative impacts on native peoples. In addition, it is clear that Ortiz understands that native peoples are not singled out merely because they are native. No simple racism is involved here. He notes, for example, that uranium mining, at which he once worked, is a highly hazardous activity involving high levels of radiation. But the combined economic motives of developers and the needs of the state for this natural resource lead to the exploitation of more than just natives. In a telling passage he writes:

> I never heard anybody [at the mining operation] talk about the hazards of radiation, if there were any. In retrospect, it seems to me that the company deliberately did not tell us anything. Why bother? --the workers were only Indians, Mexicans, Okies, Arkies, ex-coal miners from West Virginia, and ex-oilfield workers from the Gulf who had come to New Mexico looking for work since there was no work elsewhere. That seems to me to have been the reason why the mill superintendent did not tell us anything.

Miners

Miners and miner communities, ethnic or racial group identification notwithstanding, are particularly vulnerable to energy resource development. A vibrant, intact mining community today could be an abandoned ghost town tomorrow, depending on the viability of the natural resource being mined. The depletion of the natural resource (ore, gas, oil, uranium, etc.) usually negates the raison d'etre of the community existence. Although discontinuity characterizes a number of mining communities, in Chapter 5 Yount focuses on stability and continuity among miners in energy development communities. Her general point in discussing the different groups comprising energy development communities ("boomtowns") is that they tend to segregate themselves by occupation. Moreover, within occupations individuals tend to interact only with those who do the same or similar kinds of jobs. They segregate themselves because "those in similar occupations . . . share common interests and feel comfortable with each other." To corroborate this point, one of her respondents stated, "You get coal miners together, they talk coal mining," and so forth. The miners themselves tend to feel that they are not highly regarded in a community, either as individuals or as a group. One miner attributed the stereotype of miners as "rowdy" and "troublemakers" to the way they are characterized on television. He felt that miners are perceived as "trash." Consequently, this stereotype has caused some miners to internalize a negative image of themselves: "Well, I'm good enough to work underground . . . but I'm not good enough to eat in your cafe. . . . Most coal miners . . . associate with other coal miners. They don't have the same type of social clique as most people do."

In relation to the model, coal miners definitely possess what one could describe as a "culture." Self-descriptions elicit such characterizations as "hell-raisers," "hard-drinkers," and "tough." Their "culture" is derived from the underground environment in which they work. Such an environment "is extraordinarily dangerous and uncomfortable (dark, dirty, wet, and cold)"; it "requires skill with heavy machinery" and "a great deal of physical strength and endurance." Social relations revolve around contending with supervisors who use the "carrot and stick" method of interaction with their men. Moreover, the working relationship among miners involves a competition/cooperation dilemma, where they compete with each other for good work assignments while being scrutinized by both supervisor and coworkers. Together these factors breed anger, fear, frustration, and depression.

Beyond these negative factors, however, are positive ones that contribute to a sense of community among them--a community that develops an insider/outsider set of attitudes. The insiders' attitudes do not differ markedly from those of outsiders who characterize miners in stereotypic terms. "Toughness" is one of those stereotypes, one that Yount deals with extensively. For example, one miner put it this way: "Miners . . . pretty well figure they are working probably [in] one of the harshest environments there is, and I can cut it. . . . Maybe I'm a little better [than anyone else]." To bolster this tough character image, both supervisors and workers regularly engage in "pep" talks defining themselves as "mean" and "bad," as opposed to "cry-babies" and "sissies."

Miners are known, empirically and stereotypically, to frequent bars where they often drink until they are inebriated. To the outsider, frequenting bars supports the stereotype of the "hard-drinking miner." For miners, however, the bar has an altogether different function. Yount puts it this way:

> In the bar, miners carry on the business of working, discussing work plans and cementing relationships with those on the job, where the ability to get along is crucial. For example, buying a coworker a drink is a common method of resolving conflicts originating at work.

In her chapter, Yount pays a great deal of attention to those factors that make for community among miners. Without the in-depth participant observation that Yount utilizes to construct community among miners, one would never understand the "axis of variation" that characterizes such a community.

My overall argument on this score, of course, is that the application of the sociocultural model would systematically uncover all these variations and continuities in any community with a specific and definite culture, whether it is a (subculture) mining community or a (dominant culture) "managerial community." In respect to miners, theirs constitutes a definite subculture that could be better understood by the larger culture. The sociocultural model could expedite that understanding.

Ranchers

Jobes's chapter (Chapter 6) is chiefly concerned with the gemeinschaft dimensions of ranching communities. He notes that ranching communities are rare, for "they probably exist in only a few rural sections of the United States, and they are not perfect examples of the ideal type" any more than most urban settings totally lack some gemeinschaft characteristics. "However, they exist and fundamentally differ from the ubiquitous gesellschaft society of which most of us are a part." Their rarity notwithstanding, the thrust of Jobes's analysis revolves around the issue of the impact of natural resource development on ranching communities. He notes that, if studied at all, ranching communities tend to receive post facto attention, i.e., after the disruption of these communities by the incursion of development forces.

What is the content and context of ranching communities? What constitutes ranching subculture?

> Residents drive pickup trucks, ride horses, and wear jeans, cowboy boots, and hats even if they don't ranch. . . . Direct, open and frill-less conversation is typical, particularly among men. Traditional roles and values are regarded as virtuous, although some rugged shunning of convention is tolerated, if not necessarily appreciated. These and other substantively apparent characteristics distinguish ranchers from most urban dwellers.

The occupational aspect of ranching activity involves grazing animals over a large and rough span of land. "Forty or more acres frequently are required for grazing each cow and her calf," and cattle are usually handled twice a year: first, for reproduction (breeding), castration of bulls (to control reproduction), branding (for identification), inoculation, and separation; second, for rounding up and sending or taking to market. In order to accomplish these tasks, ranchers frequently hire workers on a temporary basis. These workers, still part of the ranching community, mend fences and do the branding, castrating, and all the tasks associated with raising, maintaining, and selling cattle.

The major conclusion drawn by Jobes from his analysis is that

> the characteristics of small, isolated, stable
> communities . . . are qualitatively different from
> those of other communities. Thus, the lifestyles of
> their residents differ. Although communities may
> exhibit the same type of [stable] interaction and
> organization for decades, they are fragile when
> exposed to rapid [energy-related natural resource]
> development. They are small, face-to-face, person-
> ally familiar systems based upon sharing mutually
> valued activities over extended periods, preferably
> two or more generations.

However, the introduction of energy resource development schemes in these communities can disrupt them
completely in less than a decade. This disruption is
experienced where there are large and relatively mobile
populations unfamiliar with or contemptuous of rancher
lifestyles.

Ranching communities, like ethnic/racial, and miner
communities, could be greatly aided by the application
of the sociocultural model before development incursion
takes place. It would help generate the kind (both
quality and quantity) of knowledge about a host community that would minimize, if not eliminate, the negative sociocultural impacts that usually occur when
energy resource development forces enter a community.

In conclusion, the sociocultural model is a heuristic device that can be used by both the developers and
those that may be affected by development to identify
and deal with crucial sociocultural components of a
community. Both sides may work out political problems
and identify potentially divisive issues before they
occur.

In the same vein, the model can be applied by the
state to analyze community-based subcultures. This
would enhance the state's ability to manage conflict in
the development process. The state's ultimate responsibility to develop resources is best met in a cooperative rather than a conflictful situation. Through the
use of this heuristic device, the state could provide
meaningful information to citizen groups, developers,
and all other interested parties. Acting as an arbiter
in negotiations, the state might use the subcultural
information to understand the problems and requirements
of different peoples. This would assure less conflict
and the probability of more cooperative development.

NOTES

1. This approach considers the state's internal
policy as the product of historically evolved internal

imperatives which play a major role in the state's policy and action in the international system of states.

2. While American social scientists tended to plunge headlong into the sea of society-centered explanations of political and social action, continental Europeans well understood the dangers lurking in these waters. That is not to suggest that American social scientists in general neither understood nor appreciated state-focused causation of the internal sociopolitical phenomena. (And, of course, a number of American social scientists continued to call attention to and utilize macrotheoretical, state-focused explanations of internal political dynamics.) Perhaps they understood the causal relationships quite well.

3. The dramatic reality of this reciprocal relationship can be seen in the United States' role in the Middle East, especially its protective--or defensive--role in assuring that the oil fields in this area remain open to American (and western European) oil companies. It should not be forgotten that more than once the elite in the Defense and State Departments, with assent from the Executive, have made it clear that military force would be used against any state (in the Middle East itself or the U.S.S.R.) that attempted to cut off the American oil supply.

4. In general, a two-pronged approach can be identified among these theorists who admonish us to "bring the state back in": They reemphasize the state's internal, autonomous power, and they explicate the hierarchy of power among states in the international system. The rationale for their admonishment stems from the noting that the ability of particular states, especially the superpowers, to act autonomously within their borders is closely connected with their ability to do so in the international system. Of course, this line of reasoning must take into account counterevidence that a state may in fact exhibit complete control over its internal affairs, but may have little or no influence in the international system. Moreover, some "weak" states may be supplied by "strong" ones with the means of maintaining internal control that benefits the strong state. "Client," "satellite," "dependent," and "proxy" are terms used to describe states that may exert strong internal control, but may have little or no power or influence in the international system of states.

5. State versus society-centered questions do not often become public issues in totalitarian states.

6. I do not wish here to pursue the argument of whether the American state is always the dominant actor in the resource development process. (I do, however, assume that if it came to a struggle over whether state

or society-centered interests should predominate, the former would win hands down.)

REFERENCES

Bell, D. 1973. *The Coming of Post-industrial Society: A Venture in Social Forecasting*. New York: Basic Books.
Bernard, J. 1981. *The Female World*. New York: Free Press.
Cose, E., ed. 1979. *Energy and Equity: Some Social Concerns*. Washington, D.C.: Joint Center for Political Studies.
Denver Research Institute and Resource Planning Associates. 1979. *Socioeconomic Impacts of Western Energy Resource Development*. 4 vols. Denver: Denver Research Institute and Resource Planning Associates.
Erikson, K. 1976. *Everything in Its Path: The Destruction of Community in the Buffalo Creek Flood*. New York: Simon and Schuster.
Evans, P. B., D. Rueschemeyer, and T. Skocpol, eds. 1985. *Bringing the State Back In*. New York: Cambridge University Press.
Finsterbusch, K., and C. P. Wolf, eds. 1977. *Methodology of Social Impact Assessment*. Stroudsburg, Pa.: Dowden, Hutchinson & Ross.
Gilligan, C. 1983. *In a Different Voice: Psychological Theory and Women's Development*. Cambridge, Mass.: Harvard University Press.
Hall, R. L. Forthcoming. *A State of Fear: Ethnicity in the Modern World*.
Millett, K. 1970. *Sexual Politics*. New York: Doubleday.
Moore, W. E. 1968. Social change. In *International Encyclopedia of the Social Sciences*, ed. D. L. Sills, 14:365-75. New York: Macmillan.
Nordlinger, E. A. 1981. *On the Autonomy of the Democratic State*. Cambridge, Mass.: Harvard University Press.
Olsen, M. E., and D. J. Merwin. 1977. Towards a methodology for conducting social impact assessments using quality of life indicators. In *Methodology of Social Impact Assessment*, ed. K. Finsterbusch and C. P. Wolf. Stroudsburg, Pa.: Dowden, Hutchinson & Ross.
Skocpol, T. 1981. Bringing the state back in. *Items*. Social Science Research Council.

12
Cultural Assessment of
Rural Resource Impacts:
An Addendum

Pamela D. Elkind-Savatsky
Judith D. Kaufman

In the preceding eleven chapters, we have argued that the social impacts resulting from rural resource development are experienced differently by diverse groups of people. Social impact assessment conducted on a purely regional or even a community level thus stands to miss many of the impacts experienced by significant portions of the population. Chapters by Chertok, Gale, Hall, and others have indicated that due to the dynamics of the economic system, the state, and politics, population groups are affected differently. This, our authors agree, is the result of a class stratification system where persons from minority racial or ethnic groups, as well as women, the aged, and the poor, are treated differentially. Within the stratification system, population groupings holding attitudes, norms, and values at variance with the majority beliefs are further subjected to unequal impacts from development projects. These groups have been identified as subcultures in our volume.

To simplistically state our contention: An approach to social impact assessment that integrates cultural diversity within a political economy perspective is essential. Though we acknowledge the primacy of conflicts over resources between all peoples, the manner in which persons resolve conflicts and create lifestyles with limited resources is spelled out by their cultures. The elements of their cultures require analysis in order to comprehend how particular groups might be affected by the political workings of the state and the majority culture in the distribution of resources.

Raymond Hall (Chapters 3 and 11) has demonstrated that culture is a basis of identification and also the sharing of values and attitudes. A number of components promote solidarity within culture, including history, geography, religion, and language. These can also be used to identify similarities and differences between subcultures. For example, the components of ethnic subcultures, because of the distinctive worldviews, define and explain the ethnic groups differently from one another. Furthermore, every state has a developed culture based upon the history of its various processes and dominant entities. Both minority and majority (state) cultural groups may be studied through Hall's components.

The literature reviews and case studies presented in this volume have demonstrated incidents of impact from a variety of projects within rural areas. They have also pointed to population groupings that are significantly different in value orientation and normative structure from majority persons within the society. These subcultural groupings appear to be affected by the developments in different ways from the dominant culture. Yet, little attention has previously been paid to the dynamics within and between subcultures, and between the subcultures and the majority culture, that foster an inequity of impact distribution.

These dynamics are reinforced by the state according to both Gale and Hall (Chapters 2, 3, 11). Although the state's role is to organize, mediate, and regulate in the public interest, the state does not necessarily use its power to insure the rights of each group. Since the state and its most powerful groups tend to be merged, it generally serves the needs of those dominant groups rather than the needs of diverse nonpowerful minority subcultures. Through the predominant state culture, federal policies, centralized regulatory systems, etc., a status system is fostered adhering to development ideology. Dominant and powerful interest groups espousing the development ideology are served. The state, attempting to preserve a free market economy, infuses the culture with a development orientation. Positive and negative consequences of development distribute themselves according to status and the stratification or class systems reinforced by state culture. Even in state culture, as demonstrated by Gale, however, there are various levels. Specific projects are likely to be touted, supported, or rejected by local, regional, state, or federal government agencies according to the specific interests, beliefs, and needs of that state organizational level.

The state utilizes the components of culture "as instruments of control" (Hall:Chapter 3) through such mechanisms as a ban on the use of a language or the practice of a religion, the isolation of population groups, or an interpretation of history. One example of this might be the treatment of the Indians of the Old West. The stereotyping of the Indian--first as a noble savage and subsequently as a drunken, ineffectual reservation dweller--has served to isolate, alienate, and control Native American minority cultures. In opposition to this, however, cultural groupings with a language, religion, history, or particular economic orientation consistent with the state system are given the advantages of the power placed in the state.

Raymond Hall has thus conceptualized a heuristic device which should, if properly specified, explain a good deal of the types and degrees of impact experienced by the various subpopulations of a region undergoing rural resource development. In Chapter 11, he has further specified the elements of the cultural model. Referring to the case studies in this volume, Hall has demonstrated his heuristic concept of cultural impact with respect to various subcultural groupings. He has also contrasted this conceptual approach to another model in order to show the need for cultural assessment. Yet the next step, that of operationalizing the conceptual approach, is left for another time and place.

As a practical demonstration of the way different components of culture enter into development analysis, we have opted to take a look at one of the components, language. Our intention is to use language to illustrate how, in our case studies, it is an indicator and a meaningful component of culture to be assessed in development analysis.

Language patterns, conversations, styles of communication, and the content of language may be studied to better understand the differences between cultural groupings. The symbols subgroups share and their lifestyles that differ from mass society are articulated through the use of language. Thus, language is an important element in the study of subcultures as a major cultural impact assessment variable.

Simon Ortiz (Chapter 9) repeats the words of his father, "I went outside that morning. . . . To be with the dawn, to say a few words in prayer for myself, for everyone, for the day, for the earth." But his father and their neighbors in the Acoma Pueblo "spoke about the strange dawn they had witnessed," describing the light as "something that danced on a wind which passed through them." They later found it to be an atomic bomb explosion. Ortiz in this short description has demonstrated cultural diversity in symbolism and conceptualization as seen in language. Few members of the majority culture regularly discuss their interaction with the dawn or think about light dancing on the wind and passing through one's body. The orientation is obviously quite different from the scientific/mechanistic description of an atomic explosion reported in the literature of the majority culture.

Even in nonethnic American settings, language suggests shared differences in values and attitudes. Kristen Yount (Chapter 5) quotes one respondent as saying, "You get coal miners together, they talk mining. You get teachers together, they'll talk teaching. . . . If a guy was born and raised in a coal mine and that's all he knows, there is no way he is going to feel comfortable sitting around with a bunch of professional people talking." This respondent, like others in Yount's study, believes that people talk about familiar subjects and choose to be with others sharing those same interests. Persons whose entire lives are dominated by an occupation, such as miners or farmers, select others with similar work and lifestyles as friends. In fact, the most common topic in Meeker is work: "More coal is mined in the bars than in the mines." Because of the various stressors associated with mining and the problems of potential danger and the need for mutual reliance, there appears a need for toughness which is observable in speech, attitude, and behavior. Conversation often portrays the toughness of attitude. Miners play practical jokes, tell sexual and ethnic jokes, and "continually 'rag,' 'razz,' 'thrash,' tease, and insult each other in a humorous manner" generally unacceptable in the external society. Razzing and "kidding around" manage situations by toughening up miners, pointing to problems and expressing emotion or releasing tension without hostility. Compliments or expressions of emotion detract from the tough image and make one emotionally vulnerable. Sarcasm is used instead of praise or compliments. Thus, for the miners the use of language and the style of expression differ from those of the general population. Furthermore, they differentiate the miners from other persons in their proximity. The shared symbolism and style unite the occupational group--they define the subcultural group.

Patrick Jobes (Chapter 6) comes to a similar conclusion with respect to the all-inclusive lifestyle of the ranchers. They see themselves as hardworking "heroes," a sort of romantic image: "I've worked seven days a week most of my life, but it has been here, the most beautiful place a person could ever live." These persons share life with others in a rural setting that is fairly stable. Each conversation with a neighbor or shopkeeper reflects the wholeness of interaction between the lives of community members. They share the experiences of the seasonal activities and rituals surrounding the ranches. They experience interdependence of living in a small community whose well-being rests on the dominant industry which constitutes a total lifestyle and commitment. As Jobes illustrates, when development causes growth in the community and replacement of the dominant work setting and lifestyle, these changes are reflected in both the content and the style of conversation.

If the minority group is characterized by a different language, not just a different use of the dominant language, the impact of development on language is even more apparent, as is the cultural significance of this impact. Ortiz describes the colonization of Indian lands. This includes the forcing of children to leave their homes and attend English schools. It was believed by the new settlers that one needed to speak English to be a good American. Thus, the values of the transported culture could be transmitted through the proper language.

In the case of 900 Yupik-speaking Eskimos in two villages of St. Lawrence Island, Alaska, Little and Robbins (Chapter 8) demonstrate a fairly preserved culture which would be affected by a change in the natural resource structure. The two villages are linked by kinship, friendship, and common language. Life is organized around the hunt for mammals. The entire system of logic of these people is embodied in the various requirements of sharing. Efficiency is not a concept well understood by the Yupik. They divide mammals as they are hunted, therefore spending much time moving resources and visiting rather than, as any efficient American would, waiting to the end of the hunt and then merely delivering goods one time. In fact, a more scientific orientation would suggest that if all hunts were equal, they would not have to share and could avoid all of the inefficient trips that are at the very basis of their culture. Their language reflects the values behind the rituals of sharing.

As we have previously stated, language is merely one of the components of a cultural model. In observing language, the social impact assessor should also consider how that language interacts with and reflects the other components of culture. In fact, the previous discussion has revealed the impossibility of treating language in isolation from the other cultural indicators. For example, in the Yupik case the language reflects the basic economic system of the people. The majority group language does not embody the terms necessary to carry on their daily economic endeavor. Language demonstrates the value system of the Yupik, Pueblos, women, miners, etc., in our cases, but these values have often been developed through a history of events. Women have a history of second-class citizenry, as we see in the work of Moen and Schnaiberg. Their patterns of communication reflect a value system held by the whole of society and developed over centuries. Ortiz demonstrates interaction with the Native American history by returning to the verbalized phrase, "It has happened before, and it will happen again." Spiritual or religious elements are also evidenced in the use of language. The early animistic religion of the Yupiks and their embodiment of Christianity through its sharing orientation can both be observed and comprehended through their language patterns. Similarly, the Native American elder whose spiritual life involves a communion with nature is evidenced in the rhythm and articulation patterns of speech. These are especially poignant in prayer. The prayer reflects natural surroundings, geographically bounded. These geographical elements are also apparent in the speech of the farmers, ranchers, and miners, all occupational groupings dependent upon rural resources.

The interactions among the components illustrate the dynamic nature of subcultures. Due to the interrelatedness of the various components of a subculture, any change in a single component affects the structure of the whole. To comprehend the potential impacts of development on a society, it is essential that the impact assessor examine the total dynamics of change both within individual subcultures and between the subcultures and the state culture. Our conceptual approach is designed to facilitate this effort by employing a political economy explanation for subcultural differentiation and by creating a wholistic understanding of subcultural change.

How would the subcultural assessment of rural resource development be accomplished? Assessing the potential impacts of rural development projects is both an art and a science. Though the assessor often deals with cultural issues in a fairly impressionistic manner, it is also possible to devise scientific approaches for evaluating cultural components. Raymond Hall has pointed to some of the shortcomings of highly specified quantitative modeling of cultural components. He has taken the first step toward solving these problems. Hall has given us a heuristic device or conceptual approach which, with a good deal of specification, could provide assessors with more than a heuristic tool.

It is possible that many of the indicators of economic, historical, linguistic, religious, and geographic components of culture could be mapped and integrated into descriptive elements of models. Linguists, for example, have generated matrices of language types which demonstrate a variety of elements within the population. Furthermore, basic content analysis of communication from recorded open-ended interviews would lead the assessor to an understanding of important values shared by persons within subgroups or subcultures of the assessment area. Such endeavors might yield a melding of the art and science necessary to demonstrate the very special composition of subcultures. This work is crucial in order to provide assessments with the information necessary to demonstrate to policymakers the significant differences between various subgroups being affected differentially by rural resource development projects.

Index

Age-based subcultures, 3, 8-9, 110(n4), 120, 139, 164, 193, 283.
  children/youth, 9, 106-109, 195
  elderly, 105-106, 108-109, 139, 170, 191, 193, 195, 202, 252(n6), 283

Boomtown, 9, 89, 91-110, 119-139, 147, 161, 164-165, 167-179, 180(n3), 227, 232, 240, 271-272, 276

Class, 4-7, 17-32, 34, 38, 41-46, 48-49, 52-57, 58(n2), 79, 108, 141(n10), 164-165, 169, 171, 236, 238-240, 242, 246-247, 249-250, 252(n5), 263-265, 272, 283-284, 287
  dominant, 7, 19-20, 28, 31, 41-46, 49, 52-54, 57, 58(n2). See also Group, dominant.
  elite, 17, 20-22, 25, 38, 43, 56, 77-79, 84, 231, 233, 240
  subordinate, 7, 41-45, 53-55, 58(n2-3). See also Group, subordinate.
Community, definitions of, 6-7
Concept. See Model, (socio)cultural.

Conceptual model/tool. See Model, (socio)cultural.
Cultural components, 2, 7-8, 10-12, 62, 64, 65(table), 66(table), 67-69, 79, 82(figure), 85(n3), 181, 261, 264-266, 267(figure), 268, 270, 275, 279, 283-285.
  economy, 2, 5, 7, 64, 65(table), 66(table), 68, 85(n3), 268, 285, 287-288.
  ethnicity, 2-3, 66(table), 67-70, 73-75, 84, 264-266, 268, 270
  gender, 2-3, 66(table), 67, 69, 84, 155-156, 266, 268, 272
  geography, 2, 6, 8, 10, 33-34, 64, 65(table), 66(table), 68, 75, 84, 85(n3), 158, 208, 266, 268, 270, 273-275, 283, 288
  history, 2-4, 8, 10, 12, 23, 25-26, 30-33, 48, 64, 65(table), 66(table), 67-68, 70, 72, 75-76, 78, 84, 85(n3), 128, 130, 141, 152, 154, 156, 162, 166, 186-187, 221-228, 231, 250, 266, 268, 270, 275, 279, 283-285, 287-288

289

language, 2, 8, 12, 64,
  65(table), 66(table),
  67-69, 72-73, 85(n3),
  161, 266, 268-270,
  275, 283-288
 patterns of domination/
  control (political
  impact), 66(table),
  67-69
 race, 2-3, 68-70, 84,
  266, 268, 270
 religion, 2, 5, 7-8, 10,
  28, 64, 65(table),
  66(table), 67-69, 72-
  73, 84, 85(n3), 120,
  171, 176, 202-203,
  222-223, 266, 268,
  270, 274-275, 283-285,
  287-288
Culture, 2-3, 7-9, 28, 33,
  52, 63-64, 65(table),
  66(table), 70-72, 74-
  76, 79-81, 83-84,
  85(n2-3), 166, 185-
  186, 189-190, 203,
  210-211, 216-217, 223-
  224, 229, 233, 235-
  237, 239, 242, 249,
  250, 266, 270-272,
  275-278, 283-285, 287.
  See also Subculture.
 components. See Cultural
  components.
 dominant, 2, 8, 28, 63,
  71, 74, 75, 84, 278.
  See also Culture,
  majority; Culture,
  state.
 elements. See Cultural
  components.
 ethnic, 8, 62-64, 65
  (table), 68-70, 75-76,
  80, 85(n3)
 majority, 283-285. See
  also Culture, domi-
  nant; Culture, state.
 state, 8, 63-64, 66
  (table), 68-69, 284,
  288. See also Culture,
  dominant; Culture,
  majority.
 variables. See Cultural
  components.

Economy, political. See
  Political economy.
Environment, 11, 17, 22,
  27, 32-33, 38, 42-44,
  48, 52, 62-64, 77-78,
  131-134, 136, 155,
  186-187, 201, 208,
  210-212, 216-217, 236-
  240, 249-251, 266, 277
Environmental impact. See
  Impact, environmental.
Ethnic/racial subcultures,
  2-3, 9, 12, 34, 79-80,
  139, 164, 266-267,
  269-270, 279, 283-284
 Afro-American. See Eth-
  nic/racial subcul-
  tures, black (Afro-
  American).
 Asian-American, 70-71,
  73-75, 78, 83
 black (Afro-American),
  68, 70-71, 73-74, 78,
  81, 83, 140, 274
 Chicano (Mexican-Ameri-
  can), 68, 71, 73-74,
  78, 81, 83, 224-225,
  274, 276
 Eskimo, 9, 12, 185-204,
  207-218, 287. See also
  Ethnic/racial sub-
  cultures, Native
  American.
 Hispanic, 68, 70, 73
 Indian. See Ethnic/
  racial subcultures,
  Native American.
 Mexican-American. See
  Ethnic/racial sub-
  cultures, Chicano
  (Mexican-American).
 Native American, 9-10,
  63, 68, 70-74, 81, 83,
  185-217, 221-228, 261,
  272-276, 284-285, 287-
  288. See also Ethnic/
  racial subcultures,
  Eskimo.

Gemeinschaft, 7, 145-148,
  150, 158, 161, 166-
  167, 173, 175-176,
  178-179, 180(n3), 278

Gender-based subcultures, 2-3, 7-10, 12, 34, 80, 120, 139, 161-162, 164, 166-167, 171, 173, 175-176, 178, 180(n1), 266, 268-272
  female (women), 3, 7, 10-12, 75-76, 79, 81, 83-84, 93-94, 110, 155, 161-179, 180(n1), 193-194, 202, 238, 242-246, 252(n6), 266, 270-272, 287
  male (men), 3, 10, 75-76, 83-84, 92-94, 161-162, 164-166, 171-172, 174-179, 180(n1), 187, 190, 194-195, 202, 247, 266, 270-272
  men. See Gender-based subcultures, male (men).
  women. See Gender-based subcultures, female (women).
Gesellschaft, 7, 146, 148, 158, 166-167, 173, 176-179, 278
Group. See also Class and Subculture.
  dominant, 2, 8, 21, 42, 44-45, 57, 65, 69-70, 73-74, 78-79, 83-84, 209, 284. See also Class, dominant.
  subordinate, 7-8, 41-42, 44-45, 52, 57, 65. See also Class, subordinate.

Hegemony, 8, 27-30, 43
Heuristic, 1, 7, 9, 11-12, 81, 261, 266, 279, 285, 288. See also Model, (socio)-cultural.

Impact
  environmental, 51, 55, 62, 79, 85(n1), 96, 105, 186, 217
  social, 1, 9, 12, 57-58(n1), 78, 80, 89, 120, 146-147, 164-165, 177, 185-186, 212-213, 227, 261-262, 264, 266, 271, 283, 287
Inequality, 2-5, 7-8, 10, 12, 17-24, 29, 32, 34, 62, 68, 70, 74, 162, 164, 248, 253(n8). See also Inequity.
Inequity, 1-5, 7-12, 97, 239, 284. See also Inequality.
In-migrant, 11, 43, 149, 165, 168, 232, 235-237, 239, 241-242. See also In-migration.
In-migration, 11, 146, 157, 176, 235, 237, 239, 252. See also In-migrant.

Model, (socio)cultural, 1, 7-9, 11-12, 61, 77, 79, 81, 82(figure), 84, 261, 264-266, 267 (figure), 268-279, 285, 287. See also Heuristic.

Occupational subcultures, 2-3, 8-10, 12, 22-26, 34, 76, 77, 79-80, 83-84, 119-120, 122-125, 127-132, 138-139, 140(n4), 149, 155, 158, 161, 165-166, 209, 235-237, 243, 265-266, 269, 276-278, 286-287
  agriculturalists, 100-102, 152. See also Occupational subcultures, farmers; Occupational subcultures, ranchers.
  business persons, 83, 98-100, 104, 120-123, 126-127, 129, 138, 140(n2), 149, 165, 238
  construction workers, 92-95, 120, 122, 127, 140(n2), 165, 168-169, 172, 271. See also Occupational subcultures, energy workers.

energy workers, 119-120, 122-129, 135, 138-139, 140(n2). See also Occupational subcultures, construction workers; Occupational subcultures, miners; Occupational subcultures, oil rig workers.
farmers, 8, 79, 81, 100-103, 121, 123-124, 130, 165, 223, 232, 248, 261, 286, 288. See also Occupational subcultures, agriculturalists.
housewives/homemakers, 94, 122, 138, 141(n9), 163-166, 168-169, 171, 174-175, 177, 238, 244-246, 271-272
miners, 8, 10, 76, 79, 81, 95, 120, 122-124, 127-130, 132-139, 140(n2), 141(n6), 169, 174, 223-225, 227, 261, 270, 276-279, 285-288. See also Occupational subcultures, energy workers.
oil rig workers, 120, 122, 124, 127, 129, 139, 140(n2), 141(n10). See also Occupational subcultures, energy workers.
professionals, 97, 120-124, 126-128, 140(n2), 149-150, 168, 174, 245, 249, 286
ranchers, 10, 77, 79, 81, 100-104, 120-123, 126-127, 129-130, 138-139, 145-158, 165-167, 261, 266, 270, 278-279, 286, 288. See also Occupational subcultures, agriculturalists.
Out-migration, 146, 231, 233, 251

Political economy, 2-4, 12, 69, 75, 283, 288

Resources, 3, 8-9, 23, 26, 30-34, 38, 40-41, 49-50, 53-55, 61, 68, 75, 79, 81, 83, 91, 145-146, 174, 177, 179, 185-187, 190-193, 198-199, 205-207, 209-211, 213, 215-217, 226, 233, 240, 247-248, 261-262, 264, 268, 279, 283, 287-288
economic, 53, 174, 177, 179, 215
energy, 91, 145, 185, 210, 226
natural, 33, 38, 61, 81, 185-187, 191, 209-211, 213, 216-217, 233, 261-262, 264, 268
Rural residents
long-term, 92, 95, 124
longtime (longtimers), 93-94, 96-108, 110(n4), 120, 165, 168-170, 174-176, 180(n3). See also Rural residents, oldtimers.
newcomers, 9, 55, 92-95, 98-99, 103, 108, 110(n2,4), 120, 125, 148-150, 153, 157, 168-170, 172, 174-176, 178, 180(n3), 229, 235, 237-250, 252(n4)
oldtimers, 11, 95, 108, 110(n2), 148, 157, 237-244, 247-250, 252(n3). See also Rural residents, longtime (longtimers).

Social impact. See Impact, social.
State, the, 1, 7-8, 37, 42, 51, 54-56, 62-64, 66(table), 67-70, 74-75, 83, 85(n4), 178, 230-231, 261-265, 268, 275, 279-281(n1-6), 283-285, 288

Stratification, 4-6, 17, 22-24, 26, 30-33, 84, 149-150, 251, 283-284
Subculture, 2, 3, 7-9, 11-12, 43, 52, 56, 76-77, 79, 81, 119-120, 128, 138, 158, 161, 272, 277-279, 283-285, 288. See also Culture and Group.
  age-based. See Age-based subcultures.
  ethnic/racial. See Ethnic/racial subcultures.
  gender-based. See Gender-based subcultures.
  occupational. See Occupational subcultures.